PUBLICATIONS OF THE DEPARTMENT OF ROMANCE LANGUAGES
UNIVERSITY OF NORTH CAROLINA

General Editor: ALDO SCAGLIONE

Editorial Board: JUAN BAUTISTA AVALLE-ARCE, PABLO GIL CASADO, FRED M. CLARK, GEORGE BERNARD DANIEL, JANET W. DÍAZ, ALVA V. EBERSOLE, AUGUSTIN MAISSEN, EDWARD D. MONTGOMERY, FREDERICK W. VOGLER

NORTH CAROLINA STUDIES IN THE
ROMANCE LANGUAGES AND LITERATURES

ESSAYS; TEXTS, TEXTUAL STUDIES AND TRANSLATIONS; SYMPOSIA

Founder: URBAN TIGNER HOLMES

Editor: JUAN BAUTISTA AVALLE-ARCE
Associate Editor: FREDERICK W. VOGLER

Other publications of the Department: *Estudios de Hispanófila, Hispanófila, Romance Notes, Studia Raeto-Romanica*

Distributed by:

INTERNATIONAL SCHOLARLY BOOK SERVICE, INC.
P. O. BOX 4347
Portland, Oregon 97208
U. S. A.

NORTH CAROLINA STUDIES IN THE
ROMANCE LANGUAGES AND LITERATURES
Number 132

THE *AUTO SACRAMENTAL*
AND THE PARABLE
IN
SPANISH GOLDEN AGE LITERATURE

THE *AUTO SACRAMENTAL* AND THE PARABLE
IN
SPANISH GOLDEN AGE LITERATURE

BY

DONALD THADDEUS DIETZ

CHAPEL HILL

NORTH CAROLINA STUDIES IN THE ROMANCE
LANGUAGES AND LITERATURES
U.N.C. DEPARTMENT OF ROMANCE LANGUAGES
1973

ISBN: 978-0-8078-9132-2

DEPÓSITO LEGAL: V. 3.567 - 1973

ARTES GRÁFICAS SOLER, S. A. - JÁVEA, 28 - VALENCIA (8) - 1973

CONTENTS

	Pages
PREFACE	9
CHAPTER I: TWO LITERARY GENRES: THEIR NATURE AND PURPOSE	13
— II: THE NON-KINGDOM PARABLE *AUTOS*	33
— III: THE KINGDOM PARABLE *AUTOS*	84
— IV: GENERAL OBSERVATIONS AND CONCLUSIONS.	170
LIST OF REFERENCES	194
INDEX	200

PREFACE

It is a fact among students of Spanish literature that relatively little of literary value is known concerning the *auto sacramental*. The following work proposes to fill in some measure this obvious *hueco* that exists in the study of Spanish literature. It does so by bringing together for consideration all those one-act allegorical dramas written during the sixteenth and seventeenth centuries in Spain which have as their bases one of the New Testament parables. More importantly however, it attempts to uncover stages in the aesthetic development of the *autos* through a comparative analysis of the various sacramental pieces set thematically and chronologically within a parabolic grouping. Just how the *auto sacramental* developed over the centuries from its relatively simple and uncomplicated dramatic form to its highly refined and complex allegorical structure is another goal of the present volume.

Although the studies of Bruce W. Wardropper, Jean-Louis Flecniakoska, Angel Valbuena Prat, and Alexander A. Parker afford an historical and literary comprehension of the nature and development of the sacramental drama, the works of the above mentioned can serve only as an introduction because of either their general nature or limited scope. In the detailed analysis of the influence of early religious poetry and Jesuit drama upon the *auto sacramental*, Flecniakoska confines his study to the *autos* before 1635 and thus eliminates any of the Calderonian plays. Wardropper does virtually the same as Flecniakoska when he concentrates upon those *autos* written before 1648 and thus excludes from his discussion Calderón's most important and significant sacramental pieces, those from the latter-half of the author's life. Angel Valbuena Prat has done extensive work on Calderón and his sacramental plays but his contribution has been chiefly in the areas of compilation and cataloguing rather than literary analysis. Another who has researched Calderón is Alexander A. Parker. The latter not only arrives at a meaningful insight into the nature of the *auto sacramental* through the work of its greatest genius, but he also presents a fine example of scholarship in his detailed exposé of the *autos* which he treats. However, even Parker's study has its limitations in that it only deals with three of Calderón's allegorical plays, and students of Spanish literature anxiously await Parker's fulfillment of his promise to make further similar investigations.

Although the following study considers those one-act allegorical dramas that treat of one or the other of the Gospel parables, I have found it desirable and useful to exclude those plays from outside the Peninsula not written in the Spanish vernacular but that would otherwise qualify for the present work. Full-length dramas of more than an act written on one of the Gospel parables are also viewed as being outside the realm of this inquiry and will appear cited in the notes only if they relate to *autos* under consideration in the text. My efforts to gather together those *autos sacramentales* treating of the Gospel parables have been greatly facilitated by the catalogues of La Barrera y Leirado, Alenda y Mira, Julián Paz, Medel del Castillo, and the information of the early Jesuit plays provided by García Soriano and Jean-Louis Flecniakoska.

In the consideration of the parable *autos* which makes up the major portion of this study, I have attempted not to burden the text with unnecessary bibliographical data, which I reserve for the notes. Whenever possible, I have employed the most readily available editions of the *autos sacramentales*, making extensive use of Pedroso's collection found in the *Biblioteca de Autores Españoles*. I have also relied heavily on the Academia edition of Lope's plays as well as on Angel Valbuena Prat's collection of the Calderonian drama.

I would like to acknowledge H. Reynolds Stone and Ruth Lee Kennedy who aided me while I was at the University of Arizona. I am particularly grateful to William M. Whitby for his assistance in the acquisition of the necessary manuscripts from the Spanish libraries. My sincerest appreciation is due also to Ball State University and the Faculty Publications Committee and especially Richard W. Burkhardt, Dean of Faculties, who so generously provided financial guarantees for the publication of this work.

D. T. D.

To Kathy

Chapter I

TWO LITERARY GENRES: THEIR NATURE AND PURPOSE

Before undertaking a study of the parable as it appears in the *auto sacramental*, it is well to examine the nature and purpose of both the *auto* and the parable. Just precisely what are the *auto sacramental* and the parable and why do they exist?

The road to an acceptable definition of the *auto sacramental* has been a long and difficult one. Scholars and critics have offered many alternatives as to the essence of the one act religious drama of the Renaissance. The development of the definition of the *auto sacramental* revolves around what one critic calls, the "hecho histórico" and the "hecho literario."[1] A definition based on the "historical fact" emphasizes more the time element, when and for what occasion were the *autos* written; a definition centered around the "literary fact," on the other hand, concerns itself more with the literary aspect, what is the *auto* and of what does it consist.

In 1865, Eduardo González Pedroso gave to the Hispanic world the first modern edition of the *autos sacramentales*. In the prologue which introduced his collection, González Pedroso was the first of the modern critics of the sacramental play to base his definition almost exclusively on the "hecho histórico." Stressing the fact that the plays were written for and performed on the festival of the Corpus Christi, he defined the *autos sacramentales* as

---

[1] Bruce W. Wardropper, *Introducción al teatro religioso del siglo de oro: Evolución del auto sacramental, 1500-1648* (Madrid: Revista de Occidente, 1958), pp. 19-30.

Dramas sagrados en un acto, que tienen por objeto elogiar las excelencias del sacramento de la Eucaristía, o de los cuales consta, por lo menos, que se representaron en la festividad del Corpus.[2]

This definition offered by the first modern compiler of the *autos sacramentales* greatly influenced critics and students of Spanish literature for more than fifty years. Others who attempted to define the *auto* agreed with González Pedroso that what made a dramatic piece of one act an *auto* was that it be presented on the feast of the Corpus Christi. However, one significant note appears in the definitions of González Pedroso's successors. They all place new emphasis on the play's theme which must have "una conexión estrecha con el culto del Santísimo Sacramento."[3]

To view the *auto* only from its historical circumstances, as did González Pedroso and his immediate successors, proved to be highly inadequate. It certainly is not valid to say that, because a piece is composed and given on a particular day and in honor of a particular feast, it is then to be called an *auto*. In such a case any play of one act such as the comic *pasos* of Lope de Rueda or the light-hearted *entremeses* of Cervantes could classify as an *auto* were it to be performed on the Festival Day. With regard to the problem of the theme being closely related to the Eucharist, what is to be said of all those *autos* that have little or nothing to do with the Eucharistic theme, but deal rather with the Virgin or some of the other saints? Indeed, González Pedroso has been negatively criticized because his definition is not consistent with the choice of *autos* that appear in his collection. In fact, the very first selection in his edition deals not with the Eucharist either directly or indirectly, but rather with a saint of the Church, St. Martin.[4]

---

[2] Eduardo González Pedroso, his prologue to *Los autos sacramentales desde su origen hasta fines del siglo XVII. Biblioteca de Autores Españoles*, LVIII, viii.

[3] See also Henri Mérimée, *L'Art dramatique à Valencia* (Paris: Imprimerie et Librairie Edouard Privat, 1913), p. 193.

[4] In a footnote to this play by Gil Vicente, the editor admits that the play has nothing at all to do with the Eucharist. However, he maintains that the play should be included in his collection because "ésta fue representada *durante la procesión del Corpus del año 1504, en la iglesia de las Caldas de Lisboa...*." With this note, González Pedroso offers even more evidence

An attempt to see the sacramental drama from its essentially literary aspects was made by two contemporary scholars, Angel Valbuena Prat and Alexander A. Parker. In his monumental work on Calderón and the *auto sacramental*, published in 1924, Angel Valbuena Prat attempted to discover the true nature of the *auto*.[5] Striving to see the *auto sacramental* in its essence and keeping in mind the inadequacies of his predecessors, Valbuena saw the *auto* as "una composición dramática (en una jornada), *alegórica* y relativa, generalmente, a la Comunión."[6] Although some were to take issue with and try to expand on Valbuena's idea of the *auto*, all those who attempted to define the *auto* thereafter recognized its allegorical nature.[7]

However important and influential Don Angel Valbuena's definition of the sacramental play proved to be, the Spanish scholar did little to clarify the question concerning the presence or absence of the Eucharistic theme; also, in recognizing the *auto* as allegory, he failed to analyze the function of allegory. The lot for the completion of these tasks fell to another *calderonista*, Alexander A. Parker. Parker in his masterful study, *The Allegorical Drama of Calderon*, published in 1943, begins the second chapter of his book by resolving the previously unanswerable question of the theme. He does so by distinguishing between the *asunto* and the *argumento*. The *asunto* is the play's underlying theme. The *argumento* is its plot. Employing traditional scholastic theology, Parker states that, since the Eucharist is at the basis of all Catholic doctrine, "the *asunto* of every *auto* is therefore the Eucharist, but the *argumento* can very from one to the other: it

---

on how he considered the time factor to be the most important in his definition. See his collection, p. 3. ·

[5] Ángel Valbuena Prat, "Los autos sacramentales de Calderón: Clasificación y análisis," *Revue Hispanique*, LXI (1924), 1-302.

[6] *Ibid.*, p. 7.

[7] Nicolás González Ruiz wished to expand on Valbuena's definition of the *auto* and especially on the clause, "relativa, generalmente, a la Comunión". He does so by considering not only those dramas that deal with the Sacrament as *autos sacramentales* but also those that pertain to the Virgin. See his definition of the *auto sacramental* in the general introduction found at the beginning of his collection, *Piezas maestras del teatro teológico español* (2 vols.; *Biblioteca de Autores Cristianos*, Madrid: La Editorial Católica, S. A., 1953), Vol. I, p. 19.

can be any *historia divina* — historical, legendary, or fictitious — provided that it throws some light on some aspect of the *asunto*."[8]

After making the distinction between the theme which is always the Sacrament, and the plot, which may embrace any one of the many aspects of Catholic teaching, Parker undertakes his second task, that of analyzing the function of allegory. Using as his basis for discussion the Calderonian *auto*, he carefully studies the four stages of progression in the composition of the *auto* and elucidates how, through the medium of allegory, the imagined concept or idea in the author's mind (*concepto imaginado*) becomes the real or formalized image of the stage (*concepto práctico*):

> Allegory is the medium by which the "concepto" becomes "cuerpo," which transforms "lo no visible" into "lo animado"; the medium, that is to say, by which the conceptual order is given a concrete expression that makes it more directly accessible to human experience, this concrete expression (or visible, living "reality") being the dramatic action.[9]

After the pioneering work of Angel Valbuena Prat and Alexander A. Parker on the Calderonian *auto*, Bruce W. Wardropper and Jean-Louis Flecniakoska have reviewed the *auto* appearing before Calderón.[10] Although Wardropper and Flecniakoska both follow in the tradition of their contemporary predecessors in seeing the *auto* as allegory, the former scholar deserves special mention. In his *Introducción al teatro religioso del siglo de oro*, Wardropper clearly showed the intrinsic relationships among allegory, the *auto*, and the liturgy of the Church. He points out that the sacramental plays grew out of the earlier liturgical functions of the Corpus Christi procession with its hideous and awesome *tarasca* and its primitive *rôques*. The *tarasca*, a monstrous serpent figure with large mouth, often symbolized some evil force, perhaps the

---

[8] Alexander A. Parker, *The Allegorical Drama of Calderon* (Oxford: The Dolphin Book Co. Ltd., 1943), p. 59.
[9] *Ibid.*, p. 79.
[10] Wardropper, *op. cit.* (above, note 1). Jean-Louis Flecniakoska, *La Formation de l'auto religieux en Espagne avant Calderon, 1550-1635* (Montpellier: Imprimerie Paul Déran, 1961), especially pages 393-427, on the *auto* and allegory.

devil, while the *rôques* drawn on carts were crude still-life representations of biblical figures.[11] In an earlier article published in 1950, Wardropper compared the allegorical nature of the Eucharist as a sacrament with that of the *auto*.[12] He states that, according to Thomas Aquinas, a sacrament by definition is a sign, and the purpose of a sign is to discover the unknown by means of the known. Wardropper concludes that "the allegorical structure of the *auto sacramental* is perfectly consonant with the nature of the world of sacraments."[13]

In the light of contemporary scholarship on the *auto sacramental* beginning with Valbuena Prat and Alexander A. Parker and culminating in the more recent studies of Bruce W. Wardropper and Jean-Louis Flecniakoska, there can be no doubt that the nature and essence of the *auto sacramental* is allegorical. However, in tracing the development of the *auto*'s definition as viewed by the critics, one must be careful not to conclude that Valbuena Prat was the first to see allegory in the sacramental play. Calderón himself was very much aware of the substance of the literary genre which he perfected. Calderón defines the sacramental play as

> Sermones
> puestos en verso, en idea
> representable cuestiones
> de la Sacra Teología
> que no alcanzan mis razones
> a explicar ni comprender
> y el regocijo dispone
> en aplauso de este día.[14]

The Spanish literati of the eighteenth and nineteenth centuries also understood the allegorical nature of the *auto sacramental*. Ignacio Luzán in his *Arte poética* (1737) says the *autos* "son otra

---

[11] Wardropper, 31-52.
[12] Bruce W. Wardropper, "The Search for a Dramatic Formula for the Auto Sacramental," *PMLA* LXV (December, 1950), 1196-1211.
[13] *Ibid.*, pp. 1197-1198.
[14] Calderón de la Barca, found in the *loa* to *La segunda esposa o triunfar muriendo* in *Obras completas*, edited by Ángel Valbuena Prat (3 vols.; Madrid: Ediciones de Aguilar, S. A., 1952), Vol. III, p. 427. This is the edition from which subsequent passages will be cited, here-after referred to as "*Obras* ...."

especie de Poesía dramática conocida sólo en España: y su artificio se reduce a formar una alegórica representación en obsequio del sacrosanto misterio de la Eucaristía." [15] Indeed, the Neoclassicists of the eighteenth and early nineteenth centuries were so aware of the allegorical elements of the Eucharistic drama that they aimed their venomous arrows directly at the drama's abstractions and personifications. Nicolás Fernández de Moratín offers an example of the nineteenth century critics' scorn for the inverisimilitudes and anachronisms of the allegorical figures:

> ¿Es posible que hable la Primavera? ¿Ha oído usted en su vida una palabra al Apetito? ¿Sabe usted cómo es el metal de voz de la Rosa? ... ¿Juzgará nadie posible que se junten a hablar personajes divinos y humanos de muy distintos siglos y diversas naciones, v. gr., la Trinidad Suprema, el demonio, San Pablo, Adán, San Agustín, Jeremías y otros tales, cometiendo horrorosos e insufribles anacronismos? [16]

Even the stringent traditionalist of the nineteenth century, Menéndez Pelayo, influenced greatly by the Neoclassic affinity for the three dramatic unities, reacted negatively against the excessive use of "personificaciones morales y las ideas puras." [17] It was amid this hostile atmosphere of nineteenth-century criticism that González Pedroso dared to publish the first modern collection of the *auto sacramental*, and perhaps it was precisely because he desired to avoid the "touchy" problem of the allegory that he consciously omitted it from his definition.

If the problem of determining the essential quality of the *auto sacramental* can eventually be resolved in the realization of the *auto*'s allegorical nature, the equally puzzling question of the essence of the parable can only be understood when the parable is not viewed as allegory but as analogy.

The problem that arises with regard to the parable is that, beginning with the evangelists themselves and continuing down

---

[15] Ignacio Luzán, *La poética, o reglas de la poesía general y de sus principales especies* (1737), as quoted by Parker, p. 20.

[16] Nicolás Fernández de Moratín, *Desengaño al teatro español* (1763), quoted by Parker, p. 24.

[17] Marcelino Menéndez Pelayo, *Calderón y su teatro* (Buenos Aires: Emecé Editores, S. A., 1912), pp. 81-128.

through the Church until as late as the nineteenth century, the parable has traditionally been interpreted allegorically. Thus, the parable itself has come to be considered as allegory. The eminent German biblical exegete, Joachim Jeremias, attributes the allegorical trend in parable interpretation to four major factors.[18] First, Jeremias points to the Hellenistic world and the Greeks' fondness of interpreting the myths as vehicles of esoteric knowledge.[19] Secondly, the evangelists themselves tended to treat the parables of Jesus allegorically, and there are four gospel parables that have received a detailed allegorical interpretation.[20] A third factor which Jeremias lists as contributing to the allegorical interpretation of the parable is the "hardening theory." The "hardening theory" based on Mark's puzzling passage (4:11-13), proposes that Jesus used the parables with the intention of concealing in mystery his teachings from the hostile among his listeners. If Christ's parables were mysterious utterings of hidden meaning and concealed truths, then it is understandable how the parables became fertile fields ready to be tilled and cultivated by the individual exegete, who wished to reap their hidden fruit. Finally, Jeremias offers as the fourth reason that enhanced the allegorical mode of parable interpretation, "the Primitive Church." The parables "lived" in the very early Church and were the content of missionary activities and assemblies. The Church freely collected and arranged the parables according to subject material for catechetical instruction.

Coming after the apostles and forming part of the "Primitive Church" of which Jeremias speaks, the Church fathers nurtured the young institution through its tumultuous first five centuries of life. No single force did more to implant the allegorical approach

---

[18] Joachim Jeremias, *Die Gleichnisse Jesu* (Zurich, 1954). In the present study, references come from the English translation by S. H. Hooke, *The Parables of Jesus* (New York: Charles Scribner's Sons, 1962). See especially pages 13-23.

[19] For an excellent account of the Hellenistic influences on Christian scriptural interpretation, see Richard P. C. Hanson, *Allegory and Event: A Study of the Sources and Significance of Origen's Interpretation of Scripture* (Richmond, Virginia: John Knox Press, 1959), pp. 9-97.

[20] The four parables are: the Parable of the Weeds (Math., 13:37-43); the Parable of the Net (Math., 13:49-50); the Parable of the Sower (Mark, 4:14-20); and the Parable of the Good Shepherd (John, 10:7-18).

deep in the heart of scriptural studies than did the early Church fathers, particularly those of the influential Alexandrian school. Men such as Irenaeus (c. 130-c. 200), Tertulian (160-220), Clement (150-215), and Augustine (354-430), zealously followed in the footsteps of the Greek philosopher, Philo of Alexandria, "whose allegorizing ingenuity in the first century B. C. enabled him to reconcile the faith of Israel with Greek philosophy." [21] Although opposed by the Antiochene school lead by its greatest proponent, John Chrysostom (347-407), the Alexandrian tradition with its reverence for allegory prevailed over the good sense of the Antiochene.

One man stands out among the fathers of the Alexandrian school — Origen (185-254). Origen devised an elaborate theory of scriptural interpretation whereby he held that scripture contained three senses. Just as man has a body, a soul, and a spirit, so scripture has a literal meaning, a moral one, and a spiritual one. [22] Take as an example the mustard seed of the Gospel parable (Math. 13:31). According to Origen, the literal sense is obviously the grain of mustard. On the moral level the mustard seed means faith and on the spiritual, the kingdom of God. [23]

If Valbuena Prat and Alexander Parker succeeded in redefining the nature of the *auto sacramental* in terms of the "hecho literario" instead of the "hecho histórico," Adolf Jülicher threw new light on the essence of the Gospel parable by unequivocally rejecting the traditional allegorical method of scriptural exegesis. Jülicher maintained that the parables were not vehicles of esoteric mysteries but rather "were designed for immediate effect, products of the moment, and deeply rooted in the peculiarity of the moment." [24] C. H. Dodd and A. T. Cadoux continued the work of the German scholar by also rejecting allegory as a basis for

---

[21] For a brief but excellent account of the history of biblical interpretation, see Archer M. Hunter, *Interpreting the Parables* (London: SCM Press Ltd., 1960), pp. 21-41.

[22] For the best study of Origen's theory of scriptural interpretation, see Hanson.

[23] Hunter, 25.

[24] Adolf Jülicher, *Die Gleichnisreden Jesu* (2 vols.; Tubingen, 1899), I, 91. Quoted by Geraiant Vaughan Jones, *The Art and Truth of the Parables: A Study in Their Literary Form and Modern Interpretation* (London: S. P. C. K., 1964), p. 17.

the parable and by attempting to study the parable in its original form.[25] Dodd states in this manner the problem that confronts the exegete:

> The task of the interpreter of the parables is to find out, if he can, the setting of a parable in the situation contemplated by the Gospels and hence the application which would suggest itself to one who stood in the situation.[26]

The "form critics" believed that before they attempted an interpretation of the parable, they first had to divorce themselves from allegorical tradition and had to discover the original form of the parable passage by tracing its history and development. In proposing to arrive at the parables' original form, they set before themselves a formidable task. For besides allegory they faced the problems of semantics and translations, the oriental love of embellishment and exaggeration, the addition of nature stories and folkloric themes, etc.[27]

In rejecting the allegorical method of interpreting the parable and in searching for the original scriptural passage, the "form critics" denied any belief that the parable in its essential form is allegory. For them, the parable is closely akin to the analogy and is a simile or comparison rather than a metaphor. However, in their discussions and definitions of the nature of the parable, the "form critics" very often did not understand what was meant by the various figures of speech and thus they intermingled ideas and terminology. For example, Dodd seems to equate metaphor and simile when he states that "at its simplest the parable is metaphor or simile drawn from the nature of common life."[28] Denzer also inadvertently expresses the same confusion of metaphor and simile when he says that "an allegory ... is a succession of metaphors or unexpressed comparisons."[29] As one scholar has

---

[25] Charles H. Dodd, *The Parables of the Kingdom* (New York: Scribners' Sons, 1961) and A. T. Cadoux, *Parables of Jesus: Their Art and Use* (London: James Clarke and Co., 1931).

[26] Dodd, 14. See also pp. 1-20 for Dodd's rejection of the allegorical method of parable interpretation.

[27] Jeremias, 23-103.

[28] Dodd, 5.

[29] George A. Denzer, *The Parables of the Kingdom: A Presentation and Defense of the Absolute Mercy Theory of the Kingdom Parables with a*

pointed out, "much academic argument about whether or not the parables are allegories would have been unnecessary if those engaged in it had been men of letters or philosophers of art rather than, or as well as, theologians...."[30]

What then are the two basic elements that differentiate the parable from the other figures of speech and cause it to be essentially unlike allegory? Geraiant Vaughan Jones, who studies the parable in its literary aspects, makes this distinction between similitude and allegory:

> The difference between similitude and allegory is that the latter does not, as it were, set one thing by the side of another but substitutes one thing for another. It must be interpreted point by point, and every symbol must represent something else and must occupy its place in a coherent pattern. It is a kind of code. A fable is not allegory; the dog is a dog, the bridge is a bridge, the stream is a stream, and the bone is a bone. None of these symbols stand for anything else. The dog does not represent a certain kind of person any more than the bone represents any particular desirable object. It is the story as a whole that enforces the point.[31]

A. M. Hunter singles out a second basic factor that differentiates the parable and the allegory:

> Parable must be "life-like" — must hold a mirror up to life. By contrast the allegory, need not conform to the laws of "life-likeness" and probability and may stray off into "never-never" world where eagles can plant vines and stars become bulls.[32]

Although the *auto sacramental* and the parable have distinct natures in that they are different figures of speech, nevertheless, they share the same objective, that of imparting a religious or

---

Review and Criticism of Modern Catholic Opinion (Washington, D. C.: The Catholic University of America Press, 1945), p. 8.

[30] Jones, 108.

[31] *Ibid.*, p. 88.

[32] Hunter, 10. Also see A. Berkeley Mickelsen's graphic listing of six other points that differentiate the simile and parable from the metaphor and allegory in his *Interpreting the Bible* (Grand Rapids, Michigan: Eerdman's, 1963), pp. 213 and 230.

moral truth. From the time of Lope de Vega, the *auto* has always been written "a honor y gloria del pan." [33] Lope saw the *auto* mainly as an instrument for the instruction of theology and the explanation of matters of faith especially with regard to the Sacrament. Calderón de la Barca, who was even more aware than Lope of the didactic value of the sacramental drama, called his religious masterpieces, as was stated above — "sermones puestos en verso." [34] Calderón believed that a sermon acted possesses greater didactic value than a sermon preached:

>   ... perciben menos
> los oídos que los ojos... [35]
> ... ...
> ... no tiene el oirlo
> la fuerza que tendrá el verlo. [36]

Even though Lope de Vega, Calderón de la Barca, and the other *auto* dramatists intended to instruct the people with their one-act sacramental plays, did the Spaniard in the street grasp the message veiled in the allegory? Recent scholars of the *auto* unanimously agree that those who watched the plays understood the allegorical action unfolding before them. In an article on Calderón and his symbolic theater, W. J. Entwistle says that the debates in the universities, particularly at Salamanca, the sermons heard from the pulpits, and the passionate theological discussions in vogue at the time — all aided in familiarizing the Spaniard with the themes dramatized in the *autos*. [37] Moreover, Parker feels

---

[33] Lope de Vega, *Loa entre un villano y una labradora* in *Obras de Lope de Vega publicadas por la Real Academia Española* (13 vols.; Madrid: Sucesores de Rivadeneyra, 1890-1902), Vol. II, p. 141. This is the edition from which subsequent passages will be cited, hereafter referred to as "*Obras*...."

[34] See above, p. 17.

[35] Calderón de la Barca, *Las espigas de Ruth* in *Obras*..., Vol. III, p. 1089. Quoted also in Parker, p. 66.

[36] Calderón de la Barca, *Sueños hay que verdad son* in *Obras*..., Vol. III, p. 1213. Quoted also in Parker, p. 66.

[37] W. J. Entwistle, "Calderón et le théâtre symbolique," *Bulletin Hispanique*, LII (1950), 48. See also Ángel Valbuena Prat, "Los autos calderonianos en el ambiente teológico español," *Clavileño*, No. 15 (May-June, 1952), 33-35; Arturo M. Cayuela, "Los autos sacramentales de Lope de Vega, reflejo de la cultura religiosa del poeta y su tiempo," *Razón y Fe*, CVIII (1935), pp. 168-190 and pp. 330-349.

that the popularity of the *auto* after Calderón's death proved substantially that the ordinary Spaniard understood the allegory:

> The public taste demanded performance of his [Calderon's] *autos* during eighty years — after these plays had forfeited the esteem of the "intellectuals" — and would have demanded them for longer still.[38]

Finally, in his study of the Spanish Medieval allegory, Chandler A. Post affords, perhaps, the best explanation of the Spaniards' ability to comprehend the *auto sacramental* when he illustrates that allegory and the allegorical mode have always been deeply rooted in Spanish society even in the early Middle Ages.[39]

No one has yet questioned the didactic purpose of the Gospel parable. Like the *autos sacramentales*, the parables were little sermons which conveyed religious and moral truths. Christ used as the basis of his parables the everyday experiences of agriculture and production, trees and their fruits, domestic and family life, the business world, employment practices and capital investments.[40] It will be remembered that one of the essential qualities of the parable is that it be "life-like."[41]

Just as in the discussion of the didactic purpose of the *auto sacramental* the question was raised as to whether or not the Spaniards really understood the play's allegory, so, in speaking of the parable, a problem arises that threatens the parable's didactic purpose. Actually, the problem is not whether Christ uttered the parable in order to teach, but rather did he have in mind the instruction of only a few chosen ones, his apostles and a select group of his disciples. The passage in question is that of Mark (4: 11-13) in which Jesus speaks to his apostles about the purpose of his parables:

> To you it is given to know the mystery of the kingdom of God; but to those outside, all things are treated in parables, that "Seeing they may see, but not perceive;

---

[38] Parker, 13.

[39] See Post's book, *Medieval Spanish Allegory* (Cambridge: Harvard University Press, 1915). For further discussion of Post's position with regard to allegory in medieval Spanish society, see below, p. 26.

[40] Mickelsen, 219.

[41] See above, p. 22.

and hearing they may hear but not understand; lest perhaps at any time they should be converted, and their sins forgiven them." [42]

Those who interpret the above passage according to its most literal significance, that Jesus purposely hardened men's hearts by concealing his truths in mystery, belong to that school of exegetes who propound the "hardening theory." Scholars who accept the "hardening theory" explain that Jesus did, in fact, keep some from grasping the true meaning of the parable either because, in his divine justice, he wished to punish them for their rejection and disbelief, or because, in his divine mercy, he knew that they were not yet ready to comprehend the mysteries within the parable and thus he wanted to spare them unnecessary difficulties later, "lest perhaps they be converted." [43] Another group of biblical scholars accepts the "hardening theory" as an explanation for the passage of Mark but shifts the effect of the passage from a clause of purpose to a clause of consequence. They maintain that, because the unbeliever did not understand or know Christ, he therefore did not and could not understand the parables which then had an effect of hardening him. Though the parables of themselves were clear and dealt with familiar and ordinary things, they were obscure only to those who previously were blinded by their hostility. [44]

Other biblical exegetes, particularly the "form critics," completely reject the "hardening theory." They maintain that the theory is at complete variance with the ministry of Christ and that it is inconceivable that a great pedagogue would have consciously concealed from any of his hearers a single truth. Using as a basis for their conclusions language study and stylistics, the "form critics" explain the crucial passage in Mark by denying completely that Christ had ever spoken it. Jülicher attributes the passage to

---

[42] All quotations from the Bible found in this study are taken from *The Holy Bible* (New York: Benziger Brothers, Inc., 1961).

[43] For an example of one who accepts the "hardening theory" and sees in it God's punishment see Leopold Fonck, S. J., *The Parables of the Gospel*, trans. from German by E. Leahy (Ratisbon: Frederick Pustet and Co., 1915), p. 15. For an explanation based on God's divine mercy see Denzer's work already cited.

[44] Denzer, 7.

the evangelist himself who misinterpreted Christ's words or misunderstood Christ's explanation of why he spoke in parables.[45] Dodd, as well as Jeremias, maintains that the passage shows no internal evidence that it was written by the evangelist and, therefore, it probably does not contain the words of Jesus.[46] The work of the more recent biblical exegetes such as that of the "form critics," not only eliminates the problem posed by the "hardening theory" but also casts doubt on the validity of Mark's passage itself, and thus reaffirms the didactic purpose of the parable.

As a medium of religious instruction, both the *auto sacramental* and the parable have corresponding precedents in their respective cultures. Allegory, which is the very core of the *auto sacramental*, has always been regarded by the classical rhetoricians as a trope containing a doctrinal truth and has come to be known traditionally for its hortatory and prosaic qualities.[47] Commenting on the early allegorical tradition, Chandler Post in his study of Medieval Spanish allegory states:

> The tendency to allegorize is as deep rooted in the Iberian Peninsula as in any other district of Europe, nay more so, if priority in time is of any significance, for the first Christian manifestation of allegory as the setting of the whole composition is the achievement of Prudentius.[48]

Spanish sculpture and art, street decorations and many other civil and religious monuments testify to the Spaniards' love for allegory. Speaking more directly of the natural bond that existed between the Eucharistic drama and the allegorically minded Spaniard of the Renaissance, Flecniakoska states:

> Un théâtre allégorique ne détonne donc pas dans une société où l'allégorie trouve sa place dans les diverses manifestations de l'art et de la vie civile et religieuse.[49]

---

[45] Jülicher, I, 146-148.
[46] Dodd, 8. See also Jeremias, pp. 64-68.
[47] Edwin Honig, *Dark Conceit: The Making of Allegory* (New York: Oxford University Press, 1966), p. 4.
[48] Post, 15.
[49] Fleckniakoska, 394.

Flecniakoska also devotes an entire chapter in his book to the study of the "poesía a lo divino" and another chapter to the "théâtre de collèges des jésuites" to show that allegory persisted in these two genres which later influenced the *auto*. [50]

The parable, as a mode of teaching, also appears deeply rooted in past tradition. The Jewish writers of the Bible were extremely fond of figurative language and employed it profusely for its instructive value. The parable descends directly from an earlier form in Hebrew literature known as the *mâshal*. The term, *mâshal*, as found in the Old Testament particularly in the Book of Proverbs, encompasses a much broader significance than just a parable. The *mâshal* includes within the scope of its definition not only parable but also metaphor, riddle, satire, canticle, maxim, paradox, and other figurative sayings. [51] This multiple nature of the Jewish *mâshal* from which the parable comes, helped to confuse those who searched for the parable's essential significance. [52]

There arises from the discussion of the didacticism of the *auto sacramental* and the parable still another consideration. Both the sacramental drama and Christ's similitudes were said to be used as weapons against the enemy. Lope de Vega, for example, stated that he wrote the *auto* for the "confusión de la herejía y gloria de la fe." [53] Traditional scholars of the Spanish allegorical drama concur that the *auto* was "una arma de combate." González Ruiz's words serve as an apt example of this traditional point of view:

> La trinchera teatral del gran combate que capitanea San Ignacio de Loyola, la defienden Lope y Calderón. El auge del auto sacramental es una faceta brillantísima de la lucha española contra la herejía protestante. Es una forma literaria y artística de la más rotunda afirmación. [54]

---

[50] *Ibid.*, pp. 159-312.
[51] Fonck, 14-16. See also Jeremias, pp. 52-79.
[52] See above, p. 21.
[53] Lope de Vega, *Loa entre un villano y una labradora* in *Obras...*, Vol. II, p. 141.
[54] González Ruiz, prologue to his *Piezas maestras...*, I, 21-22. See also his article "El auto sacramental, martillo y espada" in *Teatro* (March, 1953), No. 5, pp. 47-48.

While studying Calderón, Entwistle became so convinced that the *auto* was used as a weapon that he concluded by saying most of the Calderonian sacramental dramas were "generalmente dirigidos contra alguien." Entwistle saw in each of the Calderonian *autos* an expression of the author's threefold article of faith — "Creo en Dios, humanado, sacramentado." Each of Calderón's *autos* in effect constitutes an attack against the three chief opponents of the Church, the Gentiles who deny the one true God by worshipping many, the Jews who refuse to accept the incarnate Messiah, and the Protestants who overlook the important doctrine of transubstantiation, the basis of the Eucharist.[55]

Some critics reject the traditional idea of the *autos sacramentales* as defensive weapons in favor of a more positive approach.[56] More in keeping with the didactic purpose of the sacramental play, they hold that the *autos* do not defend the Eucharist and the other Catholic doctrines by directly attacking the Protestant heresies; but rather they afford another opportunity to instruct the *vulgo* in their religion. Thus, the *autos sacramentales* became for these critics an open manifestation of reform within the Church itself that actually started long before the Protestant Revolt.[57] The *auto* was not a negative weapon to be used against the Protestant Revolt but rather a positive instrument of Catholic Reform — a mode of instruction.

With regard to the parable and its use as a weapon, there occurred this same transformation from the negative approach to the more positive. Those who upheld the "hardening theory" believed that Christ uttered the parables in defense against the hostile Jews who were always ready to condemn him. This negative approach was rejected in favor of the more positive one by those who viewed the parable not as a weapon that concealed

---

[55] William J. Entwistle, "La controversia en los autos de Calderón," *NRFH*, II (July-September, 1948), 223-238. See also Beryl Smalley, who sees "allegory as a weapon in polemic with the antagonists of Christianity and in controversy among Christians at a time when the Church was still persecuted and her dogmas still fluid," in *The Study of the Bible in the Middle Ages* (Notre Dame, Indiana: University of Notre Dame Press, 1964), p. 9.

[56] Wardropper, *Introducción al teatro*..., pp. 110-118. See also, Marcel Bataillon, "Essai d'explication de l'auto sacramental," *Bulletin Hispanique*, XLII, No. 3 (1940), 193-212.

[57] Wardropper, *Introducción al teatro*..., p. 115.

hidden meaning but as a figure of speech having "the character of an argument, in that it entices the hearer to a judgement upon the situation depicted, and then challenges him, directly by implication, to apply that judgement to the matter at hand." [58] Occasionally, when the parable does not involve self-criticism, it is an extempore rebuke by which the one rebuked receives the point in the parabolic material. In short, the parables were not "undisguised condemnations or attacks, but, nevertheless sufficiently pertinent to make those for whom they were intended apply them, even if resentfully or reluctantly, to themselves." [59]

Having reviewed the nature and purpose of the *auto sacramental* and the parable at some length it is interesting to note that some have challenged the artistic and aesthetic value of these two literary genres on the very basis of their figurative nature or their didactic purpose.

Although some scholars have based their objections on the *auto*'s didacticism, [60] the *auto sacramental*, as drama, has been attacked most often because of its allegorical nature. Nicolás González Ruiz has stated that "el auto sacramental era casi una parte de la leyenda negra." [61] Certainly González Ruiz's statement proves to be true of eighteenth-century Spain when the Neoclassicists chastized the sacramental drama for its "metáforas violentas y anacronismos horribles." [62] The same members of the eighteenth century school of *buen gusto* also objected to the mixing of "lo sagrado con lo profano" and bitterly opposed religion on the stage.

Perhaps the most surprising opposition to the worth of the sacramental plays as drama came from the eminent and influential Menéndez Pelayo. [63] When confronted with the question, "si lo

---

[58] Dodd, 11.
[59] Jones, 114.
[60] Gerald Brenan compares the *zarzuela* and the *auto* and concludes that "the *auto* has, therefore, a much stricter and more intellectual form and contains as a rule more argument and less 'poetry' " (*The Literature of the Spanish People* [Cambridge: The University Press, 1951], p. 297).
[61] González Ruiz, prologue to his *Piezas maestras*..., p. 21.
[62] See above, p. 18.
[63] Bruce W. Wardropper states that Menéndez Pelayo was highly eclectic as a critic and favored the order and unity promulgated by the Neoclassicists. See his article, "Menéndez Pelayo on Calderon," *Criticism*, VII, No. 4 (1965), pp. 363-372.

sobrenatural, lo invisible, y con mucha mayor razón las abstracciones, las personificaciones morales, las ideas puras, los atributos divinos, las pasiones en abstracto, las virtudes, y los vicios, etc., caben en el arte?" Menéndez Pelayo answered, "el arte no puede limitarse a lo humano, ni mucho menos, a lo plástico, y figurativo." [64] But when Menéndez Pelayo asked himself whether or not the abstractions and personifications are within the realm of drama, he replied:

> Casi me atrevería a contestar que no. La dramática, tal como todas las escuelas la han entendido, tal como ha aparecido en todos los teatros y en todas las civilizaciones del mundo vive de pasiones, de afectos, de caracteres humanos; no es más que la vida humana en acción y en espectáculo. Construir un drama con figuras simbólicas, construir un drama con personajes abstractos, es un verdadero alarde de ingenio, perdonable solo a título de excepción y singularidad. [65]

Although not to the same extent as with the *auto sacramental*, the artistic value of the parable has also come under attack, not so much because of its figurative nature as because of its didactic purpose. A. T. Cadoux affords a splendid example of the criticism leveled against the artistic value of the parable because of its pedagogic function:

> It is not art in the highest form, because it is harnessed for service and conflict. The parables of Jesus are the work of an artist devoting himself to the answer of demands more humanly imperative than the call of beauty. [66]

Joachim Jeremias also balittles the parables as literature because they correct, reprove, and attack, and "they are not, therefore, primarily literary productions." [67]

What can be said of these objections against the *auto sacramental* and the Gospel parable? One only has to refer to the

---

[64] Menéndez Pelayo, 84-85.
[65] Menéndez Pelayo, 84-85. Bonilla y San Martín also doubts that allegory makes drama. See his *Las Bacantes o del origen del teatro* (Madrid: Rivadeneyra, 1921), pp. 117-118.
[66] Cadoux, 11.
[67] Jeremias, 21.

modern studies so often cited in this chapter. With regard to the sacramental play, Parker, in answer to the objections of the Neoclassicists and the denial of Menéndez Pelayo of the allegory's place in drama, discusses the dramatic function of the *auto's* allegory in which "there can be thus (*pace* Moratín) no question of historical anachronisms." [68] It will also be remembered that Parker observed the close bond between the sacramental plays and the liturgy and thus convincingly answered the eighteenth century criticism against the dramatization and instruction of religion on the stage which was then accustomed to "corregir las costumbres ridiculizándolas." [69]

Because most biblical scholars have been interested in the theology of the parable, few have studied the parable as literature. One who did, however, is Geraiant Vaughan Jones. [70] He elaborated on the didactic value of the parable and emphasized the remarkable gift of imagination and extemporization of the parable's narrator. He speaks of the parable's structure and balance and of its technique. One such technique is the shock effect of improbable traits, such as those who accept the wedding invitation from the king and then fail to come, or the employer who hires laborers at different hours and then pays them equal wages. It is the improbable trait in the parable that drives its meaning home. Still another of the techniques found in the parable and discussed by Jones is the parable's ability to obtain the approving interest of the listener until the tables are turned on him. In his book, Jones also calls the parable a *comedie humaine* in which the characters, as the Prodigal Son and the Good Samaritan, become so "alive" and familiar that they are no longer fictitious, but living characters, much in the manner of Don Quixote or Sancho Panza. "The parables, as the most characteristic method of teaching and disputation practised by Jesus, are a particular kind of literary genre." [71]

---

[68] Parker, 76. See also, especially, pp. 58-109, for a discussion of the *auto* as drama in which all of the problems concerning the Spanish sacramental plays are treated.

[69] See above, p. 18.

[70] See especially Jones, pp. 110-132. Also Colman Barry, "The Literary and Artistic Beauty of Christ's Parables," *Catholic Biblical Quarterly*, X (1948), 376-383.

[71] Jones, 57.

This first chapter has discussed at length the nature and purpose of the *auto sacramental* and the Gospel parable. Subsequent chapters will explore those one-act religious dramas of the sixteenth and seventeenth century Spanish literature which dramatize one or the other of the New Testament parables. The actual number of parable *autos* is relatively small. Furthermore, there are only ten of the numerous parables found in the Gospels that serve as the theme for the sacramental dramas. The task of studying the parable *autos* is simplified by dividing them into two groups, those dealing of the "kingdom parables" and those that do not, the "non-kingdom parables." The "kingdom parables" are those parables that have been interpreted by scriptural scholars as allegorically representing God's celestial kingdom, Heaven, or his earthly kingdom, the Church. Although scholars are not in agreement as to which of the Gospel parables belong to the class designated as the "kingdom parables," most all would agree that at least such parables as the Parable of the Weeds (Math., 13:24-30), the Parable of the Sower (Math., 13:3-25), the Parable of the Vinedressers (Math., 21:33-46), the Parable of the Laborers in the Vineyard (Math., 20:1-16), the Parable of the Great Supper (Math., 22:1-14), the Parable of the Treasure and the Pearl (Math., 13:44-46) all undoubtedly belong to the "kingdom parables." [72]

---

[72] Fonck in his *The Parables of the Gospel* approaches his entire study from the point of view that all the Gospel parables may be considered at least indirectly as treating of God's kingdom to come. Fonck thus considers all parables as "kingdom parables." Other books that study some or all of the parables from the point of view of "the kingdom" are: R. Knox, *The Mystery of the Kingdom* (London, 1937); G. C. Morgan, *The Parables of the Kingdom* (New York: Fleming H. Revell Company, 1907); Franz M. Moschner, *The Kingdom of Heaven in the Parables* (St. Louis: B. Herder, 1960); Dodd, *op. cit.* (above, note 25).

CHAPTER II

THE NON-KINGDOM PARABLE *AUTOS*

Before studying the non-kingdom parable *autos* set aside for this chapter and in order to better understand how the Gospel parable became ready material for the *auto* dramatist, it is well to recall briefly certain conclusions that came to light in the introductory chapter. With regard to the nature of the parable, it will be remembered that the modern and contemporary scholars beginning with Jülicher, Dodd and the rest of the form critics, have come to consider the Gospel parable as something other than allegory, namely analogy and simile. However, in the consideration of the parable *auto* what is important and what must now be stressed is that, until the very late nineteenth century with the coming of Jülicher, scriptural scholars continued to view the parable according to the traditional allegorical mode inherited from the early Church, especially the Alexandrian school. Indeed, in the sixteenth and seventeenth centuries while all of Europe was involved in the intellectual currents of the Renaissance, the Protestant Revolt, and the Reformation, the traditional method of scriptural interpretation of the Middle Ages somehow miraculously triumphed in spite of the fact that "the spirit of the Reformation is diametrically opposed to the authoritative interpretation of the Bible" and that great reformers such as Luther, Calvin, Wycliff, and others gave new impetus to scriptural interpretation based on "the plain and more obvious meaning of Scripture." [1] While

---

[1] Robert M. Grant, *The Bible in the Church* (New York: MacMillan Co., 1954), p. 109.

the Protestant reformers were intent upon arriving at a more precise interpretation of Scripture, they so strove to fit Scripture into their predisposed article of faith that "in theory every man now became, with the Holy Spirit's help, his own interpreter of Holy Writ."[2] Scriptural scholars such as Erasmus and other humanists who valued the classical and reverenced the traditional authorities defended the allegorical method of biblical exegesis.[3] During this same period, Spain, aware of her role as the great defender of the faith, deviated little from the traditional norm of scriptural interpretation.[4]

In an attempt to arrive at a better comprehension of why the *auto* dramatists found the parables good subject matter for their dramas, two other conclusions from the first chapter must be kept in mind, namely that the essence of the *auto sacramental* lies in its allegorical nature and that the Spanish people, through their culture, were orientated to accept allegory and symbolism as a way of life.[5] In spite of the fact that the Bible was interpreted figuratively in Spain as in the rest of Europe, nevertheless it was readily understood by the Spanish people who were acquainted with the traditional scriptural interpretations.[6] Writing of Calderón's frequent and often subtle allusions to the Bible, Sebastián Bartrina states: "Calderón pudo obrar así porque sus contemporáneos conocían la Biblia y cogían enseguida las alusiones vaporosas y sutiles."[7] Flecniakoska finds the ancient Alexandrian mode

---

[2] Hunter, 31.

[3] Grant, 120-21.

[4] The Jesuit Juan de Maldonado (1533-1583) comments on the allegorical interpretation of the Prodigal Son Parable which is especially useful "predicando al pueblo sencillo y creyente" (*Comentarios a los cuatro evangelios* [3 vols.; "Biblioteca de Autores Cristianos"; Madrid: La Editorial Católica, S. A., 1954-1956], Vol. II, p. 670). Although Maldonado admits the usefulness of allegory in preaching and although he presents in his commentaries the various interpretations of the Church fathers, he constantly warns against over-allegorization. For an example of Maldonado's admonition against too much allegory in scriptural interpretation see Vol. I, p. 761.

[5] See Chapter I of this study, p. 26.

[6] Juan Antonio Monroy has an excellent chapter in which he shows that, in spite of ecclesiastical sanctions, the Bible did circulate in the vernacular throughout Renaissance Spain. See his *La Biblia en el Quijote* (Madrid: Editorial V. Suárez, 1963), pp. 25-52.

[7] Sebastián Bartrina Gassiot, *La Biblia y Calderón* (Madrid: Editorial Ifiba, 1957), p. 34.

of biblical interpretation indispensable to the Spanish sacramental dramatists:

> L'allégorie *in facto* n'a pas été inventée par nos auteurs dramatiques; ils l'avaient héritée des Pères de l'Eglise sans qu'il y ait jamais eu de véritable interruption. [8]

Flecniakoska also maintains that if one is to understand the *autos sacramentales*, then one must be familiar with the allegory of the Church fathers particularly those of the Alexandrian school:

> Si nous voulons comprendre le théâtre religieux allégorique, c'est avec la méthode exégétique d'Alexandrie que nous devons l'aborder et non pas avec une âme de rhéteur. [9]

The Prodigal Son

The first group of *autos sacramentales* that merit consideration under the category of the non-kingdom parables is that dealing with the well-known biblical account of the ungrateful son who leaves father and home only to return penitent after having frivolously squandered his inherited wealth. Concerning the Parable of the Prodigal Son, Mariscal de Gante writes in his early study of the *auto sacramental*: "Es uno de los asuntos más tratados en el drama sacramental." [10] Indeed, the Prodigal Son not only enjoyed great popularity in the sacramental drama of Spain but it also appears as a frequent theme in dramatic literature throughout the rest of Europe as well. [11] In the fourth volume of his extensive collection of early *autos sacramentales*, Leo Rouanet lists and discusses dramatic pieces of various European countries that have as their basis the Parable of the Prodigal Son. [12]

---

[8] Flecniakoska, 426.
[9] *Ibid.*, p. 400.
[10] Jaime Mariscal de Gante, *Los autos sacramentales desde sus orígenes hasta mediados del siglo XVIII* (Madrid: Renacimiento, 1911), p. 124.
[11] J. P. W. Crawford, *The Spanish Drama before Lope de Vega* (Philadelphia, 1922), p. 105.
[12] Leo Rouanet, *Colección de autos, farsas, y coloquios del siglo XVI* (4 vols.; Madrid: Biblioteca Hispánica, 1901), IV, 261-68.

The Parable of the Prodigal Son serves as basis for several *autos sacramentales* found in the literature of sixteenth and seventeenth century Spain. The first and presumably the earliest of these sacramental plays, the *Aucto del hijo pródigo*, appears printed for the first time in the Rouanet collection.[13] The *auto* has the distinction of being the only one found in the entire Rouanet collection that deals with a New Testament parable. Like all of the early *autos* appearing in the four volumes of the Rouanet anthology, the *Aucto del hijo pródigo* was probably written between 1550-1575 and, like most of the *autos* in the collection, by an anonymous cleric.[14]

In their respective catalogues, Julián Paz and Alenda y Mira cite a second *auto* on the Prodigal Son appearing just before the close of the sixteenth century, Alonso Ramón's *Auto del hijo pródigo* written in 1599.[15] Although La Barrera does not mention Ramón's play, the *auto* does exist in manuscript at the Biblioteca Nacional in Madrid.[16]

Three other *autos sacramentales* dealing with the Prodigal Son appeared in the seventeenth century. Early in the 1600's, Lope de Vega wrote his *El hijo pródigo* and included it in his famous *El peregrino en su patria* published in Seville in 1604.[17] Another sacramental drama that can be dated to the early part of the seventeenth century is José Valdivielso's *Auto del hijo pródigo* first appearing in *Doze autos sacramentales* published at Toledo

---

[13] *Ibid.*, Vol. II, pp. 294-313.

[14] José María Aicardo, "Autos anteriores a Lope de Vega," *Razón y Fe*, VI (1903), 20-33.

[15] Julián Paz, *Catálogo de las piezas de teatro que se conservan en el Departamento de Manuscritos de la Biblioteca Nacional* (2 vols.; Madrid: Blass, S. A., 1934-35), I, 252; Jenaro Alenda y Mira, "Catálogo de autos sacramentales historiales y alegóricos," *Boletín de la Real Academia Española*, V (1918), 105.

[16] Cayetano Alberto de la Barrera y Leirado, *Catálogo bibliográfico y biográfico del teatro antiguo español desde sus orígenes hasta mediados del siglo XVIII* (Madrid: M. Rivadeneyra, 1860). For the complete bibliographical data on the manuscript see Flecniakoska, p. 484.

[17] Lope's *auto* is more readily available in the Academia edition, *Obras...*, Vol. II, pp. 55-71. All quotations appearing in this study on Lope's *Pródigo* are taken from this edition.

in 1622.[18] Although it is true that Valdivielso could have written his *auto* anytime before its initial publication in 1622, an allusion in the drama to Sancho of Cervantes' *Quijote* fairly well establishes that Valdivielso must have penned his play sometime after 1605, the date of Cervantes' first edition of his masterpiece.[19]

A third *auto* dealing with the Prodigal Son must also have appeared in the middle of the seventeenth century. La Barrera and Alenda make reference to an *auto* by Manuel Vidal Salvador, *El hijo pródigo*.[20] Neither La Barrera nor Alenda provide the bibliographical and descriptive data that usually accompanies their listings. La Barrera only mentions that Vidal Salvador's *auto* follows the earlier plays of Lope and Valdivielso on the Prodigal. In an earlier section of La Barrera's catalogue, one finds a brief biography of Vidal Salvador in which the date of the latter's death is listed as 1698.[21]

Because the *Auto del hijo pródigo* written by Alonso Ramón in 1599 resembles its predecessor, the anonymous *auto* of the Rouanet edition, and because I have been unable to locate any copies of Vidal Salvador's drama on the Prodigal, the following study will be limited to a discussion of the anonymous Rouanet *auto* and of those by Lope and Valdivielso.

In the case of all three *autos*, the anonymous *Aucto del hijo pródigo* in Rouanet, the *Pródigo* of Lope and that of Valdivielso, critics have noted and stressed their rigid adherence to the biblical story. Speaking generally of all the *autos* in the Rouanet collection, José María Aicardo maintains that the anonymous clerics were exact in portraying the biblical accounts in their religious dramas.[22] Commenting specifically of Lope's *El hijo pródigo*, Marcelino Menéndez Pelayo not only shows how Lope faithfully followed the scriptural account but also states that because Lope did so he failed to capture the human aspect of the parable as well as

---

[18] The *auto* is more readily available in Pedroso's collection, *Los autos sacramentales desde...*, pp. 216-30. All quotations appearing in this study on Valdivielso's *Pródigo* come from Pedroso's edition.
[19] See Pedroso's footnote to his edition of Valdivielso's *auto*, p. 222.
[20] La Barrera y Leirado, 596; Alenda y Mira, *Boletín de la Real Academia Española*, V, 105.
[21] La Barrera y Leirado, 476-77.
[22] Aicardo, "Autos anteriores...," *Razón y Fe*, VI, 29-30.

did Luis Miranda in his full-length *comedia*.[23] In his study on the *auto sacramental* before Calderón, Bruce Wardropper states that Valdivielso so religiously tried to follow the Gospel story that he failed to make any concessions whatsoever in his drama:

> El fin primordial de Valdivielso en este *auto* ha sido reproducir alegóricamente la línea general de la parábola sin omitir nada: el cuento de Jesucristo le fue tan sagrado que no concebía variación por motivos dramáticos.[24]

Admittedly, the three *autos* under discussion basically dramatize the main parts of the Gospel parable. All three *autos* depict the ungrateful son asking from his tearful and admonishing father his inheritance, the Prodigal's frivolous squandering and total loss of his acquired wealth, his subsequent struggle to survive by begging the job of a lowly swineherd and, finally, the son's repentance and return to his awaiting father who willingly forgives in spite of the envy of his older son, the Prodigal's brother. Nevertheless, I cannot agree without reservation with Aicardo, Menéndez Pelayo, and Wardropper, who overstate their case. Although they are right in assuming that the *auto* writers on the Prodigal did dramatize the main parts of the Gospel story, the above critics are misleading when they fail to point out adequately the many significant variations from the Gospel story present in the Prodigal *autos*. The discussion that follows will demonstrate how the anonymous writer of the Rouanet *auto*, Lope de Vega, and Valdivielso deviated from the Gospel story in their sacramental plays by expanding upon incidents as well as characters and how these innovations reflect varying approaches and points of view of the same New Testament parable.

In the early *Aucto del hijo pródigo*, found in the Rouanet edition, the unknown author introduces two incidents very early into his drama that do not in any way relate to the biblical parable. First, the mother of the Prodigal appears in one of the

---

[23] Marcelino Menéndez Pelayo, *Estudios sobre el teatro de Lope de Vega*, edited and annotated by A. Bonilla y San Martín (Madrid: Librería General de Victoriano Suárez, 1919), I, 49. The *comedia* referred to by Menéndez Pelayo is that of Luis Miranda, *La comedia pródiga*, published in Sevilla in 1554.

[24] Wardropper, *Introducción al teatro religioso*..., p. 288.

early scenes. She is a spirited woman, who not only pleads with her son to reconsider his decision, but what is more significant, she spends a great deal of her time scolding her husband for failing to understand their son and for being too restrictive. Nowhere does Scripture mention the Prodigal's mother, nor in fact, does the evangelist mention any woman in his account. Shortly after the appearance of the Prodigal's mother, the anonymous author introduces his second innovation, a sly Portuguese dog vender who attempts to make a shady deal by selling the Prodigal some marvellous dogs that "se posen mantener/de a caniña que faran" (v. 261) and that "fazen música que e gloria" (v. 278).[25] The addition of these two innovations into the early part of the play gives the *auto* a characteristic tone of realism that is maintained throughout the entire play and that reflects the author's realistic approach to the Gospel parable. What exemplifies a true-to-life situation more than a husband and wife quarreling over the rearing and disciplining of their children? With regard to the Portuguese dog seller, he reflects the historical situation not only in his crude actions but also in his vulgar language. Commenting on the *portugués* and other similar *bobo* types characteristic of the earlier Spanish *autos*, Aicardo states, "nos ponen en contacto con el pueblo de antaño."[26] The presence in the Rouanet *auto* of such domestic and social situations has caused Flecniakoska to consider this early *auto* on the Prodigal Son a satire on the customs and luxury of the times rather than a religious drama.[27]

Besides the two very real characters of the permissive mother and the cheating dog vender, the complete absence of any truly allegorical figures enhances even more the *auto*'s realism. The Italian scholar Sorrento, commenting on this lack of allegorical figures in the Rouanet *auto* states: "I caratteri del Prodigo, del padre e della madre sono messi in opposizione con brio e verità. Non ci sono figure allegoriche."[28] It is interesting to note that

---

[25] Quotations from the anonymous *auto* on the Prodigal are taken from Rouanet, Vol. II, pp. 296-313.
[26] Aicardo, "Autos anteriores...," *Razón y Fe*, V, 323.
[27] Flecniakoska, 316.
[28] Luigi Sorrento, "I *Trionfi* del Petrarca *a lo divino* e l'allegoria religiosa negli *autos*," *Estudios eruditos in memoriam de Adolfo Bonilla y San Martín (1875-1926)* (Madrid: Imprenta Jaime Rates, 1930), II, 404-405.

Alenda in observing the absence of allegory in the Rouanet *auto* arrived at the same conclusion as did Flecniakoska with regard to the profane nature of this early sacramental play:

> Pertenecen al siglo XVI todos los personajes de esta obra: de manera que perdiendo el carácter de composición sagrada más bien parece un drama profano destinado a inculcar la lección moral de la parábola.[29]

Exactly to what extent the realistic personages of the Rouanet *auto* contrast with the allegorical figures of the Lope and of the Valdivielso *autos* on the Prodigal will become evident in subsequent discussion.

Like his anonymous predecessor, Lope de Vega, although adhering to the four principle movements of the Gospel parable, also departed from the original scriptural account in his *Hijo pródigo* published in 1604. Lope not only added new elements early into his drama but, what is of greater significance, he greatly expanded and actually emphasized the second part of the Gospel parable.

Lope's first innovation or variation of the Gospel story comes at the very beginning of his *auto*. Whereas the biblical account begins abruptly with the son requesting his share of his father's wealth (v. 12), Lope begins his drama with a discussion of the Prodigal and the extremely important allegorical figure, Juventud. The Prodigal's youth tempts him to take what is his share of his father's money and encourages him to free himself from the paternalistic fetters to which he is bound so that he may enjoy the pleasures of the world. In introducing the allegorical Juventud in conversation with the Prodigal, Lope strengthens the abrupt beginning of the parable as it is in the Gospel and makes it more dramatically suitable.

The systematic manner in which Juventud lures and entices the Prodigal in the opening scenes of Lope's play reflects how well Lope succeeds in effectively dramatizing the parable's beginning. First, Juventud reminds the Prodigal that he is getting old and that he better enjoy life while he still possesses the vigor of youth:

---

[29] Alenda y Mira, *Boletín de la Real Academia Española*, V, 104-05.

> Cuando en otra edad estés
> Sujeto a la enfermedad,
> Al tiempo, á la autoridad,
> Al gobierno, al interés,
> No podrás salir un punto
> De aquel reloj concertado
> Con que vive un hombre honrado
> Para sus gustos difunto.
> (p. 59)

Still warning the Prodigal of his waning youth, Juventud uses a slightly different approach:

> Todos disculpan á amor
> En poca edad y una vez.
> Si viejo has de andar con plumas,
> ¿No es mejor en esta edad,
> Mientras tienes mi amistad,
> Que no cuando me consumas?
> (p. 59)

Having approached the question of the Prodigal's age by appealing to his sensuality, Juventud continues by reminding the Prodigal of the rewards of being a *galán* and the joys of having mastered the art of gambling:

> Al mozo que va galán
> Codíciale la mujer,
> Á todos causa placer,
> Mil bendiciones le dan,
> Sálenle mil casamientos,
> Promete mil esperanzas,
> Halla empréstidos, fianzas,
> Convites, ofrecimientos.
> ... ...
> Juega, empresta, da barato,
> Dicen que es noble en efeto,
> Que el que da siempre es discreto,
> Si es bestia en ingenio y trato.
> (p. 59)

After arousing the Prodigal's interest in love, women, and gambling, all of which can best be enjoyed in youth, Juventud proceeds in his next and perhaps most important temptation. She assures the Prodigal that neither women, love, nor success at gambling can be had without money:

> Cuenta por muerto al mancebo
> Que sin dinero camina.
> ... ...
> Bríos sin dinero son
> Como sin fuerza el león,
> O como el ave sin alas.
> (p. 59)

The scene having been dramatically set, Lope introduces the Prodigal's father, Cristalio, whose name obviously symbolizes Christ. However, along with Cristalio, enters Invidio, the Prodigal's older brother, whose name is also symbolic. Invidio's early appearance in the story represents Lope's second departure from the original scriptural account. In Scripture as also in the Rouanet *auto*, the older son does not appear until the very end of the parable. Lope's inclusion of the Prodigal's older brother into the start of the play not only heightens the conflict of the Prodigal's dramatic departure from home but it also makes more credible the older son's role as the envious brother at the end of the parable.

Besides the two innovations of the allegorical Juventud and the early apperance of the envious brother, Lope expands and develops even more the parable's second part in which, once again, the biblical account is extremely brief: "And not many days later, the younger son gathered up his wealth, and took his journey into the far country; and there he squandered his fortune in loose living" (v. 13). In his sacramental play, Lope ramifies this brief verse of the evangelist by allegorically dramatizing how the son spent his fortune in loose living.

Exactly how Lope succeeded in dramatizing this second part of the parable story may best be seen by comparing Lope's allegorical scenes with the blunt realism of the earlier Rouanet *auto*. In the Rouanet *auto*, the Prodigal is seduced by two harlots, Platina and her sister simply known as Moça. The two women desire only the Prodigal's money and in return are willing to sell themselves. One says to the other: "Mientras durare el dinero,/

mostrármele e alaguera,/ amigable y plazentera,/ hasta que mi majadero tenga la bolsa ligera" (v. 307-11).

The two girls also speak of the Prodigal who is accustomed to sitting in at the gambling table (vv. 320-21) and who has agreed to throw a banquet in their honor (vv. 317-318), although, in fact, the audience never sees the Prodigal gamble nor witnesses the lavish banquet of which the women only speak.

In Lope's *Hijo Pródigo*, the two plotting bawds never appear but rather the author introduces a whole host of allegorical figures. The realistic *mujer* and *moça* are replaced by the abstract and figurative Lascivia and Deleite who seduce the Prodigal with the aid of the other allegorical personages such as Engaño, Lisonja, and Locura. Whereas in the Rouanet *auto* the two women only speak of the Prodigal's affection for gambling, the passion becomes alive in Lope's play in its personification, Juego.

With regard to the banquet mentioned by the two bawds in the Rouanet *auto*, Lope once again allegorically dramatizes it before the audience. Actually, the banquet scene becomes for Lope the focal point of his whole dream. Lope delights in portraying the Prodigal and Deleite as the typical *galán* and *dama* found in almost any of his secular dramas. Having partaken of the meal and imbued with the wine of *olvido*, the two lovers enjoy the fruits of love, while in the background is the ever present chanting of the *músicos*, or chorus, who not only sing the praises of love but ominously lament the Prodigal's forthcoming fate.

Lope obviously took pleasure in and was attracted to the second part of the parable, for it is not only the most expanded part of his drama but also the most poetic. Although Aicardo does not agree with my position when he says: "A mi parecer, la vida desenfrenada del Pródigo está representada con una extensión proporcionada a todo el resto del auto,"[30] I offer Lope's relatively abrupt ending to his drama as final proof that he not only preferred dramatizing the Prodigal's life away from home but actually emphasized this part of the parable story. In Lope's *auto*, the Prodigal accepts the job of a swineherd but suddenly decides he was better off before and returns to his father, who awaits him

---

[30] Aicardo, "Autos sacramentales de Lope de Vega," *Razón y Fe*, XXI (1908), 38.

with open arms. The final scenes of the play are swift and undeveloped and contrast sharply with the earlier elaborate allegorization. Lope falls short in his dramatic development exactly where the Gospel parable is most emphatic, in its last part, in which the penitent Prodigal returns to his anxious father (vv. 15-32).

Even though José Valdivielso also basically adhered to the Gospel account in his *Auto del hijo pródigo* published in 1622, like the author of the Rouanet *auto* and Lope de Vega, he also introduced certain innovations into his sacramental play that are not found in Scripture. In the earlier stages of his drama, Valdivielso patterns his sacramental play after that of Lope. Although Valdivielso begins his drama with the Prodigal immediately asking his share of the father's wealth, as does the evangelist in his Gospel, nevertheless, Valdivielso shortly thereafter introduces Juventud, who then functions much as does Lope's allegorical counterpart. Also much like Lope, Valdivielso allegorizes in great detail the Prodigal's downfall, how he is carried off into the deceiving world by his wild youth in the company of Lascivia and Olvido and how, after gambling with Juego, he becomes involved in an amorous affair and finally weds Placer. However, unlike Lope, Valdivielso does not cease to expand his allegorical dramatization with the Prodigal's downfall, but rather he continues to allegorize the Prodigal's repentance and return to his father.

Valdivielso successfully and effectively dramatized the last part of the Gospel parable exactly where Lope fell short. In Valdivielso, the Prodigal does not just suddenly become aware of his plight while tending the swine and return to his previous riches, but rather he is counseled by his conscience into acknowledging his sin and accepting final repentance. Valdivielso's introduction of a new allegorical personage, Inspiración, who constantly reminds and plagues the Prodigal to acnowledge his guilt and return penitently to the all-merciful father not only enables the author to dramatize effectively the Prodigal's mental struggle, but it also allows him to introduce important theological questions, such as the danger and gravity of the sin of despair, from which the Prodigal would have no recourse or the death of the Prodigal's sinful soul through the loss of sanctifying grace (p. 224).

Typical of the manner in which Inspiración moves the Prodigal to accept repentance and indicative of how the author allegorically dramatizes the last part of the Gospel story, is the appearance late in the *auto* of three allegorical carts. The first cart representing death comes upon the scene while Inspiración and the Prodigal are discussing the latter's desperation and his desire to die. The cart depicts a large sepulchre in which appear all types of humanity from the Pope and King down to the lowliest of humanity. While they behold the cart of death, Inspiración reflects on the Medieval theme of *ubi sunt* because everything on the cart "resuelve en la sepultura / Salud, donaire, nobleza, / Gala, gracia, gentileza, / Fuerzas, aviso, hermosura" (p. 225). The cart of death really prepares the scene for the *carro del infierno* which immediately follows it. Huge flames of fire and billows of smoke surround the cart of hell and, while they behold the terrifying scene, Inspiración reminds the Prodigal what will await him should he have his wish and die in despair. Later when the Prodigal, having served as swineherd, contemplates returning to his father but still fears to do so, Inspiración reveals to him the third cart, that of mercy. The *carro de misericordia* depicts a child affixed to a cross, above which appear four angels each holding in his hand some item symbolic of mercy. One of the angels holds a ring and another a white robe symbolic of the friendship between father and son. Still another angel carries sandals "hechas de ejemplos de los santos" (p. 288), while the fourth nestles within his arms, a calf which is to be offered in sacrifice for the remission of sin. In the Gospel story, the father bedecks his returning son with a ring, a robe, and sandals, and then offers a calf in sacrifice as thanksgiving to God for his son's return.

The role of Inspiración as the conscience and guiding light of the Prodigal as well as the appearance of the three allegorical carts of death, hell, and mercy illustrate Valdivielso's theological concern in his approach to the Gospel parable in his drama. The traditional interpretation of the Parable of the Prodigal Son by scriptural scholars has always focused upon the doctrine of repentance and forgiveness. Juan de Maldonado expresses this traditional idea of the theme of the Gospel parable in his *Comentarios a los cuatro evangelios*: "Hay en el cielo mayor gozo por un solo pecador que se convierte que por noventa y nueve justos que no necesitan convertirse." [31] Valdivielso was undoubtedly aware of the traditional viewpoint of the parable and he desired to convey it to his audience. This is why, unlike Lope, Valdivielso dramatized and actually emphasized the last part of the Gospel story in his religious play. Wardropper also observes this affection for the theme of repentance and forgiveness present in all of Valdivielso's plays as he notes a basic difference in the theological approach of Valdivielso and his eminent successor Calderón: "Si Calderón es el poeta de la Redención mediante el dogma, Valdivielso lo es mediante el arrepentimiento sincero del pecador." [32]

Besides the extensive allegorization in his drama of the last part of the Gospel story, the role and function of some of the minor characters further demonstrate José Valdivielso's theological approach to the original scriptural passage. Valdivielso's most original creation, Inspiración, has already been discussed above, especially with regard to its role as the Prodigal's conscience which encourages final repentance. However, Inspiración appears in almost every scene of the drama from its very beginning. [33] In the earlier stages of the play as the Prodigal's conscience, she is the baroque figure who accompanies the Prodigal through his journey of sin and who makes her presence felt by never uttering more than a few brief but important lines. The few lines, always baroque, have the effect of warning the Prodigal of hidden deceptions in the words and promises of his evil adversaries. For example, when Lascivia and Olvido urge the Prodigal to drink the cup of pleasure which will quench his passionate thirst, Inspiración succinctly warns: "No te podrá hartar jamás, / Pues, mientras bebieres más, / Matarás menos tu sed" (p. 220). Later, when the Prodigal speaks of the "heaven" he will possess upon giving the ring to Deleite in marriage, Inspiración reminds him that in wedding himself to Deleite he divorces himself from Heaven: "Si le das, pues del te alejas; / que el cielo das, pues le dejas, / Y al que le hizo para tí" (p. 220).

Valdivielso's treatment of the swineherd also illustrates his theological approach to the Prodigal Parable. In the Rouanet

---

[31] Maldonado, II, 648.
[32] Wardropper, *Introducción al teatro religioso* ..., p. 286.
[33] See above, p. 44.

auto, Porquero simply takes pity on the Prodigal and offers him a job tending the pigs. Lope has two swineherds in his *auto* both of whom are significantly named: Montano (mountain) who proclaims in tender poetic utterances the beauties of nature (*beatus ille*) and at the same time rejects the deceits of courtly life (*menosprecio de corte*) and Belardo whose name is significant because of its relationship to the pig he tends. Montano and Belardo when they first appear in the drama lament the fact that, because they have to divide their attention between the pigs and the sheep, they have lost some of their finest sheep to thieves and robbers. When the Prodigal later appears, they welcome him because by hiring the Prodigal for the pigs they can personally attend to the sheep which they prize more. Later, if the Prodigal proves himself worthy, he too can be privileged to watch the sheep. Montano states to his friend Belardo: "Si guarda bien, al que viene / Le doy ovejas y cabras" (p. 70). Valdivielso, like Lope, also has two swineherds, Chaparro and his master who is simply called Amo, but who clearly represents the devil. Chaparro, Amo's servant, complains of his job and threatens to leave it. Amo at first tries to dissuade him but agrees to let Chaparro go when the Prodigal enters and asks for the position. Not only does the Prodigal's conscience, Inspiración, try to warn the Prodigal of the Amo's diabolical nature but also Chaparro attempts to dissuade the Prodigal by relating to him the many miseries and unfulfilled promises that he experienced working under the Amo. In depicting this scene of the Gospel story as he does and in introducing the allegorical Amo as the devil, Valdivielso once again adheres closely to the traditional interpretation which suggests the swine to be various devils and the farm or sty as an extension of the devil's power and dwelling place.[34]

There is one final, minor character that should be mentioned in this discussion because it too reflects Valdivielso's interests in theology and his approach to the scriptural parable. As was seen above, whereas in the Rouanet *auto* the Prodigal's older brother only appears once in the drama at its very end as in the Gospel account, in Lope, the audience sees him enter early into the drama as well as at the very end. However, outside of Lope's

---

[34] For the various allegorical interpretations of the Prodigal Son Parable promulgated by the Church fathers, see Maldonado, Vol. II, pp. 648-672.

early introduction into the drama of the older son and his symbolic name of "Invidio," Lope's *hijo mayor* functions in the play much as does the counterpart in the Rouanet *auto*. In Valdivielso's *auto*, although the older son laments his plight much in the manner of the Rouanet work and that of Lope, the reader, nevertheless, is conveyed the feeling that the older son laments more the Prodigal's unjust treatment of his own father rather than the fact that his father neglected him. Note that Valdivielso did not call his *hijo mayor*, Invidio, as did Lope, but rather significantly Justino (justice). In Justino's first and only appearance outside of the expected final scene, he is seen in his father's vineyard discussing his brother with Labricio, his working friend. In this discussion, although he does envy his brother to some extent (p. 222), nevertheless, Justino is more perturbed by the fact that his younger brother could be so disrespectful to their beloved father, who has given them so many blessings. Labricio closes their discussion and the scene with these words indicative of Valdivielso's interpretation of the role of the *hijo mayor* in the parable and in his drama: "Que á los malos sus gustos / No duran, ni las penas á los justos" (p. 222). Later in the final scene, Justino again expresses his desire that justice be done rather than that his envy be satisfied. In his final discourse addressed to his father he parenthetically adds: "Pienso que cumpliendo al justo / Lo que me ordenaste de mí" (p. 230).

Before moving on to those *autos* treating of another Gospel parable, that of the Lost Sheep, which, as it will be seen, relates to the parable on the Prodigal, it is well to review briefly some of the conclusions from the discussion above. Although scholars have stressed the strict adherence of the *autos* to the original Gospel account, the authors of the Prodigal *autos* did in fact introduce new scenes and personages not found in the original scriptural tale. Further, it was observed that the innovations often reflect the author's particular approach to the parable. For example, the true-to-life incidents of the quarrelling mother and the crooked dog vender, together with the complete absence of any truly allegorical figures in the Rouanet *auto*, contrast greatly with the allegory and personifications found in the *autos* of Lope and Valdivielso and point to the author's realistic approach to the parable. However, even the two allegorical dramatizations of Lope and Valdivielso reflect differing points of view of the Gospel story. Lope, interested more in the Prodigal's adventurous escapades of love and intrigues away from home, extensively depicts the second part of the parable, and shows little interest in that part of the parable which follows. Valdivielso, on the other hand, desired to convey to the audience the theology of repentance and forgiveness and thus was attracted to the last phase of the Gospel story.

Of greater significance than the authors' varying approaches to the Gospel parable in the sacramental plays, is the role and development of some of the minor characters as seen in the three *autos*. Lope as well as Valdivielso took the two bawds of the Rouanet *auto* and developed them into a whole host of allegorical figures who acted out before the eyes of the *público* the Prodigal's downfall. With regard to two other minor characters, Hijo Mayor and Porquero, in the Rouanet *auto*, they only appear once, and they function in the manner of the Gospel figures, while in Lope and Valdivielso both the older son and the swineherd appear twice. The early appearance of the *hijo mayor* gives some insight into his character and makes his characteristic attitude at the end of the play more acceptable; and the early discussion of the two swineherds discloses to the audience exactly why they were glad to accept the Prodigal when he approached them later in the story. Finally, it came to light in the discussion above, that Lope and Valdivielso introduce important new minor characters in their sacramental plays not found in the Rouanet *auto*. Both authors present Juventud and effectively use this allegorical figure to dramatize visibly the Prodigal's inner struggle and to show why the Prodigal left his father. With his innovation of the minor character, Inspiración, who never leaves the Prodigal's side even during his sinful spree, Valdivielso goes yet another step further in dramatizing the Prodigal's inner struggle because, in every scene of the drama, Valdivielso carefully pits the two moral forces of good and evil against each other.

The Lost Sheep

Another popular theme found in the sacramental dramas of Spain is the Parable of the Lost Sheep centering about the good and loving shepherd who leaves the ninety-nine faithful of his flock and goes in search of the one lost sheep; "and when he has found it, he lays it upon his shoulder rejoicing" (Luke, 15: 5-6). The early *églogas* of Gómez Manrique, Juan del Encina, and Garcilaso de la Vega had already popularized the pastoral motif in dramatic literature, and the Parable of the Lost Sheep with its shepherds and rustic setting enabled the *auto* dramatists to manipulate an already popular theme.[35]

That I should consider the Parable of the Lost Sheep after the Parable of the Prodigal Son is appropriate, since the two parables are closely related. Not only did the evangelist include both parables within the very same chapter but both convey the identical doctrinal message of the need for repentance and forgiveness and of Christ's delight "over one sinner who repents."[36] In fact, the evangelist places a closely related third parable in with those of the Prodigal and the Lost Sheep. The third parable depicts a woman who, having lost one of her ten coins, lights up and sweeps out her house in search for the one missing drachma and who, after having found it, gathers together her neighbors and friends in celebration.[37] In his *auto* on the Prodigal studied in detail above, José Valdivielso, fully aware of the related message of the three scriptural passages, makes direct reference to all three parables within the same verse. In one of Valdivielso's last scenes, the Prodigal's father, anxiously awaiting his son's repentance and return, recalls for the audience the many times he is pictured in scripture as the forgiving Christ:

> Ya me introduce dama,
> Que la casa trastorna
> Por la perdida drama
> Que, hallada, en sí la torna;
> ... ...
> Ya un pastor represento,
> Con que á el teatro asombro,
> Viéndome entrar sangriento

---

[35] González Ruiz in his "Introducción" to *Piezas maestras*..., p. xxxvi, writes of the early *autos* on the Parable of the Lost Sheep: "Pastores, zagales, balidos de ovejas, tintineo de esquilas, canciones ingenuas, el pandero y el tamboril ... estos autos sacramentales son poco más que églogas del Nacimiento."
[36] Luke, Chapter 15.
[37] The Parable of the Lost Coin, Luke, 15: 8-10.

Con la ovejuela al hombro;
Y hoy, de un hijo perdido,
Un padre represento enternecido. (p. 229)

The first of the four *autos sacramentales* treating of the Parable of the Lost Sheep dates to the sixteenth century when it was presented in a Jesuit college at Villagarcía. The play claims no known author and bears the simple title of *Auto de la oveja perdida*. The *auto* is found in manuscript form in the *Códice de los jesuítas* and first appeared in printed form in Pedroso's collection.[38] The anonymous Villagarcía *auto* closely resembles another sixteenth century *auto* of the same name written by Juan de Timoneda. Timoneda's *Oveja perdida* first appeared in his *Ternario spiritual* of 1558 in Valencia and again in his *Ternarios sacramentales* of 1575, also in Valencia.[39] The Villagarcía *auto* and that of Timoneda so closely follows the same pattern that there has been some discussion as to which of the two *autos* can claim to be the original. At least one scholar, Soriano, has seen enough alternations in the two *autos* to conclude that "se ha de descartar, por tanto, la hipótesis de que un texto sea copia del otro, sino ambos refundiciones de un original anterior, perdido o desconocido hasta ahora."[40] Having examined and studied the two *autos* as they appear in the Pedroso edition, I frankly do not observe any substantial differences in the two dramas to warrant Soriano's conclusion. If, in fact, the two sacramental plays were substantially different from each other, this would not alone

---

[38] The manuscripts of the *Códice de los jesuítas* are housed in the Biblioteca de la Real Academia de la Historia at Madrid. Bibliographical data on the manuscript of the *Oveja perdida* is found in Flecniakoska, p. 489. The *auto* is also reproduced in footnotes to Timoneda's *auto* of the same title in Pedroso, pp. 76-88.

[39] Timoneda's *auto* is found in Pedroso who reproduces the play from a copy made of the *Ternarios* (1575) by Agustín Durán. Timoneda's play also appears in an annotated edition with introduction and glossary by Dr. D. Antonio García Boiza, *Auto de la oveja perdida* (Salamanca: M. Pérez Criado, 1921). García Boiza uses Pedroso's edition as the basis of his text "teniendo en cuenta la índole vulgarizadora de esta edición" (p. 43). The *auto* also appears in a copy from the *Ternario spiritual* (1558) in P. Félix Olmedo, "Un nuevo *Ternario* de Juan de Timoneda," *Razón y Fe*, XLVII, 483-497. References to Timoneda's play found in this study come from Pedroso's edition, pp. 76-88.

[40] Justo García Soriano, *El teatro universitario y humanístico en España* (Toledo, 1945), p. 234.

eliminate the possibility that the one written first served as model for the second, without the necessary existence of a third *auto* upon which both were based.

Lope de Vega affords two other examples of *autos sacramentales* treating of the Parable of the Lost Sheep. Lope's two *autos* are distinct from one another, the first, *El pastor lobo y la cabaña celestial*, is patterned after the Villagarcía and Timoneda *autos*.[41] Lope's second *auto*, *La oveja perdida*, is different from any of the preceding three autos on the Lost Sheep. Although the date of Lope's *La oveja perdida* is not certain, his *El pastor lobo y la cabaña celestial* was written in 1624.[42]

Since three of the four sacramental plays, the Villagarcía *auto*, Timoneda's *Oveja perdida*, and Lope's *El pastor lobo y la cabaña celestial* treat of the Lost Sheep Parable in more or less the same manner, I will discuss, first, the two identical *autos* found in Pedroso, and then I will point out important variations in Lope's *El pastor lobo*. Finally, this portion of my study will conclude by analyzing Lope's second *auto*, *La oveja perdida*, whose treatment of the Gospel parable is strikingly different from that of the other three.

The anonymous Villagarcía play and that of Timoneda not only present the same allegorical figures, but they are also identical in their dramatization of the scriptural story. Apetito (carnal desires) lures away the Oveja (the soul) from Custodio (the soul's guardian angel). Custodio goes in search of the lost sheep which by now is well down the wide and flowery path of evil. (The

---

[41] Francisco Medel del Castillo, in his *Indice general alfabético de todos los títulos de comedias que se han escrito por varios autores antiguos y modernos y de los autos sacramentales y alegóricos así de D. Pedro Calderón de la Barca como de otros autores clásicos* (Madrid: Imprenta de Alfonso de Mora, 1735, p. 132) lists the *auto*, *El pastor lobo y la cabaña celestial*, as having been written by Mira de Amescua. Emilio Cotarelo y Mori ("Mira de Amescua y su teatro" *Boletín de la Real Academia Española*, XVIII, 75) mentions Medel del Castillo's reference to an *auto* written by Mira de Amescua with the same title as Lope's *El pastor lobo* but he states that Medel del Castillo's reference is the only one he has ever found of such an *auto*. Menéndez Pelayo says that the *auto* is definitely Lope's in his "Observaciones Preliminares" to *Obras de Lope de Vega*, II, lxvii.

[42] A list of dates of some of Lope's *autos* are found in Flecniakoska's article, "Les rôles de Satan dans les *autos* de Lope de Vega", *Bulletin Hispanique*, LXVI (1964), 44.

road to hell is always depicted as wide and green in contrast to the narrow path leading to heaven always full of thorns, thistles, and sharp-piercing stones.) Custodio is joined in his search by Miguel, the archangel, San Pedro, and finally by Christ himself, Cristóbal Pascual. This heavenly troop later recovers the Oveja bound by ropes and in a state of despair and exhaustion. Both dramas end with the celestial group liberating the Oveja which Cristóbal triumphantly and rejoicingly carries off on his shoulders.

Several points of these two almost identical dramatizations of the Lost Sheep Parable merit further consideration. It will be recalled that in the anonymous *auto* found in Rouanet the two bawds only talk of seducing the Prodigal and that the audience never actually sees the seduction. So, too, in the Villagarcía *auto* and that of Timoneda, the audience never really sees dramatized before it Apetito's tempting and luring of the Oveja. In fact, the only time Apetito appears in the plays, he spends most of the time arguing with Custodio over which of them has the right to lead the sheep. Only after Apetito and Custodio finally decide in their argument that the Oveja must exercise her free will and choose between them, does the audience see Apetito make an attempt to lure the Oveja:

> Yo luego le doy que coma—
> Toma del pan: ¡re, re, re!
> Que lo futuro no asoma,
> Y al fin, fin, más vale un *toma*
> Que después dos *te daré*. (p. 80)

In this scene in which Apetito coaxes the Oveja, the Oveja is somewhere off to the side and never appears on the scene. In fact, the Oveja Perdida for whom the plays are named, never enters them as a dramatic figure. This entire scene in which Apetito appears and utters a few enticing words to an unseen figure is at best a half-hearted attempt by the authors in their respective dramas to dramatize the Oveja's temptation and fall. The authors were obviously not interested in taking advantage of the dramatic situation afforded by the temptation scene nor even concerned with portraying the Oveja, who never appears.

In contrast to the brief and undramatic portrayal of the Oveja's temptation and fall, the two early *autos* present two rather lengthy scenes, both of which are laden with theology. In the first scene, Miguel, commander-in-chief of the angelic hosts, questions Custodio about the whereabouts of the Oveja. After Custodio's explanation of what had happened and Miguel's boast of how he had once conquered his diabolic rival in a fierce and fiery battle, the two angels proceed to trace in detail the various steps the soul takes into sin.[43] The theological note having been set with the angels' discourse on sin, the following scene involves even more theology when Cristóbal Pascual appears with Peter. Cristóbal is depicted as the good shepherd, who, concerned for the welfare of his flock, establishes upon the rock of Peter his Church, in which the sheep can find refuge and shelter from the ravenous wolves and lions. In failing to capitalize on the dramatic opportunity afforded by the temptation scene and in depicting, instead, the two following scenes that center around the idea of sin and the Church's power to forgive, the authors sacrificed drama for theology.

In picturing Christ as the Good Shepherd who knows his flock and whose flock knows him (p. 83), the authors took advantage of the close affinity of the Lost Sheep parable with another parable found in the Gospel of St. John.[44] In this same scene of the two *autos* in which Cristóbal establishes his Church, the authors drew heavily from other parts of Scripture as well. Note how ingeniously the authors tied in still another pastoral theme found in the words of St. John's last chapter of his Gospel, "Feed my lambs, feed my sheep."[45] Peter receives the mandate to provide for the flock but first he has to confess his faith and love to the Master three times, the same number of times Peter had earlier denied him (p. 84). In this same scene, there are other key ideas drawn from other parts of Scripture that relate closely to either Christ's founding of his Church or to the parable's theme of forgiveness. For example, the Church has the authority to forgive, for whatever it binds on earth shall be bound also in heaven; and Peter and his successors in the Church must not

---

[43] Mariscal de Gante points out that the tracing of the steps the sinner takes into sin is a popular theme in the *autos*. See his discussion of Timoneda's *auto* in his *Los autos sacramentales desde...*, pp. 64-69.

[44] The parable is that of the Good Shepherd (John, 10:1-21).

[45] John, 21:15-23.

only forgive seven times but "seventy times seven" (Math., 18: 22). As was mentioned above, in his *auto* on the Prodigal, Valdivielso only alluded to other scriptural passages. In the Christ and Peter scene of the Villagarcía and the Timoneda *autos*, the other related biblical passages fit more directly into the *autos*' dramatic action. Cristóbal actually appears as the Good Shepherd, and Peter receives Christ's command to nourish his flock. The delicate art of effectively entwining sundry scriptural passages of similar themes into the *auto*'s dramatic action is masterfully handled by Calderón, as it will be observed especially in the study of the kingdom-parable *autos*.

Although Lope de Vega's *El Pastor lobo* resembles the Villagarcía and the Timoneda *autos* in its allegorical dramatization in that it, too, depicts Christ (Pastor Cordero) searching for the sinful soul (Cordera), nowhere are there found the two scenes of the angels discussing the steps to sin nor Christ founding his Church upon the rock of Peter. More a poet-dramatist than a theologian, Lope exploited the dramatic potentiality of the Lost Sheep Parable where the two earlier *autos* had failed.

In the two earlier *autos* studied above, Apetito appears only once in what is really a half-hearted attempt to portray Apetito's role in tempting the Oveja. In Lope's work, Apetito appears many times and plays a direct part in bringing about the Cordera's downfall. In fact, Lope strengthened the temptation scene by multiplying threefold the one evil personage, Apetito, much in the manner that he had expanded the two bawds of the Rouanet *auto* on the Prodigal into a whole host of allegorical figures. In this parable on the Lost Sheep, Lope introduces Descuido and Lobo. Lobo, who is the Devil himself and whose name appears in the title, actually replaces Apetito as the central figure of evil. It is Lobo who begins the *auto* with a long monologue in which he laments his bitter destiny and swears to take revenge by waging a relentless war against God, his all-powerful adversary. Unlike the cruel and insensitive Devil of the Middle Age literature, Lobo is rather typically depicted as a keen and astute student of human nature, well aware of his diabolic role in the Divine plan. [46]

---

[46] Fleckniakoska, *Bulletin Hispanique*, LXVI, 30-44.

Having increased the evil forces to the Lobo, Apetito, and Descuido and having set the stage with the Devil's monologue in which revenge and relentless war are the key note, Lope was then ready to exploit the temptation scene. Just as Lope preferred to portray the wild spree of the Prodigal, so he delighted in dramatizing before the audience that part most neglected by the earlier two *autos* — how the *oveja* became an *oveja perdida*.

Lope is at his best in portraying the seduction scene which resembles those in many of his profane dramas. There are the loyal and good husband, Cordero, and his faithful and true wife, Cordera. Cordero nourishes his spouse with the bread of life, and Cordera, deeply in love with her husband, often withdraws into the heavenly hut to contemplate his goodness (pp. 193-94).[47] While Cordera is within the *cabaña celestial* thinking of her beloved, Apetito disguised as Mercurio, attempts to obtain entrance into the heavenly hut by convincing Cuidado, who is guarding the hut, that he is an angel — all in the tradition of the *capa y espada* play. Employing his bewitching powers, Apetito finally lulls Cuidado to sleep. Cuidado, significantly, represents the Cordera's reason and understanding, which is overcome by passion.[48] A kidnapping scene follows in which Lobo enters the hut, steals the wife of Cordero, and carries her off in his arms in spite of her shouts and screams of resistance.[49] The action heightens as Cuidado, realizing Apetito's true identity and what has happened, goes off to inform the Cordero.

The scene changes to the mount of hell, situated opposite the *cabaña celestial*. Lobo is seen trying to change Cordera's will and seduce her while a chorus of *músicos* lulls her to sleep. Confident that the sleeping Cordera is in his power, Lobo places her in his hut. At this point, Cuidado and Pastor Cordero turn the tables on Apetito and Lobo and steal back the Cordera, who in her sleep, makes known to the Cordero her fidelity and innocence.

---

[47] References to Lope's *El pastor lobo* are taken from Pedroso, pp. 190-201.

[48] That Cuidado represents reason and understanding can be seen in Apetito's own words to the Lobo: "Mal conoces esta vara/ Y los deleites propuestos:/ Entra, que ya están dormidos/ La Razón y Entendimiento" (p. 196).

[49] See below, pp. 57-58 and pp. 61-62.

The play ends with the Devil once again lamenting his inevitable failure while Pastor Cordero carries the Cordera on his shoulders up the narrow and thorny road to the *cabaña celestial*. Finally, just before the curtain descends, Pastor Cordero reveals to his wife and to the audience the true nature of the heavenly *cabaña* which suddenly appears glorious and radiant, bedecked with the Blessed Sacrament. On the other hand, on the opposite hill, the dwelling of the Lobo, once flowery and green, now becomes a mass of giant flames.[50]

Besides the fact that Lope dramatized the Cordera's seduction and that the two theology-laden scenes present in the earlier *autos* are absent in Lope's drama, there is another basic factor found in the seduction scene of Lope's sacramental drama that reveals its author as a better poet than a theologian. In the two early *autos*, although the temptation is extremely brief and undeveloped, Apetito's few words, quoted above, show that Apetito enticed and tempted the Oveja.[51] It will also be remembered that Apetito and Custodio agreed in their conversation and argument before the fall that the Oveja had the right to choose between them and that the use of her free will must be preserved. That the Oveja ultimately gave in to the temptation is obvious from the plot of the plays. That the Oveja fell of her own doing is also explicit when later, after she is found, she must willingly repent and be cleansed by the sacraments, especially that of penance, before she is worthy to be carried off on Cristóbal's shoulders.

In Lope's adaptation of the Gospel parable, Cordera is not tempted but seduced. Cordera is seized by force and carried off from the *cabaña celestial* by the raging Lobo. Nor for one moment does Cordera give in to the desires of the Lobo. In fact, with Cordera's seduction, Lope denies the most essential Roman Catholic doctrine of free will. Unlike the Apetito of the earlier two *autos*, Lobo denies that Cordera has any choice in the matter:

---

[50] Speaking of Lope's effective finale to his *autos* Wardropper says: "La técnica de la apoteosis — una tentativa de aliar el arte escultórico al drama para dejar en la memoria del espectador una visión simbólica — es la mayor contribución de Lope al auto sacramental." See his *Introducción al teatro*..., p. 281.

[51] The quotation is cited above, p. 53.

"Entra, que ya no hay Cordero. / Ya estás en poder del Lobo: / No tienes, Alma, remedio" (p. 197). Cordera herself not only incessantly resists Lobo's attempt to possess her but she never once blames herself and admits guilt. Rather she blames her seduction on Cuidado, her reason and understanding, who fell asleep under the influence of Apetito. After having been rescued by the Cordero, Cordera proclaims her innocence in her sleep and casts the blame on Ciudado:

> Conozco que mi Cuidado
> Fué, por escuchar, culpado,
> A unos traidores fingidos;
> Que, si no les diera oídos,
> No hubieran al Alma enterado.   (p. 199)

Lope seems unable to write good drama without sacrificing theology. This is precisely one of the reasons why Lope never reached the heights of Calderón as a writer of the *auto sacramental.*

Lope's second *auto* on the Lost Sheep Parable, *La oveja perdida*, differs greatly from his *El pastor lobo* and the early Villagarcía and Timoneda *autos*. Although the play begins much like Lope's earlier drama with the Devil, this time called Luzbel, lamenting his tragic destiny and complaining of God's favoritism toward man, whose past deeds in history seem to deserve the same condemnation which the Devil himself has received, Luzbel is joined by three completely new personages, Culpa, Murmuración, and Adulación. Culpa, the Devil's right hand man and a *gracioso* type, goads Luzbel and causes the Devil to be even more remorseful by reminding him of his tragic fate: "¿Qué haces? Siempre has de estar / Solo, enojado y secreto" (p. 610). [52] On the other hand, Murmuración and Adulación are completely friendly to the Devil. They boast of their power to destroy man (p. 612), and they swear to aid Luzbel in bringing about Oveja's downfall. Later when Cristo, Pedro, and San Juan appear, the two allegorical figures of gossip and flattery play their roles to perfection. [53] Murmuración chides Cristo for being born in a lowly

---

[52] References to Lope's *La oveja perdida* are taken from *Obras de Lope de Vega*, Vol. II, pp. 609-624.

[53] Although the Apostle, Peter, has precedence because of his appearance in the earlier *autos*, St. John's appearance is curious. Perhaps, Lope had in

state, amid the shepherds whom he can govern easily (p. 613). She also chides Peter by reminding him that he had denied Christ and that he once cut off the ear of a man "quien armas no tenía" (p. 613). Nor does Murmuración permit St. John to escape her venomous tongue. St. John, the evangelist, always appears in the play with a scribe's quill. Murmuración plays upon the Spanish word, *pluma*, which not only denotes pen but also is used idiomatically to connote a dandy, especially in the expression, "*andar con plumas*" (p. 613). Adulación also plays her role well for she is always willing to whisper honeyed words to all with whom she comes in contact. For example, when Cristo first comes upon the scene, Adulación greets him with a breathtaking host of titles (p. 613). This entire first part of Lope's *La oveja perdida*, in which the forces of evil are pitted against those of good in a battle of words and wit, is well constructed and well dramatized.

The second part of Lope's *La oveja perdida*, the temptation scene, brings to mind Lope's rendition of the Prodigal's downfall discussed at length above.[54] Like the Pródigo, the Oveja expresses concern for her waning youth and desires to flee from the narrow and rough path of the *buen pastor* in order to enjoy the ripe green pastures of pleasure (p. 614). While the Oveja is being tempted by Murmuración, Adulación, and the other evil figures, she continually ignores the warnings and counsels of Memoria, a conscience figure recalling Inspiración of Valdivielso's *Pródigo*. When the Oveja finally surrenders herself to the temptation, she is led away to Villaviciosa, an allegorical city where "se vive sin ley: / Hay siempre fiestas y juegos" (p. 616). It will be recalled that, in Lope's *Pródigo*, the Prodigal was similarly led down the street of Novedad and that Juego actually appears as an allegorical figure in the drama.[55] Having arrived at Villaviciosa, the Oveja peers into one of the rich huts and sees a lavish banquet table at which Gula (gluttony) is feasting. The Oveja asks to

---

mind St. John's closely related Parable of the Good Shepherd when he wrote his drama and therefore included the evangelist himself in the play.

[54] The similarities of Lope's *Pródigo* and the *Oveja* brought to light in the paragraph that follows would seem to back up Menéndez Pelayo's contention that the *La oveja perdida* was definitely written by Lope. See above, n. 41.

[55] See Lope's *Pródigo* in *Obras*..., p. 62.

partake of the banquet meal but the *músicos* answer that Gula cannot share "porque todo es menester, / Lo que tengo y lo que quito, / Para dar á mi apetito / Lascivamente á comer" (p. 616). The Oveja then spots another allegorical figure, Avaricia, bedecked with huge sacks of money. Once again the Oveja's plea to share the money is turned down and the *músicos* chant:

> Dar no quiero, dar no quiero,
> Porque vivo de pedir,
> Aunque poderoso soy,
> Y á pobre ninguno doy;
> Que mi fin es recibir.   (p. 617)

The banquet scene in Lope's *Pródigo* in which the two lovers, Prodigal and Deleite, celebrate their marriage is closely related to the dramatic action. However, it is difficult to see exactly how the banquet scene and the following scene with Avaricia fit into the *auto* dramatically. In refusing to permit the Oveja to share in their wealth and pleasure, both Gula and Avaricia only contribute to the Oveja's disillusion and weaken the case for the other evil spirits who are trying to convince the Oveja that worldly pleasures are good and can be had for the asking.

In contrast to the well developed first part, the third and final part of Lope's *La oveja perdida* is poorly written. Here Lope freely mixes the metaphors in such a manner that the drama becomes confusing. For example, Cristo refers to himself as the Good Shepherd while in the very next stanza the chorus of *músicos* hail him as the *pescadorcito*, fisher of men (p. 619). The confusion of metaphors becomes even more pronounced when, in the very next scene, the Oveja, Luzbel and his companions are hunters hunting for pleasures. The hunters are equipped with bows and arrows and have at their disposal trained horses and "los mejores perros" (pp. 619-20). Although the horse and the bow and arrow clearly symbolize love and unbridled passions, the mixing of these symbols of the hunting scene with the biblical references of Christ, the Good Shepherd, and Christ, the Fisher of men, found in the preceding stanzas, tends only to confuse the dramatic action of the *auto*. Besides containing unrelated metaphors, in its latter stages, Lope's *auto* also becomes artificial and unwieldy. The *auto's* dramatic artificiality is seen particularly in the abrupt manner in which Oveja frees herself from the evil forces and returns to Cristo's flock. While hunting, the Oveja becomes tired, lies down to rest, and falls asleep. Just as Luzbel is gloating over the conquest of the Oveja, Memoria whispers a few words to the sleeping Oveja, who immediately awakens and shouts the name of Jesus. Upon hearing the sacred name, Luzbel and his evil friends disappear and the Oveja now is willing to repent. At this point, with the Oveja's return, instead of quickly drawing to a close, the drama rambles on depicting various scenes, such as the one which portrays the Oveja riding high on Cristo's shoulders or another which sees Luzbel engaging in a long harangue against Spanish society (pp. 622-23).[56]

In comparing Lope's second dramatization of the Lost Sheep Parable with the first, there is one fact that stands out. In his *La oveja perdida,* Lope was undoubtedly more conscious of the theological and doctrinal aspects of the Gospel parable. Lope's attempt to preserve orthodoxy is best seen in the all-important temptation scene. Unlike the first *auto* where Lobo abducts Cordera, the second auto depicts Luzbel and the evil forces tempting the Oveja, who freely and willingly succumbs to the temptation. Lope thus preserved the important doctrine of free will. Later, when, again unlike the Cordera of the first *auto*, the Oveja admits her guilt and weeps over her sin, Lope follows another sound Catholic doctrine, which maintains that forgiveness is only possible with true repentance and sorrow. Note also the manner in which the Oveja with the prompting of Memoria, who not only represents the Oveja's conscience but also the memory of God, in whose image and likeness the Oveja is made, renounces the evil powers by uttering the name of Jesus. Although the practice is not exactly orthodox doctrine, the name, Jesus, has been traditionally invoked in times of temptation and great moral danger. In Lope's drama, the invocation of the sacred name

---

[56] The presence of unrelated metaphors together with the loosely dramatized last part of Lope's *auto* are, perhaps, the factors that prompted Aicardo to reach the following conclusion concerning Lope's *La oveja perdida*: "Es el poema más primitivo y más imperfecto que de su clase poseemos: poema endeble, a pesar de algunos trozos de buenísima versificación, pues al fin es de Lope." See his "Autos sacramentales de Lope de Vega," *Razón y Fe,* XXI (1908), 450.

brought immediate results as Luzbel and his companions are seen fleeing while declaring in unison: "Ese nombre nos vence" (p. 620).

Besides the theological and traditional teachings found in the temptation scene, which contrasts greatly with the seduction scene of *El pastor Lobo,* there are other parts of Lope's *La oveja perdida* which contain bits of doctrinal teachings not found in his previous *auto.* For example, in the early scenes, the doctrine of the Trinity is forcibly brought out in the melodious and repetitive song of the chorus: "No cese el eterno canto/ Alabando al Uno y Trino,/ del Santo, Santo y divino,/ Del Pastor hermoso y Santo" (p. 612). Even the poorly dramatized last part of Lope's *La oveja perdida* succeeds in conveying the doctrinal message of the Gospel parable more than does his first *auto* not only by depicting to a greater extent the true sorrow felt by the Oveja and the goodness and fogiveness of Cristo but also by contrasting the Devil's inevitable and tragic defeat with Cristo's glorious triumph.

The Good Samaritan

A third group of *autos sacramentales* that falls within the scope of this chapter concerning the non-kingdom parable *autos* consists of those plays based on the account of the Good Samaritan.[57] Although the relation of the Parable of the Good Samaritan with that of the Prodigal Son and of the Lost Sheep may not be readily apparent to one who simply reads the Gospel narration of the parable, the Good Samaritan Parable does, in fact, relate to the two previously discussed parables when one takes into account the Good Samaritan's traditional allegorical interpretation.[58] The man in route from Jerusalem to Jerico who is ambushed by a band of thieves has been viewed as mankind, who comes from God's paradise (Jerusalem) and, in life's journey,

---

[57] Luke, 10:25-37.

[58] For the parable as it has been interpreted traditionally see Juan de Maldonado, Vol. II, pp. 550-51; Luis de la Puente, *Meditaciones de los misterios de nuestra santa fe* (2 vols.; tenth edition; Madrid: Editorial Apostolado de la Prensa, S. A., 1953), Vol. I, pp. 967-974. La Puente's *Meditaciones* were first printed in 1605.

falls down into the city of darkness (Jerico). The thieves represent the various evils and demons that man encounters in his journey and that take from him all his spiritual and physical talents. The Levite and the priest, who are the first to see the robber's victim, pass him by, admitting that they are unable to help man because they represent, respectively, Natural Law and the Written Law of Moses and of the Prophets. Without the help of Divine Law, the Laws of Nature and of the Prophets are unable to effect man's salvation. Finally the Good Samaritan (Christ) saves man from his plight and carries him off to the inn symbolic of the Church, entrusted with the work of curing mankind's wounds. The first part of the Good Samaritan Parable, in which man goes down from Jerusalem to Jerico, where he encounters the band of evil-doers, recalls the Prodigal Son leaving his father's home and going in search of the world's pleasures. Similarly, the scene in the Good Samaritan Parable where man, stripped and beaten by the thieves, finds hope in the *buen samaritano* brings to mind the *oveja perdida* and the *buen pastor*. In fact, as the discussion below will indicate, allusions to both the Prodigal Son and the Lost Sheep parables are very much present in the dramatizations of the Good Samaritan.

The *Códice de los jesuítas* contains one of the earliest examples of a sacramental drama written concerning the Good Samaritan Parable.[59] As most of the plays in the *Códice de los jesuítas*, the *Parabola Samaritani* remains anonymous and in manuscript form.[60] In the first decades of the seventeenth century José Valdivielso penned another *auto sacramental* based primarily on the Good Samaritan, *El peregrino*. Valdivielso's play first appeared in 1622 in Toledo and was reprinted two years later at Braga.[61] In addition, there exist two versions of Calderón de la Barca's sacramental drama on the Parable of the Good Samaritan. The first version

---

[59] Another early *auto* pertaining to the sixteenth century is Gil Vicente's *Obra da Geraçao Humana* (*Deux Autos Méconnus de Gil Vicente*, ed. I. S. Révah; Lisbonne: Agrégé de l'Université, 1948), pp. 9-50. Vicente's *auto* remains outside the scope of this study because it is written entirely in Portuguese. The *auto* in Révah's edition may be found at the University of Chicago Library.

[60] The *Parabola Samaritani* is found in the Colección de Cortés of the *Códice*, No. 384. Biblioteca de la Real Academia de la Historia.

[61] See Pedroso's edition of Valdivielso's play, p. 202, n. 1.

of *Tu prójimo como a ti* appeared sometime before 1674, the date of the appearance of the second version.[62] In the extensive and most recent edition of the Calderonian *autos*, Angel Valbuena Prat presents both of the versions of *Tu prójimo como a ti*.[63]

The following discussion concerning the *autos sacramentales* written on the Parable of the Good Samaritan will consist of a twofold comparison. First, a comparison of the early *Parabola Samaritani* of the *Códice de los jesuítas* with *El peregrino* of Valdivielso will demonstrate how Valdivielso so successfully expanded the characters and events of the Gospel story that he was able to present a much more dramatic play than was the author of the anonymous Jesuit *auto*. Second, a comparison of Calderón's two writings of his *Tu prójimo como a ti* should be of particular interest "en relación con la formación de Calderón en el género del auto sacramental y en los casos de repetición de tema."[64]

The *Parabola Samaritani* of the *Códice de los jesuítas* consists of little more than a dramatic narration of the Gospel story. In the opening scene, Pecador deplores the hardships and tribulations of travelling the narrow and good road, and he expresses his desire to leave it and follow the wide road to Jerico "que es ciudad muy populosa." While on the road to Jerico, he meets the three thieves, Morguto, Maluto, and Joringo, who beat him and leave him to die in the ditch by the side of the road. Confessing their inadequacy, Levita and Sacerdote pass by the wailing Pecador. Finally the Samaritano encounters the Pecador by the wayside and carries him off to the *mesón*, symbolic of the *iglesia militante*.

The final scene of the *Parabola Samaritani*, which consists of a long dialogue between the Samaritano and the Mesonero and which in effect makes up the entire latter half of the play, is the drama's most interesting scene, although the scene, as such, contri-

---

[62] For a discussion of the two versions their dates and manuscripts, see Ángel Valbuena Prat's "Nota Preliminar" found in *Obras...*, Vol. III, p. 1409. It is observed that the titles for the two versions appearing in Valbuena differ slightly. The first version has the title: *A tu prójimo como a ti*. The title to the second version reads: *Tu prójimo como a ti*. In this study, I choose to use the latter title for the sake of conformity and simply because it is the title found in the later writing of the play.

[63] Ángel Valbuena Prat, *Obras...*, Vol. III, pp. 1409-1442 and pp. 1889-1907. References to the two *autos* are taken from Valbuena's edition.

[64] *Ibid.*, p. 1877.

butes little to the dramatic action of the play. The scene's interest lies in the fact that, in the ensuing dialogue between the Good Samaritan and the innkeeper, the former instructs the latter in various matters of faith, particularly with regard to the laws regulating the proper reception of the Eucharist.

In his *El peregrino*, Valdivielso develops the Gospel parable much in the manner as did the author of the *Parabola Samaritani*, but into almost every scene, Valdivielso introduces new characters in order to intensify his drama. Like the Pecador of the *Parabola Samaritani*, Peregrinó, his counterpart in Valdivielso's play, initiates the action by complaining to the allegorical Tierra of his labors and toils here on earth. Peregrino makes it clear that he desires to leave Tierra and begs Tierra to permit him to be free to seek the eternal reward for which he is destined:

>   PER.   ¡Suelta, madre!
>   TIER. ¡Ay, hijo amado!
>   PER.   Suelta, Tierra.
>   TIER. ¡Ay, mi consuelo!
>   PER.   Déjame que busque el cielo,
>   pues que fuí para él criado.
>   TIER. ¿De tu madre es bien te ausentes
>   con deliberación tanta?
>   (p. 81)[65]

By introducing the allegorical figure, Tierra, who resists the pleas of the Peregrino and by presenting to the audience this dramatic conflict in the opening lines of the play, Valdivielso immediately reaches greater dramatic intensity in his *auto* than does his predecessor in the *Parabola Samaritani*.

Peregrino, intent upon rebellion but exhausted from his encounter with Mother Earth, momentarily escapes his frustrations and the struggles of earthly life by falling into a deep sleep. While Peregrino sleeps, he envisions the two roads upon which man can make life's journey from earth to eternity. The allegorical Verdad describes the two roads of life while the choruses of *lo bueno* and *lo malo* accompany Verdad's descriptions with suitable

---

[65] References and quotations found in this study of Valdivielso's drama are taken from Alejandro Sanvisens, *Autos sacramentales eucarísticos* (Barcelona: Editorial Cervantes, 1952), pp. 81-99.

refrains. Again the road of good is narrow, full of thorns, thistles, and rough stones while the path to evil is wide, strewn with flowers, and filled with sweet scents.[66] This portrayal of the "dos caminos" scene in the early stages of his drama is another way in which Valdivielso augmented the dramatic action of his play. In the *Parabola Samaritani*, the theme of the "dos caminos" comes to light in Pecador's initial monologue ("buen camino es el que llevo,/ fresco, verde, y muy florido"), but the scene's dramatic potentiality is never realized as it is in Valdivielso's work.

In the *Parabola Samaritani*, after the scene in which Pecador expresses his wish to leave the straight and narrow path for the more adventurous and exciting path of pleasures, Morguto, Maluto, and Joringo enter the play and rob the Pecador. The whole scene depicting Pecador's encounter with the devil figures and his subsequent downfall is brief and undeveloped, for the author seems to have been anxious to introduce the Samaritano and the long dialogue with the Mesonero on faith and morals, which, as it was seen above, actually makes up the entire last half of the play. In contrast, Valdivielso's *auto* offers the audience a series of dramatic scenes in which Peregrino attempts to walk the straight and narrow path but constantly faces various temptations set up by the devil figures, Luzbel, Deleite, and Engaño. The first temptations Peregrino meets along the way are the Ciudad de Placer and the Venta de Honor. Each time, the Peregrino entertains the thought of abandoning the *buen camino* to visit the City of Pleasures and the Inn of Honor, but each time he listens to Verdad, who incessantly exposes the temptations for what they really are. When Peregrino finally comes to the House of Beauty, it proves to be too much of a temptation for him to overcome, and he immediately falls in love with Deleite. As Peregrino sits to eat with Deleite in the Casa de Hermosura, four covered plates are arranged before them, the plates representing the honors, riches, beauty, and pleasure awaiting the Peregrino in the new life he has chosen. But as the Peregrino uncovers each of the plates, that of honor turns out to be "un pájaro que vuela," that of riches, "un carbón," that of beauty, "una calavera," and that of pleasures, "un vacío." The Peregrino suddenly experiences a great

---

[66] See above, p. 53.

disillusionment as the evil figures flee from him and leave him alone and destitute.

Instead of the long didactic dialogue that terminates the *Parabola Samaritani*, Valdivielso's *auto* in its last stages again becomes more meaningful drama. In the dramatization of the parable's passage in which the Levite and the priest pass by the wounded man, these two parable figures never really take part in Valdivielso's drama. Verdad simply tells the wounded Peregrino that he sees Levita and Sacerdote pass and that they cannot really help him, because they possess limited remedies which are by themselves inadequate. Immediately after Verdad's announcement that Sacerdote, who symbolizes the Law of the Prophets, has just passed, Valdivielso takes the occasion to introduce another new allegorical personage, St. John the Baptist, who is the last of the great prophets. St. John, in turn, announces the coming of Christ, who then enters as the Buen Samaritano. The final scenes of Valdivielso's *auto*, in which Samaritano entrusts the Peregrino to the Iglesia, corresponding to the figure of the Mesonero in the *Parabola Samaritani*, is filled with allusions to the Good Shepherd who goes in search of the Lost Sheep. Also evident in the same scenes are occasional references to the Prodigal Son, who returns penitent to his forgiving father.

That Valdivielso had in mind his *Auto del hijo pródigo* in the writing of his *El peregrino* is clear not only because of the occasional references to the Prodigal Son contained in the last scenes of his *El peregrino* but also because of the similarity in the development of the two dramas. The opening scene of *El peregrino*, when the Peregrino asks to be freed from his mother, Tierra, recalls the Pródigo asking his father for his inheritance with the intention of leaving him. The manner in which the Peregrino goes out on his own only to fall prey to the world's pleasures, his temptations with the City of Pleasure and the Inn of Honor, and his love for Deleite bring to mind the similar adventures of the Pródigo, who encounters Juego, Juventud, and Lascivia and who falls madly in love with Placer. The allegorical personage, Verdad, who stays at the Peregrino's side throughout the entire drama, suggests a corresponding personage in Valdivielso's *Auto del hijo pródigo*, Inspiración, who functions as the Pródigo's good counselor while he undertakes his worldly and amorous adventures. The dramatic role of Verdad and Inspiración in their respective plays are strikingly similar, for each acts as a type of conscience, constantly keeping before her corresponding companion the necessity of choosing between good and evil, all of which intensifies the play's drama. Valdivielso's *peregrino* and *hijo pródigo* finally repent of their sins after experiencing similar disillusionment with the evil figures, the Peregrino in witnessing the four dishes of worldly goods turn to naught, and the Pródigo in seeing himself spent and ruined by loose and luxurious living. Having felt the emptiness of the banquet of pleasures, both the Peregrino and the Pródigo partake in the end of the meal of forgiveness — the Eucharist.

In comparing the two versions of Calderón's *Tu prójimo como a ti* found in Valbuena's collection of the Calderonian *autos*, it becomes immediately apparent that the two renditions of the Good Samaritan Parable are basically the same in structure and development. The few differences between them are of interest in determining the way in which Calderón handled the rewriting and recasting of earlier *autos* and themes.

The first significant variant in the two versions of Calderón's *Tu prójimo como a ti* takes place in the *autos*' initial scenes. In the beginning scenes of the first version, in which Culpa calls upon the other devil figures, Mundo, Lascivia, and Demonio to help bring Hombre's downfall, Culpa deplores the idea that she no longer enjoys favor with God. She expresses her jealousy over the fact that man still receives from his Creator certain *joyas*, among which are the five senses and the intellectual faculties of understanding, memory, and will. In the second version, Calderón actually dramatizes on stage how Hombre receives these gifts only mentioned in the first version, these same gifts that later are taken from him by the thieves. The second version depicts Man asking the three Laws, Levita, Sacerdote, and Sol, to give him what he needs to undertake life's journey. Levita (Natural Law) gives Hombre the lowest of his gifts, his five senses (*cinco sentidos*). Sacerdote (Written Law) endows him with the intellectual powers of reason (*entendimiento*), memory (*memoria*), and will (*voluntad*). Sol (Divine Law) bequeaths Hombre free will (*albedrío*), with which Hombre must decide how he wishes to use his other faculties. This entire early scene of the second version vividly brings to mind once again, as in Valdivielso's *El peregrino*, the Prodigal Son's requesting of his father his inheritance in order that he may enjoy the world.

The addition of the "Prodigal scene" in the second version permitted the author to augment considerably the dramatic role of his personages. In this early scene, Deseo is seen as the Hombre's tempter, persuading him to seek a better and more glorious life: "Vivamos lo que vivimos;/ veamos tierras, veamos mares,/ poblaciones, edificios,/ tratos, comercios y gentes" (pp. 1412-13). Later, as in the first version, Deseo functions as man's instinct of self-preservation and pleads with Hombre, half-dead and beaten by the highway criminals, to take courage and to seek help rather than die helpless. As a result of the "Prodigal scene" other figures receiving greater dramatic roles in Calderón's second writing than in his first are the two law figures, Levita and Sacerdote. In fact, in the first version, they appear only long enough to pass wounded Hombre lying on the roadside and, at the very end of the play, to function as two of the seven sacraments. The dramatic function of Levita and Sacerdote in this later scene of the first version will be treated in the discussion that immediately follows.

A second important difference between the two versions occurs at their very end. In the final scenes of both *autos*, Calderón depicts the wounded Hombre being taken to the Cueva de Penitencia by the Buen Samaritano. The Cave of Penance obviously represents the Church, for the cave is guarded by Pedro representing the apostle Peter, the Church's first head. To better dramatize the curing effect of the Church, Calderón introduces into the final scenes of both *autos* the symbolism of the sacraments. In the first version, because Calderón undertakes to allegorize all seven of the sacraments, he fails to achieve structural balance and, in fact, forces the allegory of the play. Calderón begins allegorizing the final scene of his first version by taking some of the personages already present in his drama and associating them with the sacraments to which they can best be related. For example, Lucero, symbolic of St. John the Baptist, who appears just before Alba (Virgin Mary) and Sol (Christ), is called upon to wash Hombre of "todas las manchas" (p. 1906), a clear reference to the sacrament of Baptism.[67] Calderón was able to take another figure, Sacerdote, appearing earlier in the play and easily relate Sacerdote to another of the Seven Sacraments, Holy Orders. However, Sacerdote's companion personage, Levita, who also is seen in an earlier scene of the drama, confirms Hombre, thus linking Levita with the Sacrament of Confirmation, an association that is not exactly clear. A fourth personage seen earlier in the drama, Noche, is called upon by Calderón to function as the Eucharist. Noche as the Eucharist is easily the best example of forced allegory for Noche, who in most of Calderón's *autos* in which she appears represents one of the devil figures, in a clumsy twist of metaphor now stands for the Eucharist:[68]

> Yo deponiendo las sombras
> de aquellas leies pasadas
> en fee de que ia es de luz
> la nueva ley que me ensalza
> dare en este blanco velo
> al enfermo una vianda
> que es pan de vida. [sic]
> (p. 1906)

For the remaining three sacraments, Calderón introduces into his first version Penitencia, Muerte, and Amor who act as Penance, Extreme Unction, and Matrimony, respectively, and each of whom has but a few limited lines in a very brief appearance.

In the corresponding final scenes of the second version, Calderón does not give to the personages already present in the play another dimension that oftentimes forces the association of the sacrament with the already established allegory, as was the case with Noche and to a lesser extent with Levita. Nor does Calderón even attempt in this scene to present all seven of the sacraments. He simply introduces three new figures who are known only by the numbers and who clearly represent Baptism, Confirmation and

---

[67] For another example of Lucero as St. John the Baptist in another of Calderón's *autos* see Chapter III of this study, especially pp. 127-129 on the dramatic function of this figure in Calderón's *La viña del Señor*.

[68] In Calderón's *La viña del Señor*, Lucero de la Noche is seen as one of the evil figures opposite Lucero del Día, the St. John the Baptist figure. See the discussion of Calderón's play found in Chapter III of the present study, pp. 121-137.

Penance. Calderón permits the three new figures to play the role of the sacraments, while at the same time he coordinates the sacramental effect of each figure with the over-all allegory. The allegorical figure representing the Sacrament of Baptism washes Hombre's wounds with her cleansing waters, that of Confirmation soothes them with linaments and oils, and that of Penance cauterizes them with her burning sting.

By introducing only three of the seven sacraments into the finale of his second version, Calderón also achieved a greater structural balance than in his first version, in that each of the sacraments effected not only a positive cure in Hombre but also a negative reaction in each of the devil figures. According to theological belief, Baptism washes away man's original sin which frustrates man and deprives him of his preternatural gifts; so also the allegorical Baptism in Calderón's drama cleanses Hombre's sores while at the same time attacking Culpa, who had mustered the evil forces which resulted in the loss of Hombre's gifts bestowed upon him by the three law figures at the beginning of the drama. Just as in theology Confirmation gives strength and courage to man so the allegorical Confirmation of Calderón's drama renews Hombre's strength and revives his spirits while at the same time counteracting Lascivia, who had earlier wooed Hombre and had stolen his heart. Theologians also hold that the Sacrament of Penance purges sin from man's soul; so the allegorical Penance burns Hombre's festering wounds while at the same time moderating Mundo, who had stolen Hombre's memories of his Creator. Although Calderón seems to have forgotten a fourth sacrament to parallel Demonio, the fourth evil figure of the drama makes it clear that he is affected by all of the sacraments, which diminish his power over man.

A third difference in the two versions of Calderón's *Tu prójimo como a ti* may not be considered as significant as those discussed above but nevertheless reflect a change in Calderón's thinking, especially with regard to the complementary nature of the three laws and ages of man. In the first version, after Culpa, Mundo, Lascivia, and Demonio rob Hombre and watch Levita and Sacerdote unsuccessfully attempt to help the wounded Hombre, the evil figures agree to stay on and to take turns guarding against anyone else who might be passing by and who might be inclined to aid their helpless victim. Culpa offers to take the first watch and does so as the allegorical figure Noche veils the scene with darkness. As Noche removes herself from the scene and as Lucero enters, Culpa, symbolic of original sin, significantly falls asleep, for Lucero not only initiates the break of day but also represents St. John, the voice in the wilderness, announcing the birth of Christ to a Virgin and preaching repentance and forgiveness through Baptism. When Lascivia comes to relieve Noche of her vigil, Lucero has already given way to Alba, who represents the Virgin Mary, triumphant over the sins of the flesh. In a scene just before the appearance of the Christ figure, Sol, Alba is seen with Gracia, who hails her in the words of the "Magnificat," the entire scene obviously representing the Angel Gabriel's visit to Mary and the announcement that Mary is to be the Mother of God.[69] Sol's entrance into the drama takes place at the precise moment that the two remaining evil figures, Demonio and Mundo, assume the vigil for the sleepy Culpa and the waning Lascivia. Demonio and Mundo have no more success at guarding their victim than did Culpa and Lascivia before them, for the two evil figures are immobilized and made powerless by Sol's splendor.

In the corresponding scenes of the second version, Calderón rearranges the entrance of the personages in such a way that the three law figures are seen as being complementary to each other and as appearing in company with the corresponding ages of man's salvation history. Levita appears on stage with Noche, symbolic of the dark ages in which primitive man was governed by Natural Law alone. Sacerdote then enters the scene with Lucero representative of St. John the Baptist, the last of the great prophets. The entire scene again refers to the second stage in mankind's salvation story in which the written law of Moses and the prophets governed God's creatures. Finally after a scene with Alba and Gracia similar to the one in the first version, Sol, the Good Samaritan, gives man a new supernatural life which initiates the culminating period in man's religious history.

---

[69] The "Magnificat" is a traditional prayer taken from the Psalms and said in praise of the Virgin Mary. Calderón was accustomed to using common Marian prayers in a scene allegorizing the Angel's visit to Mary, the Annunciation. See Chapter III of this study, n. 107, p. 153.

The harmony and continuity of man's salvation history is not only dramatized in the successive appearances of the three law figures in company with the corresponding figures of Noche-Lucero-Alba-Sol but is also expressed continuously throughout the second edition. For example, in the "Prodigal scene," after Levita, Sacerdote, and Sol have all admonished Hombre: "Amar/ a Dios aun más que a ti mismo,/ y al prójimo como a ti" (p. 1413), Hombre reflects upon the unity and harmony of the three laws:

> Con eso será más fácil
> el logro, y pues ya me miro
> de tres edades y tres
> leyes tan enriquecido,
> salgamos de aquí, Deseo.
>   (p. 1415)

Finally, exactly how closely the three periods of religious history complement each other and to what extent the three laws contribute in varying degrees to man's salvation is clearly demonstrated in the very last scene of the second version, entirely missing from the first version. In another example of the dramatic expansion of the Law figures, Levita, Sacerdote, and Sol take the stage for one final time. Levita and Sacerdote once again admit their inability to bring about man's cure independently as they had done when they passed up the wounded Hombre but nevertheless, now in the final scene, they eagerly offer Hombre the *prenda* they had promised earlier. Levita offers Hombre the bread of Melchisedec, and Sacerdote gives him the manna of Moses and of the prophets found in the desert. The bread of the ancient Melchisedec and the manna of the desert, both recorded in the Old Testament, prefigure the most perfect gift — the *hostia blanca* of the Sacrament offered to Hombre by Sol.[70]

---

[70] In the rewriting, in later years, of an earlier *auto* which was written on the Parable of the Laborers in the Vineyard and in which the law figures played a prominent role, Calderón again reveals in his later *auto* his awareness of the complementary nature of the laws, and he attempts to portray this harmony among the three laws in the recasting of an earlier theme. See the discussion of his two *autos*, *La siembra del señor* and *El día mayor de los días*, Chapter III of this study, pp. 109-117.

The Rich Man and Lazarus

The fourth and final group of sacramental plays to be included in this chapter treating of the non-kingdom parable *autos* is made up of those dramas written on the New Testament Parable of the Rich Man and Lazarus. The evangelist Luke writes of a certain rich man who used to dress in purple and fine linens and who was accustomed to feasting magnificently every day.[71] At the gate of the rich man's house there would lie a poor man named Lazarus, whose sores the dogs would lick. Lazarus would always beg the scraps from the rich man's table but the rich man always denied him even the crumbs. Finally the two men died, and, while Lazarus went to heaven to be in the company of Abraham, the rich man went to Hades. The parable ends with the rich man beseeching Abraham to permit Lazarus to cool his tongue with a drop of water and to allow Lazarus to return to earth in order to counsel the rich man's brothers to lead a good life lest they end up in Hades with him. Abraham refused both of the rich man's requests, reminding him that the gulf between heaven and hell has been fixed to prevent anyone from crossing from one side to the other and that the rich man's brothers have the Scriptures and the Prophets to guide them.

Biblical exegetes have had much to say about the fact that of all the Gospel parables, the Rich Man and Lazarus is one of the few in which some of the personages are identified by name. Many students of Scripture maintain that because the personages of the Gospel parables are usually not named, the Parable of the Rich Man and Lazarus is a true-to-life incident, the name of the rich man not being given because Christ did not want gossip concerning the rich man to spread since it was serious enough that he be condemned.[72] Maldonado refuses to accept the idea that every element in the Gospel story of the Rich Man and Lazarus comes from real life, because it is not known what happens after life here on earth, and therefore what transpires after the death of the rich man and Lazarus in the Gospel account must be parabolic. Maldonado concludes that the Parable of the Rich Man

---

[71] Luke, 17: 19-31.
[72] Maldonado, II, 693.

and Lazarus is half-history, half-parable: "A mi parecer, esta narración no es ni pura historia, ni pura parábola, sino cierta combinación de una y otra, parecida a lo que entre los poetas se llama tragicomedia." [73]

Whether or not the story of the Rich Man and Lazarus took place in real life exactly as it appears in the Gospel account in part or in its entirety, may be left for the scriptural scholars. However, the relevancy of the parable's theme in sixteenth and seventeenth century Spain cannot be doubted. In his well known work on the culture and customs of the Spanish people in the sixteenth and seventeenth centuries, Ludwig Pfandl writes concerning the importance of almsgiving:

> El amor al prójimo era un deber cristiano,
> era un caso de honor: jamás en parte alguna
> volvió a revestirse la vida medicante de
> tan gloriosa significación, de un nimbo
> religioso tan ennoblecedor. [74]

Pfandl quotes Juan Zabaleta, who writes:

> El tratar a un pobre sin cortesía
> es desacato que se hace al Rey
> de los Reyes; porque el pobre que
> pide es un hombre embiado
> del cielo, a que le ruegue de parte
> de Dios que haga una buena obra.
> Al que embía el recado ofende, quien desestima
> al recaudador. El no darle limosna es
> villanía infame, porque es ponerse de parte
> de la necesidad su enemiga, que es la parte
> mas fuerte. [75]

Of the sacramental plays of the sixteenth and seventeenth centuries I have been able to find only two that treat specifically of Luke's Parable of the Rich Man and Lazarus. Francisco de Rojas Zorrilla's *El rico avariento* dates to the first half of the

---

[73] *Ibid.*, p. 691.
[74] Ludwig Pfandl, *Cultura y costumbres del pueblo español de los siglos XVI y XVII: Introducción al siglo de oro*, trans. P. Féliz García (Barcelona: Editorial Araluce, 1929), p. 146.
[75] *Ibid.*, pp. 146-47, n. 1.

seventeenth century. Rojas Zorrilla's manuscript is in the Biblioteca Nacional in Madrid.[76] A second *auto* based entirely on Luke's parable is also in the Biblioteca Nacional at Madrid and according to the description offered by Julián Paz, it is attributed to Jacinto Cordero. However, the *auto sacramental* that I received from the Biblioteca Nacional and that was supposedly written by Jacinto Cordero turned out to be the *Auto del Rico avariento de Dn. Francisco de Rojas*.[77]

There exist other sacramental plays that definitely relate to the parabolic theme of the rich man and Lazarus although, in fact, they do not dramatize in its entirety the parable as it appears in Luke. Instead of portraying Luke's story of the rich man doomed to hell, the *autos* belonging to this second closely-related group depict the ultimate salvation of the rich man in a dramatic switch of character from the *rico avariento* to the *pobre esclavo*. The actual change in the attitude of the *rico avariento* is brought about by a miraculous dream in which the Rico witnesses how a morsel of bread thrown in a fit of anger to a poor man balances the scales of Divine justice previously tilted by an entire life-time of uncharitableness and iniquities. The most popular *auto* of this second group on the Rich Man-Lazarus theme remains Mira de Amescua's *Pedro Telonario*.[78] A second *auto*, closely patterned after Mira de Amescua's *auto*, is Felipe Godínez's *El premio de limosna y rico de Alejandría*.[79]

Another dramatic piece that would seem to pertain to this section of my study on the Parable of the Rich Man and Lazarus is shrouded in confusion. In his catalogue, La Barrera cites an *auto sacramental* written by Mira de Amescua, *El rico avariento*.[80]

---

[76] Julián Paz (*Catálogo...*, I, 481) gives the following description of Rojas Zorrilla's *auto*: 22 hoj., 4º, del s. XVII, hol. (D), 15.150. Quotations and references found in this study are taken from this manuscript.

[77] The number of the manuscript in my possession — 15.266 — corresponds to the number given by Julián Paz (*Catálogo...*, I, 481). Quotations and references found in this study are taken from this manuscript.

[78] Mira de Amescua's *auto* is found in *Teatro*, ed. Ángel Valbuena Prat (2 vols.; "Clásicos Castellanos;" Madrid: Espasa Calpe, S. A., 1943), Vol. I, pp. 157-95.

[79] Godínez's *auto* is found printed in *Navidad y Corpus Christi festejados* (Madrid, 1664).

[80] La Barrera y Leirado, 599.

Cotarelo y Mori says that La Barrera probably confuses the *auto* "con el de don Francisco de Rojas Zorrilla, o bien con la comedia, no auto, de Mira así titulada, la cual se imprimió ... en el tomo de *Autos Sacramentales* de 1655."[81] In his catalogue, Alenda questions the existence of Mira de Amescua's *El rico avariento* mentioned by La Barrera: "¿Será este mismo de *Pedro Telonario*, que es un rico avaro, y a quien en el texto se llama el *Rico de Alejandría*, como al *auto* mismo se designa, al fin, con el título de *Auto de Alejandría?*"[82]

Since this study is limited only to those sacramental pieces that specifically dramatize the Gospel parable, the remainder of this section, the last of the present chapter, will briefly compare the two plays based on the complete account of Luke's parable, Rojas Zorrilla's *El rico avariento* and the *auto* of the same name supposedly written by Cordero, henceforth referred to as the "Cordero" *auto*.

Although both *autos sacramentales* dramatizing the entire Parable of the Rich Man and Lazarus closely resemble each other in their dramatic structure, there are enough differences to suggest that Rojas Zorrilla's *El rico avariento* is a better representation of the Gospel parable than the Cordero *auto*. In the latter work, Avaricia, Gula, and Mundo initiate the play with successive monologues in which each figure boasts of his maliciousness and his power to destroy man. After several minutes and many lines, the Rico comes onto the stage, and he too engages in a long monologue, in which he takes pride in his immense wealth and entrusts his riches to the evil figures. Only after all of these figures with their long monologues have made their appearance in the drama does Caridad attempt to gain entrance into the Rico's house. In his *auto*, Rojas Zorrilla does not withhold Caridad from the drama but introduces the figure into the very beginning scene. By presenting Caridad at the very start of the play, Rojas Zorrilla immediately creates a dramatic conflict, for Caridad is seen

---

[81] Emilio Cotarelo y Mori, "Mira de Amescua y su teatro," *Boletín de la Real Academia Española*, XVIII (1931), 85. Mira de Amescua's *comedia* to which Cotarelo refers is the *Comedia famosa del Rico avariento y vida y muerte de San Lázaro* found in the *Autos sacramentales y cuatro comedias nuevas y sus loas y entremeses* (Madrid, 1655).

[82] Alenda y Mira, *Boletín de la Real Academia Española*, VII, 510.

arguing with Gula, Avaricia, and Lisonja about the Rico Avariento's need for her and her desire to see the Rico in an effort to persuade him to do good works. Instead of the long monologues of the evil figures that start the Cordero *auto*, Zorrilla's play captures the attention of his audience with a live and rapidly-moving dialogue.

The limited role of the Lucifer figure in the Cordero *auto* in contrast to its more expanded role in Rojas Zorrilla's drama provides another example of how the two *autos* differ. The author of the Cordero *auto* employs the Lucifer figure in the same way that one having read the Gospel parable would expect. Lucifer enters the *auto*'s action in the last phase of the parable's dramatization in order to claim for himself the Rico Avariento after death. In Rojas Zorrilla's play, Demonio plays a much more effective role as he not only takes the Rico's soul to Hades in a later scene but he also enters much earlier disguised as a beggar in a scene with Lázaro. In this earlier scene, in which Demonio appears disguised as a beggar, Lázaro invites Demonio to accompany him in seeking alms at the home of the Rico Avariento. In terms of drama, the entrance of Demonio into this earlier scene of Zorrilla's *auto* has two effects. First, the entire scene presents a series of sharp contrasts in which the sincere and simple character of Lázaro is seen against the deceitful and proud nature of Demonio. Lázaro blesses and praises God for the patience the Creator bestowed upon him: "La paciencia sea triaca,/ si es la pobreza, el veneno" (fol. 10). Demonio, on the other hand, curses the Lord, saying that he has received the same poverty as Lázaro but without the accompanying gift of patience: "Maldigo tu omnipotencia/ padre y Dios de la Verdad,/ pues me das necesidad/ y no me has dado paciencia" (fol. 10-11). Lázaro willingly admits his state of deprivation and realizes he had no choice in the matter, for he sees his poverty as the will of God. Demonio, on the other hand, clearly states that in his case he was once rich and that his poverty is not from God: "Pobre me puedes llamar/ pero no pobre de Dios" (fol. 11). Finally, this contrast in the personage of the two beggars is borne out in the fact that Lázaro rejoices in the hope of one day overcoming his poverty with the possession of eternal happiness while Demonio despairs in the realization of the constant anguish that awaits him in eternity:

LÁZ. Tened en Dios esperanza.
DEM. Ya no la puedo tener.
(fol. 11)

In addition to the sharp contrast presented in the characters of the two beggars, the early appearance of Demonio with Lázaro also has an effect on the dramatic structure of Rojas Zorrilla's *auto sacramental*. By disguising himself as a beggar and by staying at the side of Lázaro as he goes to visit the Rico Avariento, Demonio intends to prevent the Rico from having a change of heart and thus give alms to Lázaro; and Demonio hopes that by not receiving alms from the Rico Avariento Lázaro himself will lose hope and commit the dreaded sin of despair. Demonio himself makes known his designs to the audience in an aside:

A tres intentos atiendo,
que al pobre aunque ande pidiendo
que el que es rico no le da
y así desesperará;
y para que (aunque le sobre
al rico) su impiedad obre.
(fol. 12)

This scene of Rojas Zorrilla's *auto*, in which Demonio proposes to tempt Lázaro in a last effort to get Lázaro to fall, parallels an earlier scene in which Caridad makes a last attempt to convert the Rico Avariento to charity. When the *auto* draws to a close and when it is clear that Demonio has failed to effect Lázaro's downfall and that Caridad likewise has failed to convert the Rico Avariento to the side of the good, Caridad joins Lázaro and accompanies him to the bosom of Abraham, while Demonio sides with the Rico Avariento in preparing him for the eternal fires.

In addition to the differences found in the initial scenes and in the development of the Lucifer figures, the characterization of the Rico Avariento, particularly in the Rojas Zorrilla's play, reflects still another variation in the two *autos sacramentales*. Unlike the Cordero *auto*, Rojas Zorrilla's drama makes the Rico Avariento the central figure in the play. The constant characterization of Zorrilla's Rico Avariento as a proud glutton is particularly evident in the two scenes in which he figures most prominently — the preliminary scene with Caridad and the subsequent banquet scene with Lázaro.

In the Cordero *auto*, the Rico's confrontation with Caridad does give some insights into the Rico's love for luxury and wealth and his extreme reluctance to distribute even the minimum of his overabundance. However the Rico's character never comes out as strong in the Cordero *auto* as in Rojas Zorrilla's play where beneath the Rico's avarice and gluttony can be found a determined pride. It is the Rico's pride that prompts him to admit Caridad into his house in the first place. Caridad makes it known to the Rico that charity ranks first among God's virtues and that he who has charity, as St. Paul says, is God. The Rico hopes that by associating himself with Caridad he will be God:

> Juntos andamos los dos
> Nunca te apartes de mi,
> yo quiero tenerte a ti.
> (fol. 5)

Because the Rico's first acceptance of Caridad stemmed from his pride and his desire to be like God and not from sincere friendship, the Rico easily vacillates as he listens to the arguments brought forth by Gula and Avaricia against charity. The Rico is on the verge of rejecting Caridad completely when Caridad reminds him that, even though Job lost his fortune as Avaricia suggested, nevertheless Job "vino a ser rico después" (fol. 5). The Rico continues to vacillate between Caridad and the evil figures until Lisonja takes him into a room and shows him tables filled with the finest foods and wines, goblets and plates made of the purest silver, feathered pillows for his silk-lined bed, diamonds and pearls of the rarest type. Upon beholding his wealth and pondering the refrain uttered by the other evil figures, "Hoy hay de guardar/ si quiere tener mañana" (fol. 5), the Rico decides not to share his wealth. However, the Rico's pride prompts him to explain carefully why he is not giving of his riches, for he is quite concerned about what other people might think:

> Si ha de murmurar por fuerza
> murmúrese de que no doy,
> y no de que no lo tenga.
> (fol. 7)

Having decided to refuse Caridad's plea for charity and conversion and having satisfied any doubt as to his ability to give should he so desire, the Rico begins to justify his position by a series of rationalizations. He claims that in not giving when one is able only increases one's respectability:

> De fuerza han de estimarme
> Porque no dí, como sepan
> que puedo dar si quiero.
> No respetan al que dió,
> y al que puede dar respetan.
> (fol. 7)

Regocijo, another of the servants in the Rico's household, plays upon the psychology of the moment and immediately confirms the Rico's rationalization concerning respectability. Regocijo draws an analogy to the Rico's position stating that it is the archer who stands at the end of a street and reserves his arrows that everyone respects and not the archer who has already released his arrows.

As the scene between the Rico and Caridad draws to a close, the Rico's pride becomes even more apparent. The Rico compares himself to a statue whose head is golden, whose arms are made of silver, whose insides are of bronze, and whose legs are iron. Caridad reacts to the Rico's grand analogy by posing a simple question; "Y di, los pies de la estatua/ ¿de qué eran?" When the Rico replies, "De barro eran," Caridad answers:

> Pues rico, vuelve los ojos
> a mirar tu estatua misma,
> oro, plata, bronce, hierro,
> tierra eran antes que fueran
> metales y hay que los son
> con ejemplo experimenta
> que las bases en que estriba
> (que son los pies) son de tierra.
> (fol. 10)

Angered by Caridad's wit and her reply to his analogy of the statue, the Rico orders that Caridad be thrown out of his house. Even as Caridad is being evicted from the house, she kindly expresses her farewell to the Rico. The Rico's response to Caridad's well-wishes once again reflects his relentless pride:

> Caridad: Quiero os bien.
> Rico: No quiero que me quieran,
> que harto me quiero yo a mi.
> (fol. 10)

With the banquet scene, Rojas Zorrilla continues to paint the Rico as a proud *avariento* while the same scene in the Cordero *auto* succeeds in capturing only some of the scene's dramatic effect. In Rojas Zorrilla's play, by now the Rico is more determined than ever not to share any of his wealth. Inviting Lázaro and Demonio into his house only to tease them, the Rico seems actually to toy with the whole idea of almsgiving, for just before the entrance of the beggars, he bragged that he would never give in to their plea for charity:

> Dejadle hablar y verá
> como, aunque le oiga, no quiero
> oir su necesidad.
> (fol. 13)

In this same banquet scene the Rico again rationalizes his refusal to give to the poor. He questions why he should give to the poor if God himself, who possesses all, refuses to do so. But beyond all his rationalizations and his proud boasting, the maliciousness of the Rico's character is best reflected in three incidents that occur in this banquet scene of Rojas Zorrilla's *auto* just before both Lázaro and the Rico pass on to receive their rewards. At this stage in the drama, the Rico's determination has turned to cruel obstinacy. First, when Lázaro requests the table scraps, the Rico teases the poor man by permitting him to do no more than smell the food. Later, when Regocijo reports on the over-abundance of grain in the Rico's granaries and pleads with the man of wealth to distribute some of the food to the starving population, the Rico answers: "Llévelo el agua/ pues el agua me lo da;/ llévelo el viento también/ que el viento lo hizo granar,/ y no se lo lleve el pobre por ser mi gusto" (fol. 16). Finally, the Rico becomes disgusted with Lázaro and unleashes his dogs.

All three of the incidents described above and found in the banquet scene of Rojas Zorrilla's *auto* not only increase the dramatic intensity of the drama but also reflect the extent to which avarice and pride had carried the Rico Avariento beyond the hope of salvation. The audience, perhaps remembering Mira de Amescua's version of the theme, is now ready to accept the tragic end facing the Rico. The first two incidents, the Rico's teasing Lázaro with the food's smell and the Rico's refusal to give the over-flow of his granaries to the starving populace, are not found in the banquet scene of the Cordero *auto*. The "dog incident" can be found in the Cordero *auto* probably because it is found in the Gospel.

Chapter III

THE KINGDOM PARABLE *AUTOS*

In the introductory remarks to the last chapter it was established how the Gospel parable, steeped in the tradition of the figurative interpretation of the biblical exegetes, especially the Church fathers, provided valuable themes for the sacramental dramatists.[1] The *auto* dramatists not only took advantage of the ready-made allegory found in the traditional interpretation of the Gospel parables but they did so with the added assurance that their dramas would be understood by the people, who were familiar with the allegorical themes through sermons, religious art, etc. The "kingdom parables" have an even greater claim to the allegorical tradition. Two of the kingdom parables go back to the Gospel itself for their allegorization. Having told the story of the Sower who sows his seed that lodges in various types of soil, Jesus explains the meaning of his parable:

> When anyone hears the word of the kingdom, but does not understand it, the wicked one comes and snatches away what has been sown in his heart. This is he who has sown by the wayside. And the one sown on rocky ground, that is he who hears the word and receives it immediately with joy; yet he has no root in himself, but continues only for a time, and when trouble and persecution come because of the word, he at once falls away. And the one sown among the thorns, that is he who listens to the word; but the cares of this world and the deceitfulness of riches choke the word, and it is made

---

[1] See Chapter II, pp. 33-34.

fruitless. And the one sown upon good ground, that is he who hears the word and understands it; he bears good fruit and yields in one case a hundredfold, in another sixtyfold, and in another thirtyfold.

(Math. 13: 19-23)

In Matthew, there is a similar detailed allegory of another kingdom parable in which Jesus related the story of the wicked man who at night planted weeds among his neighbor's wheat. Note how the allegorical interpretation found in the Gospel sees the first part of the parable as presenting the state of God's earthly kingdom in which good and bad exist and how the second part shows the reward of the good in the heavenly kingdom:

> He who sows the good seed is the Son of Man. The field is the world; the good seed, the sons of the kingdom; the weeds, the sons of the wicked one; and the enemy who sowed them is the devil. But the harvest is the end of the world, and the reapers are the angels. Therefore, just as the weeds are gathered up and burnt with fire, so will it be at the end of the world. The Son of Man will send forth his angels, and they will gather out of his kingdom all scandals and those who work iniquity, and cast them into the furnace of fire, where there will be the weeping and the gnashing of teeth. Then the just will shine forth like the sun in the kingdom of their Father.
>
> (Math. 13:36-43)

Although, in fact, the evangelists record the allegorical explanation of the two parables of the Sower and the Weeds as being given by Jesus himself, some biblical exegetes such as Jeremias, who continually caution against over-allegorization in the parables, would seriously question whether or not Jesus did actually interpret the two parables or whether they even needed to be interpreted for his listeners. Jeremias argues that the explanations of the two parables found in the New Testament belonged to the evangelists themselves, who wrote many years later what Jesus had said and who then felt the need to interpret the parables adapting them to the times.[2] The problem of whether or

---

[2] Jeremias, 13-20. See also Chapter I, pp. 18-19.

not Jesus did in fact explain his parables may rightly be left to the exegetes. Significant, however, is the fact that at least two of the kingdom parables appear as allegorically interpreted in Scripture and thus deeply establish a precedence for future exegetes.

Besides the presence of detailed allegorical interpretations of two of the kingdom parables, the manner in which at least four of the kingdom parables to be included in the present study are introduced in the Gospel account also contributes to their established tradition of allegorical interpretation. The Parable of the Weeds, the Parable of the Laborers, the Parable of the Marriage Feast, and that of the Hidden Treasure all begin with the words, "the kingdom of heaven is like." This introductory phrase not only introduces the metaphoric nature of the parable with the word, "like," but also interprets the allegory by indicating that the situation in the parable is likened to the "kingdom of heaven." Again, whether or not the metamorphic introduction was really uttered by Christ or whether it was the expression used by the evangelist to introduce Jesus's parable is not relevant.[3] The fact is that the figurative introduction implying the parables' meaning is found in the Gospel and definitely influenced subsequent interpretations and views of the parables to which it was appended.

Although most scholars since Jülicher and the other "form critics" no longer view the parable as metaphor or allegory but basically as simile or analogy, nevertheless, even those who caution against too much allegorization cannot escape entirely the seemingly overwhelming influence of tradition in the allegorical approach to the parables. Hastings, for example, states that "to deny to Jesus all allegorical application of details and restrict Him to simple comparison is unwarranted."[4] Hastings adds that although in its essence the parable is not allegory "in its psychological origin the parable is closely akin to allegory."[5] Jones also confirms the mixture of parable and allegory in some of the New Testament parables.[6]

---

[3] Jeremias, 13-20.
[4] Hastings, 314.
[5] *Ibid.*
[6] Jones, 96-100.

Because the "literal and figurative are blended in such an unusual way" scriptural scholars differ as to what parables admit allegory and to what extent they do so.[7] Although this problem of selecting and sifting the allegorical from the parabolic in the New Testament parable gives rise to all combinations of classification, the kingdom parables such as the Parable of the Weeds, the Parable of the Sower, the Parable of the Vinedressers, the Parable of the Laborers of the Vineyard, the Parable of the Wedding Feast, most frequently appear among those parables admittedly containing allegorical elements.[8] On the other hand, it is interesting to note that the parables found in the *autos sacramentales* treated in the last chapter, The Prodigal Son, The Lost Sheep, The Good Samaritan, and The Rich Man and Lazarus, today no longer classify as allegories. In fact, Denzer states that the latter four parables were among those that were easily and immediately understood by Christ's listeners.[9]

Besides affording the *auto* dramatists a ready-made allegory forged by Scripture and the patristic tradition, the kingdom parables contained a great thematic richness. The wheat fields which serve as the setting for the Parables of the Sower and the Parable of the Weeds can be related to the Eucharistic theme. As it will be seen, Calderón was particularly effective in relating the themes of wheat, bread, and the Eucharist into allegorical masterpieces. Another setting seized upon by the dramatists and greatly apropos to the Eucharistic theme is the vineyards which form the setting of the Parable of the Vinedressers. The vineyards provide the wine which becomes Christ's blood through the mystery of transubstantiation, a favorite topic among dramatists. The writers of the sacramental play took advantage of the underlying theme and setting found in still another of the kingdom parables by linking the marriage feast in the parable of the same name to the Eucharistic banquet to which many are called but few come.

Thanks to the allegory found in the traditional exegesis, the *auto* dramatists discovered even greater thematic value in the kingdom parables. By presenting their dramas in accordance with

---

[7] Hastings, 314.
[8] Jones, 96-100.
[9] Denzer, 12.

the interpretation of the kingdom parables afforded by tradition, the dramatists were better able to defend the faith by lashing out against the enemies of the Church. In a great many of the *autos* to be discussed in this chapter and, in fact, in all of the sacramental dramas of Lope and Calderón, there are found the allegorical figures of Hebraísmo, Herejía, Seta, Idolatría, Apostasía, Gentilidad, and other figures hostile to the Church. While defending the faith and attacking heresies, the dramatists also fulfilled the positive function of the *auto sacramental* by pointing out the incongruities in the heresies and thus instructing the people in sound doctrine.[10] In combating heretical teachings, the dramatists were aware of Spain's particular responsibility to look after the faith and thus they extolled the country and its monarchs as the great defender of the faith.

In their defense of the faith, at times the *auto* dramatists became severe in their condemnation of some of the Church's enemies. There can be no question that in those kingdom parable *autos* in which the Jewish nation and her leaders appear as allegorical figures they receive harsh treatment in the drama's final moments. Most often, the Jews become outcast and are condemned to wander. But in one of Lope's dramas, as it will be observed, the punishment levied upon the Jews is much more severe, for Hebraísmo alone is condemned to the fires as the weeds of the good fields at harvest.[11] Certainly it is true that traditional interpretation of the kingdom parables allowed for such condemnation of the Jew who was responsible for the Savior's death, but it is also a fact that the dramatists chose their themes from Scripture of their own accord.

The Weeds

One of the earliest of the kingdom parables in the New Testament is the one describing the man who, having sowed

---

[10] For a discussion of the negative and positive goals of the *auto sacramental* see Chapter I, pp. 27-28.

[11] Flecniakoska finds unmistakable anti-Semitic feeling in the manner in which the Jew figures are treated in the *autos sacramentales* (*La Formation de l'auto religieux...*, p. 261). See also Julio Rodríguez-Puértolas, "La transposición de la realidad en los autos sacramentales de Lope de Vega," *Bulletin Hispanique*, LXXII (1970), especially, pp. 108-111.

good seed in his fields, permitted the weeds secretly planted by his enemy to grow unharmed until the harvest, when the wheat from the good seed was put into the granaries, while the weeds from the bad seed were burnt. As it has been indicated, the Parable of the Weeds, sometimes called the Parable of the Tares, is also among those parables to which the evangelists affix an allegorical explanation. [12]

In my search for those *autos sacramentales* treating of the Gospel parables, I have discovered three plays on the Parable of the Weeds. Two of the three *autos* already enjoy a certain amount of renown. Lope de Vega's *La siega* appears in several readily available editions and seems to be a favorite among editors. [13] Perhaps not as popular with editors but certainly known is Calderón de la Barca's *La semilla y la cizaña*, thanks chiefly to Angel Valbuena's excellent edition of the Calderonian *autos*. [14] The third *auto* on the Parable of the Weeds, *El juego del hombre*, is practically unknown, although it too appears printed in an edition by Louis Imbert. [15] *El juego del hombre* was written by Luis Mejía de la Cerda whose name appears at the very end of the manuscript and of whom there is little known except that he was "relator de la Real Audiencia de Valladolit." [16] The complete title of Mejía de la Cerda's *auto* as it is in the manuscript and in Imbert's edition reads: *Auto Sacramental del Juego del Hombre Fundado Sobre la Parábola del Sembrador y de la Zizaña, Mathui C (13): Simile factum est Regnum Coelorum Homini qui Seminavit Bon [um] Semen in Agro Suo. Feliciter Incipit*

---

[12] For the allegorical explanation of the Parable of the Weeds as it apears in Scripture see above, pp. 84-85.

[13] Lope's *auto* appears in the Academia edition, *Obras de Lope de Vega*, II, 309-323. The play also is reproduced in González Ruiz's *Piezas maestras...*, Vol. I, pp. 76-96, and in Alejandro Sanvisens' *Autos sacramentales...*, pp. 37-55. Quotations found in this study are taken from Pedroso's edition, pp. 171-181.

[14] Calderón de la Barca, *Obras completas*, III, 587-607. Quotations found in this study come from this edition by Valbuena.

[15] Luis Mejía de la Cerda, *Auto sacramental del juego del hombre*, ed. Louis Imbert, in *Romanic Review*, VI (July-September, 1915), 239-282. All quotations and references found in this study to Luis Mejía de la Cerda's *auto* are taken from Imbert's edition.

[16] See Imbert's introduction to Mejía de la Cerda's *auto* for remarks about the author's identity, *Romanic Review*, VI, 240.

sub Censura et Correctione Sanctae Matris Ecclesiae Catholice Romane.

All three of the *autos* on the Parable of the Weeds were presented in the seventeenth century. Although the exact date of Mejía de la Cerda's *El Juego del Hombre* is known, there is doubt as to the dates of Lope's and Calderón's plays.[17] With regard to Lope's *La siega*, in a footnote to his edition of the *auto*, Pedroso relies on evidence from the play itself to show that Lope could not have penned his drama before 1621, the year in which Philip IV ascended the Spanish throne. Lope specifically mentions the Spanish monarch in his drama.[18] Menéndez Pelayo, in his introductory remarks to the Academia edition of Lope's *autos*, conjectures that the author wrote his drama on the Parable of the Weeds sometime during the last five years of his life.[19] Using as basis his study of the devil's role in the Lopean autos, Flecniakoska assigns the exact date to Lope's *auto* as 1635, the last year of the author's life.[20]

In arriving at a precise date for the Calderonian *auto* one also encounters differences of opinion among the scholars. In his study on the life and works of Calderón, Cotarelo y Mori sets the date for *La semilla y la cizaña* at 1678.[21] Basing his conclusions on the versification of Calderón's plays which he studied in the manner of S. G. Morley and C. Bruerton of the Lopean theater, Harry Hilborn agrees with Cotarelo y Mori's date.[22] Valbuena Prat establishes the date of Calderón's *La semilla y la cizaña* on the internal evidence taken from another of Calderón's *autos*, *El cubo*

---

[17] The date, 1625, appears at the end of Imbert's edition to Mejía de la Cerda's *auto*.

[18] Pedroso, p. 180, n. 1. Imbert also concurs with Pedroso saying that Lope must have written his *La siega* between 1621-35. See Imbert's edition of *El juego del hombre*, *Romanic Review*, VI, p. 246, n. 11.

[19] See Menéndez Pelayo's introductory remarks to the Academia edition, Vol. II, p. xli.

[20] Flecniakoska, *Bulletin Hispanique*, LXVI, 44.

[21] Emilio Cotarelo y Mori, *Ensayo sobre la vida y obra de D. Pedro Calderón de la Barca* (Madrid, 1924), p. 19.

[22] Harry Hilborn, *A Chronology of Calderon's Plays* (Toronto: The University of Toronto, 1938), p. 114. In glancing at Hilborn's chronological listing, it is noted that he attributes all of the parable *autos* by Calderón, with the exception of *Los llamados y escogidos* (1648-51), to Calderón's later years.

de la Almudena, written in 1651.[23] Maintaining that the two *autos* were presented on the same day, Valbuena Prat asserts that in the latter *auto* "se alude claramente a la alegoría del auto anterior [*La semilla*] como la parábola de la siembra, en que intervienen las cuatro partes del mundo y en que se trata del tema evangélico de la semilla y la cizaña."[24] Valbuena also finds that in *La semilla* "se alude al tema de *El cubo de la Almudena*, auto que había de seguirla."[25]

Besides the reference to *El cubo de la Almudena*, pointed out by Valbuena, I find a passage in Calderón's *La semilla y la cizaña* that specifically mentions another of Calderón's *autos*, *La nave del mercader*. It is well established that Calderón penned his *La nave del mercader* in 1674.[26] It may well be that Calderón wrote his sacramental drama on the Parable of the Weeds four years after his *La nave* and that Hilborn and Cotarelo y Mori correctly gave the date of Calderón's *La semilla y la cizaña* as 1678. I quote the passage from Calderón's *auto* on the Parable that specifically refers to *La nave del mercader*:

> Aquel lejano bajel,
> que pez y ave se imagina,
> pues a un tiempo vuela y nada
> sobre las espumas rizas,
> es, si de mis conjeturas
> la ciencia nunca aprendida
> y siempre docta no engaña,
> al que otro texto publica
> *la nave del mercader*,
> que de remotas provincias
> trae el trigo por tesoro
> de sus celestiales Indias.
>
> (pp. 589-90)

---

[23] See Valbuena's introductory remarks found at the beginning of Calderón's *La semilla*, in *Obras...*, Vol. III, p. 587. Hilborn's date for the *El cubo de la Almudena* is 1651. See his chronological listing of the Calderonian *autos*, p. 114.

[24] Valbuena's introductory remarks to *La semilla*, in *Obras...*, Vol. III, p. 587.

[25] *Ibid*.

[26] Hilborn and Valbuena both agree. See Hilborn, p. 114, and Valbuena, *Obras...*, Vol. III, p. 1443.

Upon studying the three *autos* on the Parable of the Weeds, one observes that Mejía de la Cerda, Lope de Vega, and Calderón chose to develop their *autos* within the general allegorical framework found in the original Gospel account. In the discussion that follows, I will limit myself to a consideration of the extent to which the respective authors succeeded in manipulating the set allegory of the Gospel into a balanced and well-structured drama.

Of the three dramatists, Luis Mejía de la Cerda succeeded least in achieving any kind of unified and consistent allegory throughout the entirety of his drama. In the first part of his *El juego del hombre*, Mejía begins structuring his play along the traditional lines set forth in the New Testament account. Cristo, "el labrador del cielo y buen sembrador," speaks of cultivating his field and then entrusts its care to Zelo who represents the virtue of zeal and love of God.[27] Shortly after the departure of the Sembrador, Zelo grows weary of his labor and finally falls asleep waiting for the cultivated field to mature and ripen. While Zelo sleeps, the Zizañador [sic] "que es el demonio, vestido de labrador como Cristo" enters the field and plants his weeds.

In the second part of his play, Mejía loses sight of the parable's allegory and develops a kind of morality play in which the allegorical personages of Mundo and the Gustos vie for the allegiance of Hombre. The pleasures of the world prove to be too strong a match for Hombre who goes off with them in spite of the fact that Verdad, another allegorical figure, attempts to dissuade Hombre with a long sermon. Verdad's sermon affords Mejía an opportunity to satirize the various social strata from bad and irresponsible ecclesiastics to medical quacks and unscrupulous usurers (vv. 332-441). The play strays still further afield from the allegory of the drama's initial phase and of the original Gospel story when the Buen Sembrador decides to rescue Hombre from the Zizañador by volunteering to take Hombre's place in a card game initiated earlier by Hombre and at which he is losing. During the card game, in which the Sembrador stakes his life, each card represents a scene from Christ's passion, and the game ultimately

---

[27] The *Diccionario de la lengua española* (16th ed.; Madrid: Talleres de Publicaciones Herrerías, 1941), p. 280, gives the following definition of *celo*: "amor extremado y eficaz a la gloria de Dios y al bien de las almas."

ends in the Sembrador's death. The introduction of the card game, "El juego del hombre," from which the play draws its name, destroys the allegory of the parable developed in the first part of Mejía de la Cerda's play.

Having dwelt on Hombre's struggle with Mundo and the other evil figures and having developed at length "El juego del hombre," Mejía de la Cerda once again returns to the original parabolic theme in the last part of his *auto*. It is now the harvest, and the Good Sower orders Zizañador and his allies be burned, while penitent Hombre is saved by Cristo's redemption. Louis Imbert has commented, in the introduction to his edition of *El juego del hombre*, on the literary merit of the *auto*. Although I would agree with Imbert that Mejía de la Cerda's *auto* "has no great literary value," I would disagree with the second part of his statement that the *auto* "is, nevertheless, simple, dignified and well-balanced," and that "it can compare favorably with the *autos* of Lope de Vega."[28] At least it may safely be said that Mejía de la Cerda's *auto* on the Parable of the Weeds does not compare favorably with the better allegorically developed Lopean *auto* on the same Gospel parable.

Many find in Lope's *La siega* his greatest triumph as a writer of sacramental dramas. Menéndez Pelayo writes of Lope's auto: "Composición admirable, y a mi juicio la más bella entre todos los autos de Lope."[29] Even Ticknor, whose dislike for the *auto sacramental* in Spanish literature is well known, so esteemed Lope's *La siega* that he finds the play one of the "best and most solemn" of all the *autos sacramentales*.[30] Speaking more specifically of the allegory in *La siega*, Fray Modesto Sanzoles writes: "La alegoría general es una de las más sólidas y consistentes de Lope."[31]

As Sanzoles suggests in the quotation above, Lope succeeds in creating a drama consistent with the general allegory imposed by

---

[28] Louis Imbert's introductory remarks to his edition of Mejía de la Cerda's *Juego del hombre*, *Romanic Review*, VI, 240.

[29] Menéndez Pelayo in his "Observaciones Preliminares" to his *Obras*..., Vol. II, p. xli. See also Antonio Restori's praise of Lope's *auto* in his *Degli "Autos" di Lope de Vega Carpio* (Parma: R. Pellegrini Editore, 1898), p. 17.

[30] George Ticknor, *History of Spanish Literature* (3 vols.; London: John Murray, 1855), Vol. II, p. 217.

[31] Modesto de Sanzoles, "La alegoría como constante estilística de Lope de Vega en los autos sacramentales," *Revista de Literatura*, XVI (1959), 130.

Scripture. It is interesting to note the similarity between the allegory found in much of Lope's *La siega* and that found in Lope's other parable *autos* discussed in Chapter II. For example, Lope once again develops the love motif into which he introduces the familiar themes of honor and fidelity. The first part of Lope's drama centers around the love of the Esposa for the Señor de la Heredad. This first phase of Lope's *auto* resembles the initial phases of *El pastor lobo y la cabaña celestial*. It will be recalled that in *El pastor lobo*, the Cordera, the Pastor Cordero's wife, resides in the *cabaña celestial*. In the opening of the *Siega*, one can gather from the conversation of the two custodians of the wheat fields, Cuidado and Ignorancia, that the Esposa is asleep within the heavenly hut, for it is yet early morn. In their dialogue, Ignorancia laments that he and Cuidado must awaken the other laborers of the vineyard because "cuando está durmiendo el amo,/ ¿Esos cuidados le matan,/ Teniendo tan linda Esposa,/ En cuyos brasos descansa?" (p. 171). Later, in perhaps the most tender and poetic part of Lope's drama, Esposa pledges her love to the Señor de la Heredad. This introduction of the honor theme recalls similar vows of fidelity by Cordera to the Pastor Cordero.

The manner in which the two evil personages of the drama, Soberbia and Envidia, try to dishonor the Esposa and seduce her also recalls similar treatment in Lope's *autos* studied above. Like Apetito in *El pastor lobo* and Murmuración and Adulación in *La oveja perdida*, Soberbia and Envidia are astute psychologists in human affairs. They appeal first to Esposa's womanly vanity by telling her of her beauty, and then they lament that Esposa is already married to another. Finally Soberbia and Envidia deeply wound the heart of Esposa by telling her through the reading of her palm — for the two figures of evil disguise themselves as gypsies — that her husband is to die and that many of her children will be martyred. This last reference to the martyrdom of Esposa's children and in fact the entire first part of Lope's *auto* would be difficult to understand were one not to keep in mind Lope's allegorical treatment of Esposa as representing the Church who, in turn, represents the wheat of the fields or the good seed. The Church in the course of history suffers persecution and her children become the martyrs to which Soberbia and Envidia refer. Lope's allegorization of the metaphor of the Church wedded to

Christ enabled him not only to employ a popular theological theme while staying within the accepted bounds of the parable's interpretation but also to introduce the love theme so important to him.[32] That Lope was familiar with the various possible interpretations for certain aspects of the Gospel becomes clear in his words:

> En cosas que son tan altas;
> Que aquí, por alegoría,
> U de su Iglesia se trata,
> U del Reino de los Cielos
> U del Alma; que, con varias
> Razones, puede entenderse
> La Iglesia, El Reino y el Alma,
> A diferentes sentidos.
>
> (p. 172)

Having been rejected by Esposa who remains loyal to Christ and being more determined than ever to prevent the crop planted by the Señor de la Heredad from yielding a hundredfold, Soberbia and Envidia now turn their attention to the wheat fields on the other side of the *cabaña* in which Esposa safely reposes. The manner in which the two evil figures gain entrance into the wheat field by deceiving its guardian, Ignorancia, parallels Apetito's deception of Cuidado and his entrance into the *cabaña celestial* in *El pastor lobo*. Like Apetito who disguised himself as Mercurio, Soberbia and Envidia still retain their gypsy clothes with which they earlier tried to seduce Esposa. Again as in *El pastor lobo*, in which Cuidado is lulled to sleep by Apetito's fast talking, in *La siega*, Soberbia lulls Ignorancia into a deep slumber by relating to him an extremely long history of creation and the story of how the chief of the angels encountered the heavenly hosts in a fierce battle. Many such as Menéndez Pelayo and Mariscal de Gante have singled out this passage of Soberbia as the most poetic in the drama and as the first example of a true epic in the *autos sacramentales*.[33]

---

[32] The importance of the love theme in the development of Lope's *Hijo pródigo* came to light in Chapter II. See especially, p. 43.
[33] Menéndez Pelayo in his "Observaciones Preliminares" to his *Obras...*, Vol. II, p. lxii; and Mariscal de Gante, *Los autos sacramentales desde...*, p. 207.

Perhaps there is no better illustration of the critics' praise for Soberbia's epic tale of Lucifer's fall than the often quoted passage of Tomás Aguiló:

> Milton mismo se envaneciera de los pensamientos tan enérgicos y sublimes, tan verdaderamente orgullosos, que presta Lope a la Soberbia en el auto titulado *La siega*. Diríase que las ideas de Lope se atreven a competir, en elevación y grandeza con el orgullo del ángel caído.[34]

In the last part of *La siega*, unlike Mejía de la Cerda, Lope always keeps within the bounds of the parabolic allegory established in the initial phases of his drama by introducing the four figures of Hebraísmo, Herejía, Seta, and Idolatría, all of whom represent the weeds planted by the devil in the fields of the good seed. However, Lope does not expand upon these four figures nor does he capitalize upon their dramatic potentiality. Hebraísmo and the other weed figures just happen upon the drama and the audience never really sees how they were planted. After Ignorancia has been lulled to sleep, Soberbia and Envidia are only seen talking about sowing destruction as they are about to enter the garden. Once they appear, the action precipitously unfolds and Lope uses the weed figures to hurry his drama to a quick end. At first, the four figures representing various forms of religions and religious worship are at variance with the Señor and his Esposa. Later however, upon beholding the beauty of the *cabaña celestial* — again the scene recalls the closing stages of *El pastor lobo* — all become converted except Hebraísmo, who stubbornly refuses to accept the Gospel and who is burnt as chaff at the play's end.

As it has been continually observed in his *Hijo pródigo* and in his two *autos* on the Lost Sheep Parable, so too one notes in *La siega* Lope's inability to persevere in dramatizing through his entire play the extensive allegory found in the initial phases of his drama. Commenting on Lope's inability to create an allegory of any complexity, Fray Modesto de Sanzoles concludes his monograph on the Lopean *auto* by saying: "Lope no logra nunca escalar la cumbre de una perfección alegórica mayor, en cambio

---

[34] Quoted by Modesto de Sanzoles, *Revista de Literatura*, XVI, 133.

es un artista supremo en el manejo de alegorías menores." [35] Elaborating still further on this characteristic of Lope, he states:

> Construye sus alegorías casi siempre con maestría y habilidad, pero no demuestra nunca en las mayores, un dominio absoluto de su técnica. Maravilloso orfebre de miniaturas alegoricitas, no es nunca un celoso forjador de símbolos alegóricos. Juega, hábilmente, como diestro trapecista, con las alegorías menores, pero en las generales nunca se desenvuelve con holgura. [36]

Before moving to Calderón's masterful drama on the Parable of the Weeds, it would be well to point out that Lope's condemnation of the Hebraísmo in the end of his *La siega* stands out as one of the harshest treatments of the Jew found in the kingdom parable *autos*. As it will be observed later in this study, Calderón only condemned the Jews as an outcast among nations in his portrayal of the Parable of the Weeds. The powerful poetic utterance with which the Señor de la Heredad addresses the Jews leaves no doubt as to the severity of Lope's condemnation:

> ¡Oh, rebelde porfiado!
> ¿Tú solo me niegas, ¡tú,
> Que has visto tantos milagros,
> Las profecías cumplidas,
> Y que vives desterrado
> Sin templo, sin sacerdote,
> Sin rey, sin amparo humano? —
> ¡Echadle al fuego eterno!
> (p. 181)

While condemning the Jews, Lope found occassion to extol Spain and her reigning monarch for being the staunch defenders of the faith in Europe. [37] The Señor de la Heredad does so while speaking with Esposa, who represents the Church entrusted with keeping the faith on earth:

---

[35] Modesto de Sanzoles, *Revista de Literatura*, XVI, 133.
[36] *Ibid*.
[37] Although Ticknor praises Lope's *La siega*, he criticizes him for interjecting into his drama "some very misplaced compliments to the reigning royal family." See his *History...*, Vol. II, p. 217.

> Y entre los reyes de Europa
> Deberás a un quinto Carlos
> Oponerse á la herejía
> De un labrador temerario;
> Por quien á sus decendientes,
> Segundo, tercero y cuarto
> Felipes, dará otro mundo,
> Nunca visto, el cielo en pago.
>
> (p. 180) [38]

In his *La semilla y la cizaña*, Calderón succeeded in developing a balanced and well-structured allegory on the Parable of the Weeds. In fact, the *maestro* of the *autos sacramentales* united the Parable of the Weeds to the closely related Parable of the Sower and from the allegorical interpretations found in Scripture of the two parables wrote a fine sacramental drama.

The manner in which Calderón blended together the two related parables of the Weeds and the Sower into a single unified allegory is truly indicative of his remarkable ability as an *auto* writer. So meticulously did the master of the *autos sacramentales* construct his sacramental play that throughout one may perceive a symmetrical pattern centered on the number four. The drama begins with the evil figure Cizaña (Weeds), soliciting the aid of his three evil companions, Cierzo (North Wind), Ira (Locust), and Niebla (Cloud). Together the four plagues of nature represent the weeds of the parable and form the evil contingents of the play. Immediately after the play's initial scene in which the weed-figures boast of their destructive powers and their ability to spread havoc among the good seed, Calderón introduces the Sembrador (Christ) and Inocencia (Virtue or Grace) who are hastily enroute to plant the seed (Word of God) in the world. But note that, unlike Mejía de la Cerda, who depicted the world with the simple allegorical figure of Mundo, Calderón depicts it by introducing its four main parts, Asia, Africa, Europa, and América. Later, when the Sembrador wishes to form the contract whereby the continents would permit him to plant the seed, or, figuratively, listen to the word of God, each continent in turn, beginning with

---

[38] This passage influenced Pedroso's dating of Lope's *auto*. See above, p. 90.

Asia, asks to consult with its respective leader or *mayoral*. Once again four allegorical figures, Judaísmo, Paganismo, Gentilidad, and Idolatría appear, each representing the religious expression generally associated with their respective continents.

As the drama unfolds, the four destructive elements of nature are pitted against the four continents each led respectively by its *mayoral*. Each personage acts and responds to the various dramatic situations in accordance with its allegorical nature. For example, Judaísmo hardened of heart and anxious for an almighty Messiah does not understand the Sembrador's words and so entrusts his people, Asia, to the Cierzo who immediately blows away and easily dissipates all the planted seed of the Sembrador. Paganismo listens to Sembrador's words but is unable to stay awake and so willingly entrusts Africa to another evil figure, Ira, who quickly devours what little seed has begun to grow so that Paganismo can only give account later for the straw that remains. Idolatría whose land is América and who is accustomed to gazing idly upon her wealth and riches cannot help being fascinated by the beauty of Sembrador and pays no attention to his words. Thus Idolatría too entrusts the care of her people to a stranger, Cizaña, who proceeds to grow among the wheat and choke it out. Gentilidad, unlike the other three *mayorales*, at least listens to the word but, because she vacillates in doubt and fails to act upon the word, Niebla, to whom she entrusts her people, in time withers and mildews the good seed. In the final stages of his drama, in which the Sembrador is finally put to death, Calderón does not fracture his allegory like Mejía de la Cerca by portraying Christ's passion with the card game, but rather he continues with the established symmetrical pattern in a manner that truly reflects his genius. Taking the initiative in Christ's death, Judaísmo snatches from the hand of each of the other *mayorales* that which remains of the seed after the elements have destroyed it and ironically uses the remnants as an instrument to persecute Christ. Paganismo's straw stalk becomes Sembrador's sceptre. The thorns and thistles left Idolatría by Cizaña form the crown of thorns placed on the Redeemer's head. The mildewed tuft of the vacillating Gentilidad stretches across the Savior's eyes as a fit symbol of the blindfold. Finally, Judaísmo grasps in her hands the stones upon which the seed fell and from which all was blown away and hurls them at the suffering Sembrador (figure 1).

Calderón's dramatized allegory found in his *La semilla y la cizaña* is all the more amazing when one considers that it corresponds closely to the allegorical interpretation found in the evangelist.[39] Refusing to hear the word, Judaísmo, hardened of heart, corresponds to the seed that fell on the rocky ground: that is, "he who hears the word and receives it immediately with joy; yet has no root in himself" (Math. 13:20-21). Paganismo and Idolatría correspond respectively to the seeds that fell by the wayside and those that fell among the thorns; the former are trodden on by man and are eaten up by the birds of the air, while the latter become choked by the cares, riches, and pleasures of the world. At first, Gentilidad doubts and is slow to grasp the full significance of the word. However, in the end like the good seed of the Gospel parable, she accepts the word and nurtures it, and it finally grows into a strong and mature faith. It is known that Calderón was accustomed to employing the four elements of air, fire, land, and water which appear in many of his dramas and which have been studied to some extent by E. M. Wilson.[40] There does exist a corresponding similarity between the four scourges of nature, Cizaña, Cierzo, Ira, and Niebla and the allegorical figures of Tierra, Aire, Fuego, and Agua.[41]

There is no doubt that Calderón was aware of the symmetry of the drama he was constructing, for he states it clearly within the drama itself.[42] In the beginning of the *auto*, there is a rather lengthy passage in the manner of a prologue, in which Cizaña, asking his three evil companions to join against the four continents, states:

---

[39] For the allegorical interpretation of the Parable of the Weeds found in the Gospel, see the quotation from the evangelist found above, pp. 84-85.

[40] E. M. Wilson, "The Four Elements in the Imagery of Calderón," *Modern Language Review*, XXXI (1936), 34-47.

[41] In his two *autos* on the Parable of the Laborers in the Vineyards, *La siembra del señor* and *El día mayor de los días*, there is a similar treatment of the wheat theme but Calderón developed his dramas around only the three elements of Judaísmo, Apostasía, and Idolatría. For a more detailed discussion of the two *autos*, *La siembra* and *El día mayor*, see below, pp. 109-117.

Allegory of Parable in Gospel	Part of the World (Continents)	Mayorales	Plagues of Nature	Reaction to Sermon	Fruits after the Plagues	Instrument Used by Judaísmo in Passion
Seed on rocky ground. Blown away.	Asia. (Dressed as Jew on Elephant)	Judaísmo. (Hebraísmo)	Cierzo.	Refuses to believe. Remains stubborn and obstinate.	Rocks.	The rocks for stoning.
Seed by the wayside. Trodden on. Eaten up.	Africa. (Dressed as Moor on Lion)	Paganismo.	Ira.	Becomes bored. Falls asleep.	Straw.	The stalk of straw symbolic of sceptre.
Seed among the weeds. Took root but choked out.	América. (Dressed as Indian on Alligator)	Idolatría.	Cizaña.	Dwells upon externals. Becomes indifferent.	Thorns and thistles.	The crown of thorns.
Seed in good ground. Yielded a hundredfold.	Europa. (Dressed as Roman on Bull)	Gentilidad.	Niebla.	Vacillates in doubt and indecision.	Rotten grain.	The blindfold.

Fig. 1.—The Structured Allegory of *La semilla y la cizaña*.

> Y así, pues, en cuatro partes
> de la tierra nos avisa
> la letra que ha de caer
> esta Semilla, que, mixta,
> es Semilla y es Palabra,
> y la tierra dividida
> en cuatro partes está
> y somos cuatro las Iras,
> en buen duelo cuatro a cuatro
> tratemos de destruirla.
>
> (p. 590)

In the above quotation, attention is drawn particularly to the line "en buen duelo cuatro a cuatro" which reflects Calderón's awareness of the dramatic value of portraying a conflict in which the odds are even. Milton Marx in discussing the essence of drama and what constitutes good dramatic conflict writes: "In order to make the struggle or conflict exciting, which is one of the synonyms of *dramatic*, the playwright must make the odds fairly even." [43]

Within this rigid structure based on the pattern of four elements and beneath the basic allegory of the two Parables of the Weeds and the Sower, Calderón presents the story of salvation and redemption. In reality, the panoramic view of man's redemption gives life and dynamism to the allegory of the two parables portrayed by affording dramatic movement. For example, the coming of the Sembrador to plant the seed is depicted by an obvious reference to Christ's advent and birth. Lucero del Día represents St. John the Baptist who comes before the Sembrador

---

[42] For a penetrating study of the balance and structure of Calderón's dramas see chapter four, "La correlación en la estructura del teatro calderoniano," in Dámaso Alonso and Carlos Bousoño's *Seis calas en la expresión literaria española* (Madrid: Editorial Gredos, 1963), pp. 111-175. Speaking specifically of the *autos sacramentales*, Dámaso Alonso states: "No cabe duda alguna de que la construcción de los autos sacramentales, sobre todo los menos realistas o más conceptuales, es fundamentalmente correlativa. Los personajes simbólicos aparecen y actúan por parejas o ternas o cuaternas, o quinas" (p. 163). For another study on Calderonian structure and symmetry see Lucien-Paul Thomas, "Les jeux de scéné et l'architecture de idées dans le théâtre allégorique de Calderón," *Homenaje a Menéndez Pelayo*, Vol. II, pp. 501-30.

[43] Milton Marx, *The Enjoyment of Drama* (New York: Appleton-Century Crofts, Inc., 1961), p. 23.

to announce Christ's advent. The people do not heed Lucero del Día's words, and Inocencia, another allegorical figure of virtue and grace, explains that the reason the people pay no attention is because it is cold out and "hielo nos pasma" (p. 592) — Christmas comes in the cold of winter. Finally, to depict the actual arrival of the Sembrador, Calderón uses the metaphor of the ship, developed in another *auto*.[44] Christ, both the Sembrador and the *Semilla* (*trigo*), is brought to the world in the *Nave* representing the Virgin. Note how cleverly Calderón manipulates orthography of the *"nave"* to read *"ave"* thus referring the whole concept of the ship of wheat to the mother of Christ:

> Pues ser Nave en esos mares
> cuyo nombre es la armonía,
> Nave es María, claramente
> en dos sentidos se explica
> el que yo temo, supuesto
> que ninguno habrá que diga
> Nave y María que no haya
> (si a la Nave la N quita
> y al María muda el acento)
> dicho Ave y dicho María.
>
> (p. 590)

Calderón uses the second phase of Christ's life, his ministry, to depict the Sembrador's planting of the good seed. In Lope's *La siega*, one never sees dramatized how the good or bad seed are planted.[45] The Sembrador appears sitting in his boat anchored off shore and preaching to the four continents standing in the desert. When Inocencia, who accompanies the Sembrador, complains that there are not enough loaves of bread to feed the multitude Sembrador replies in an obvious reference to the Eucharist: "el bocado más pequeño/ satisfará tanto como/ si uno le

---

[44] Calderón used the ship metaphor in *El cubo de la Almudena* and *La nave del mercader*. For a discussion of the relationship of these two *autos* to Calderón's *La semilla* see above. p. 91.

[45] While praising Lope's use of allegory in his *La siega*, nevertheless Sanzoles admits that the play "no deja de tener sus fallos." Sanzoles criticizes Lope for depicting the servants, instead of the Sembrador, as the planters of the good seed. See Sanzoles's article in *Revista de Literatura*, XVI, 130.

comiera entero" (p. 596). Calderón uses the well-known scene of the multitude on the sea shore and the miracle of the loaves and the fishes, which appears in Chapter fourteen of Matthew, immediately after the chapter in which the two Parables of the Weeds and the Sower appear, to depict Christ's ministry and the manner in which he preached the Gospel and sowed the word. Note also that the *nave* which Calderón used so figuratively to represent the Virgin now becomes "un barco dentro del mar/ cátedra en que se predica" (p. 591). At the end of the *auto*, the ship takes on a third metaphoric role in the drama as the Church. The Sembrador tells Gentilidad that the two will sail together in the *Nave*, "que es la figura y la sombra/ de mi Iglesia Militante" (p. 606). With regard to the final and most important part of Christ's life, it has been indicated how Calderón effectively dramatized the redemption within the symmetrical pattern of his allegory in which the four continents and their *mayorales* all contribute to Christ's passion and death. Calderón completes his story of salvation history by depicting Christ's second coming in a scene portraying Man's final judgement.

Besides the symmetry of allegory that serves as backbone of the play and the underlying theme of salvation history, there remains still another facet that reveals the complexity of Calderón's allegorical labyrinth and the skill with which he structured his drama. Aware of the tremendous instructional value of the *auto sacramental*, Calderón uses the setting afforded by the parable of the seed-wheat, and relates it to the Eucharist. Lope neglected almost entirely the connection of the wheat to the Eucharist. Only once does Lope make any reference to the wheat and bread of the Eucharist in his *auto*: "Pues siembra Dios el trigo de Belen/ En tierra Virgen, para darles Pan" (p. 176). Mejía de la Cerda, on the other hand, did relate the parabolic theme of the wheat and the Eucharist, but only at the very end of his drama, in which Cristo appears with the host made from the wheat of the fields. Only Calderón constantly keeps before his audience the Eucharistic theme by closely integrating the wheat of the parabolic wheatfields with the bread of the Sacrament. In the early stages of Calderón's drama, one of the weed figures, Cizaña, in a lengthy discourse introduces the Eucharistic theme and ties it up closely with the allegory of the drama. First, Cizaña speaks of the Nave filled with wheat symbolic of Mary, who brought the bread of life into the world. Next, Cizaña speaks of the idea of seed or *semilla* which in the allegorical interpretation of the parable stands for the word of God. Then, bringing together the idea of the wheat-bread (*trigo-pan*) and that of the seed-word (semilla-palabra) Cizaña arrives at the matter and form of the Eucharist. The matter of a sacrament is the material sign of the sacrament. In the case of the Eucharist, the matter becomes the bread made of wheat. The form of the sacrament is defined as the words used in the sacrament itself, and thus Calderón's reference to the *semilla*, which has received its meaning from the parable as the word.[46] I now quote at length Cizaña's words in which Calderón first introduces the Eucharistic theme into his drama and relates it to the parabolic theme of wheat:

> Pues siendo así, que ya en una
> parte al texto verifica,
> que es Semilla la Palabra
> de Dios: y en otra averigua,
> que el trigo de aquella Nave,
> a quien siempre el Austro inspira
> y nunca el Abrego toca;
> también de aquesa Semilla,
> que ha de dar ciento por uno,
> si en tierra cae pura y limpia,
> quien duda (¡ay de mi!), quien duda,
> que de unión tan peregrina,
> como son Pan y Palabra;
> bien que son cosas distintas,
> siendo él Materia, ella Forma,
> se venga a hacer algún Día
> algún Grande *Sacramento*,
> cuya inmensa maravilla
> imaginada me asombra.
>
> (p. 590)

---

[46] The following is an explanation of what is meant by the "form" and the "matter" of a sacrament: "The external thing or action is called the *matter*, and the formula of words, the *form*, of the sacrament," Louis Laravoire Morrow, *My Catholic Faith* (Kenosha, Wisconsin: My Mission House, 1963), p. 266.

Another example of how Calderón kept the wheat-Eucharist theme before his audience and how he actually integrated the theme and gave it a functional role in the action of the play is found in the Sembrador's sermon. It will be recalled from the discussion above that Sembrador preached to the four continents and to their leaders, but they could not understand what he was saying. The subject of the Sembrador's sermon was precisely that of the Eucharist. In the Sembrador's sermon there is present once again the metaphoric relationship of the wheat-bread, seed-word concepts but one also finds an expansion of the concepts that reaches the very core of the doctrine of the Eucharist, the transubstantiation.[47] In the equation, *trigo-pan*, *semilla-palabra*, by changing *palabra* to the Latin word, *Verbo*, Calderón through the mouth of the Sembrador, introduces the passage from St. John's Gospel in which the "Word was made flesh."[48] Calderón then concludes his syllogism by stating that if the Word was made flesh as St. John states, then the bread is made flesh or becomes Christ's body because the two, that is the word and the bread, combine in matter and form to make the Eucharist. Once again I quote at length the passage in which Calderón in the personage of the Sembrador treats of the doctrine of transubstantiation and unites the parabolic theme with the Eucharistic:

> Luego si en latino idioma
> *Verbo* y Palabra es lo mesmo,
> y la Palabra es el Trigo
> en el pasado argumento,
> podrán Pan, *Verbo* y Palabra
> obrar algun *Sacramento*
> en que se hace Carne el Pan,
> ya que se hizo Carne el *Verbo*;
> bien que de distinto modo,
> pues fué por unión aquello;

---

[47] By "transubstantiation" is meant that "the entire substance of bread and wine is changed into our Lord's Body and Blood." See Morrow, p. 278.

[48] The passage from Scripture containing this concept of "the Word made Flesh" comes from St. John's first chapter of his Gospel. The Spanish were well acquainted with this part of St. John's Gospel since the first fourteen verses of the evangelist's first chapter were read aloud in Latin at the end of each Mass.

y mudando el Pan, Sustancia
es por conveniencia aquesto.
(p. 597)

Before moving on to the next of the kingdom parables, it is well to note that in the very last part of his *La semilla y la cizaña* Calderón did not follow the original Gospel account. In the Parable on the Weeds, the angels of the Son of Man gather together the harvest and, separating the good from the bad, they preserve the wheat and burn the chaff. It will be recalled that Lope in his *auto*, *La siega*, adhered to the Gospel account by depicting the converted Herejía, Seta, and Idolatría, as the wheat and by harshly condemning Hebraísmo to the fires of eternity. In Calderón, because of its active part in Christ's death, Judaísmo becomes a *desterrado* rejected by all the parts of the world including Asia. In picturing the Jew as rejected by society and other nations, Calderón chooses to convey to the audience the Jewish guilt by relying on the historical fact of Israel's destitution rather than risk portraying bad theology by condemning the whole Jewish nation to hell. Calderón was also cognizant of the fact that the Jews alone were not responsible for Christ's death and that, theologically speaking, Christ died for the sins of all mankind. For this reason, it was demonstrated in the discussion above how Calderón masterfully and uniquely portrayed the shared responsibility for the Savior's death as Judaísmo borrows from each of the other *mayorales* that which remains of their fruits and uses them as instruments of crucifixion symbolic of the sceptre, the crown of thorns, the blindfold, and the stones. Finally, while Judaísmo suffers destitution and Idolatría and Paganismo are left to shift for themselves, only Gentilidad receives the mandate to take over for Judaísmo and to plant the seed and spread the word of God. In entrusting the Gentiles with the Gospel, Calderón once again adheres to theology and tradition which has held from the time of Peter that Gentiles were to be included in the Church that Christ founded.[49]

---

[49] See the Acts of the Apostles, especially Chapter X.

The Laborers in the Vineyard

In my study of the kingdom parable *auto*, I move now from the Parables of the Sower and of the Weeds to the Parable of the Laborers in the Vineyard. The Gospel account of the Laborers in the Vineyard describes the well-known story of the owner who hires workers for the vineyard at different times during the day and then sees fit to pay all the hired help the same wages regardless of what hour they began working. The Parable of the Laborers in the Vineyard enters the discussion at this time because, as it will be seen, two of the three sacramental plays on this New Testament parable were written by Calderón and are similar to his *La semilla y la cizaña* in some aspects of theme and structure.

Sebastián de Horozco wrote the earliest *auto* I have found on the Laborers in the Vineyard under the title of *Representación de la parábola de Sant Mateo a los veinte capítulos de su sagrado evangelio: la qual se hizo y representó en T. en la fiesta del santíssimo sacramento por la Sta. Iglia.* [50] Although Horozco's *auto* gives the date of the drama's representation as 1548, a reference in the *auto* to the papal bull of Pope Leo X in 1517 and the Pontiff's decree a year later condemning Luther and his errors would seem to indicate that "si este suceso era reciente cuando Horozco escribía, como parece indicarlo el diálogo, quizá es la parábola mucho más antigua de lo que indica la fecha de su representación." [51] With regard to Calderón's two *autos*, Valbuena shows 1655 as the date for *La siembra del Señor* and 1678 for his second *auto* on the Parable of the Laborers in the Vineyard, *El día mayor de los días*.[52] Hilborn radically disagrees with Valbuena as to when Calderón wrote his *La siembra*, setting the *auto*'s date between 1673 and 1675, but he comes closer to meeting Valbuena's chronology of Calderon's *El día mayor* by fixing its dates between 1672-1673.[53]

---

[50] The *auto* appears in *Cancionero de Sebastián de Horozco*, ed. Antonio Martín Gamero ("Sociedad de Bibliófilos Andaluces," Vol. VII; Sevilla: Imprenta de Rafael Tarasco y Lassa, 1874), pp. 148-156. Quotations appearing in this study are taken from this edition.
[51] *Ibid.*, p. 153, n. 1.
[52] Valbuena Prat, *Obras...*, Vol. III, p. 677.
[53] Hilborn, 114.

I need not spend much time considering Horozco's *Representación a la parábola de Sant Mateo*. The *auto* may best be characterized by saying that it is the most elementary and the simplest of *autos* yet to be considered in the present study. Two peasants, two soldiers who were "captivos y prisioneros/ de las galeras de Argel" (p. 151), two solicitors for religious orders, and an old man and his son, each in his turn, are lamenting their poverty when the Padre de las Familias calls them to work in his vineyards. At the end of the day's work, all accept the same pay in spite of some short-lived grumbles from those who had begun work early in the day. Perhaps the only real worth of Horozco's drama, as Crawford suggests, lies in "the portrayal of everyday life" and of a social background "which shows unrelieved misery of the common people." [54]

Although Calderón uses the Parable of the Laborers in the Vineyard as the basis of his two dramas, *La siembra del Señor* and *El día mayor de los días*, he builds both plays around the theme of the wheat and the wheatfields much as he had done in his *La semilla y la cizaña*. The laborers, who consist of various allegorical figures representing the various stages of human and religious history, such as Adán, Moisés, or La Ley Natural and La Ley Escrita, etc., go out at different times to prepare the ground for the wheat or the Word of God. Once again, as he had done in his *La semilla y la cizaña*, Calderón integrates into his two dramas the *trigo-pan* and *semilla-palabra (verbo)* concepts and relates them to the Eucharist. A beautifully poetic passage found at the end of the Calderonian *autos* and identical in both, aptly expresses the relationship between the wheat and the Eucharist when Christ, the Word made flesh, is compared point by point with the kernel of wheat. To give only an example of the rather lengthy comparison, the grain of wheat grows in rich and fertile soil; Christ too found a rich and fertile soil in which to grow — the Virgin. The grain of wheat is subjected to all types of weather; Christ too was subjected "a las inclemencias del sol y del hielo" (p. 1655). Wheat consists of both kernel and stalk, grain and straw; so also with regard to Christ "Divinidad/ y Humanidad lo declaren" (p. 1655). In order to reap the harvest of grain, wheat is cut

---

[54] J. P. Crawford, p. 51.

down and threshed and bound; so too the Savior was cut, scourged, bound and finally died in order to produce the fruits of Redemption.[55]

Besides being similar in the wheat-Eucharist theme, in allegorical structure the two *autos* by Calderón on the Parable of the Laborers in the Vineyard also resemble *La semilla y la cizaña* especially with regard to the religion figures, this time three, Judaísmo, Idolatría, and Apostasía. The three religion figures function in the same manner as they did in *La semilla y la cizaña* by ultimately refusing the word of God and by cooperating with the devil figures, Culpa (*La siembra*) and Noche (*El día mayor*), in destroying the *trigo*. All three religion figures contribute to Christ's suffering, but once again only Judaísmo is given the responsibility for actually putting Emmanuel to death as Idolatría and Apostasía back down and try to prevent the deicide as they had done in *La semilla*.

From the consideration thus far, it becomes quite obvious that Calderón's two sacramental dramas on the Laborers in the Vineyard not only resemble his *auto* on the Parable of the Weeds and of the Sower but that they also resemble each other. However, there also exist some interesting differences between the two *autos*, *La siembra del Señor* and *El día mayor de los días*. I wish to examine these variations before moving on in my study to the next group of kingdom parable *autos*, those dealing with the Parable of the Vinedressers.

In his second dramatization of the Laborers in the Vineyard, *El día mayor de los días*, Calderón achieved greater balance and symmetry than in his first *auto* on the Gospel parable, *La siembra del Señor*. In a manner recalling the structure of his *La semilla y la cizaña*, the master of the sacramental drama develops a patterned allegory. The three laws, Ley Natural, Ley Escrita, and Ley de la Gracia, represent the laborers who are called to work in the vineyard at different stages in the religious history of mankind.

---

[55] For the passage as it appears in the *La siembra* see Valbuena Prat's edition, p. 692. For the passage as it appears in *El día mayor* see the same edition, pp. 1654-55. See also Sister M. Francis de Sales McGarry, *The Allegorical and Metaphorical Language in the "Autos Sacramentales" of Calderón* (Washington, D. C.: The Catholic University of America, 1937), pp. 117-119.

In order to construct a trio of personages around each of the *leyes*, Calderón introduces not only Adán, Moisés, and Emanuel but also Idolatría, Judaísmo, and Apostasía. Ley Natural and Ley Escrita, when they appear for the first time in the drama in their proper order, are accompanied by their respective complementary figures Adán and Moisés, as well as by Idolatría and Judaísmo, respectively. Although Ley de Gracia enters the drama for the first time with the other two law figures, she is not yet accompanied by her corresponding companion personage, Emanuel, who appears later as the Christ figure. In Calderón's *La siembra*, one does not find such neat arrangements of allegorical personages. In fact, the three *leyes* do not even enter the drama. Although Adán and Emanuel appear in Calderón's first drama, Moisés is conspicuously missing. Instead of Idolatría, Judaísmo, and Apostasía appearing with their respective *leyes* and figurative heroes, all three religion personages come on stage together.

With regard to the different ways in which Calderón introduced the religion figures of Idolatría, Judaísmo, and Apostasía into his two dramas, technically speaking it was more convenient for the author to introduce the three figures together in so far as Culpa and Sueño, the devils, could immediately turn them against Emanuel who was about to enter the drama. In his *El día mayor*, because Idolatría, Judaísmo, and Apostasía were introduced separately as the third element in their respective trios, Calderón necessarily had to devise a method to bring the religion figures together in the play without losing the *auto*'s dramatic force. This he accomplished when each of the religion figures freely leaves his respective camp and flees in search of the devil, Noche, because Idolatría could not accept one God but worshipped many, Hebraísmo accepted monotheism but rejected the Incarnation and the second person of the Trinity, Apostasía accepted monotheism and the Trinity but found difficulties with the Eucharist and the doctrine of transubstantiation (pp. 1648-50).

Besides differing as to the extent of the patterned allegory, there are certain interesting innovations in Calderón's second *auto* on the Parable of the Laborers in the Vineyard that are not present in his first drama on the same parable. *La siembra del Señor* begins as one would expect with the Padre de las Familias calling the first of the laborers, Adán, to work in the vineyard. In his *El día mayor*, Calderón begins his play by presenting Ingenio, an entirely new figure that nowhere appears in his *La siembra* nor in any other *auto* on the Gospel parables that is considered in this study. Reading from a book, Ingenio, who represents man's curiosity or ingenuity, initiates the drama by posing several questions that arise from his reading and to which he can find no solution.[56] Ingenio particularly wonders about a passage in St. John where it says that "el Grano que cae en Tierra,/ si en ella no muere, nada/ fructifica y queda él solo;/ mas que como en Tierra caiga,/ dará tan colmados Frutos/ que llenen trojes y parvas" (p. 1639).[57] Ingenio also puzzles over "el día mayor de los días," that is to say how the wheat can be planted, threshed, and made into bread all on the same day. Note how the two questions brought up by Ingenio relate closely to the Eucharist and how in fact the objective of the play will be to answer Ingenio's questions.

Disturbed and perplexed by the two questions found in his readings, Ingenio encounters Calderón's second innovation the allegorical figure, Pensamiento. Representing man's thoughts, Pensamiento thrusts himself on the pensive Ingenio who is angered by Pensamiento's intrusion and characterizes him as being a madman who flutters about toying with the imagination: "Ya sé que eres loco y no/ loco de atar, pues no hay cuerda/ imaginación que tú/ no rompas" (1637).[58] Pensamiento warns Ingenio that he will not find an easy solution to his problems and that only the Padre de las Familias, who knows everything, can help him.[59]

---

[56] More than once in his drama Calderón has employed this technique of the inquiring intellectual puzzled over some passage he has read from Scripture or from other sources. See José M. de Cossío, "Racionalismo del arte dramático de Calderón," *Cruz y Raya*, XXI (1934), pp. 37-76.

[57] The passage is found in St. John, 7:24-25.

[58] On the dramatic function of Pensamiento in the dramas of Calderón see Sturgis Leavitt, "Humor in the *Autos* of Calderón," *Hispania*, XXXIX (May, 1956), 137-44. See also Lucien-Paul Thomas, "François Bertaut et les conceptions dramatiques de Calderón," *Revue de Litterature Comparée*, IV (1924), 199-221.

[59] When coupled with Pensamiento, Ingenio often represents man's imagination or that part of man's reasoning faculty having the property of "la razón de dudar." Significantly in the *auto* under discussion, Ingenio experiences doubt and is plagued by the passage from St. John and "el día mayor de los días." See Eugenio Frutos, *La filosofía de Calderón en s s autos sacramentales* (Zaragoza: Institución "Fernando el Católico" de la Excma. Diputación Provincial, 1952), pp. 165-173.

In dramatizing the Padre de las Familias, Calderón gives to this figure a new and unique allegorical dimension. In his *El día mayor*, the Padre appears as Tiempo. Aware that God is all present and in this sense is Time itself, Calderón chooses to dramatize this attribute of the Almighty and to apply it metaphorically to the already allegorical figure of the Padre de las Familias. Pensamiento explains to Ingenio by what process the Padre de las Familias may be considered as time:

> Viendo que en su Providencia
> no hay tiempo para él pasado
> ni futuro, de manera
> que tiempo presente es todo,
> aunque varios nombres tenga,
> bien podrá hoy el Pensamiento,
> en metáfora de idea
> (no tanto en la realidad
> cuanto en lo que representa),
> darle el del tiempo en común
> en fe de que le convenga;
> pues si le consideramos
> Padre de Familias, cierta
> cosa es que ninguno es
> más Padre de todas ellas
> que el Tiempo, si le juzgamos
> Poderoso, él nos sustenta.
>   (pp. 1637-38)

In assigning the Padre de las Familias the new figurative dimension of time, Calderón also gives to this allegorical personage a dual function in the drama. Tiempo functions both as the Padre de las Familias who calls the Ley Natural, Adán, and the other laborers to the fields and also as the figure of time or "timelessness" who takes Pensamiento and Ingenio back into history by way of a flashback: "¡Ea, memorias pasadas,/ sedme presentes acuerdos/ que prueben ser Semejanza/ de la Edad de Cristo el Trigo!" (p. 1640).

With the introduction of the three new figures of Ingenio, Pensamiento, and Tiempo, one finds in Calderón's *El día mayor* a complex dramatic structure of a play within a play. On the one hand, there is the drama of salvation history in which the three *leyes* with their corresponding component figures play the main roles. And on the other hand, there is the second drama in which Ingenio and Pensamiento watch the salvation story unfolding before them. Although because of his dual role, Tiempo functions within both dramas as the Padre de las Familias and as chief interpreter for Pensamiento and Ingenio, the latter two figures never enter into the salvation story of the play except at the *auto's* very end. After each scene in the salvation drama and before another of the *leyes* enters the stage, one sees Ingenio and Pensamiento discussing with Tiempo the relevancy of what they had just witnessed but always outside the framework of the salvation-history drama. When in fact they finally enter the salvation drama near the very end of the *auto*, Ingenio and Pensamiento reject Noche in favor of the dying Emanuel. With Emanuel's death, Ingenio realizes the answers to his two questions posed at the beginning of the drama. To the puzzle of the grain that must die before it bears fruit, Ingenio sees Emanuel, the Word made flesh, die in order to effect the fruits of Redemption. Similarly Emanuel, the *semilla*, is beaten like the threshed wheat and gives his body in bread on the same day in "el día mayor de los días." As final proof of the effectiveness of the salvation drama he had witnessed and of his comprehension of the problems that plagued him, in an act of faith, Ingenio engages with the devil, Noche, in the *paridad* mentioned above, whereby Christ is compared to the kernel of wheat. In Calderón's earlier *auto*, *La siembra del Señor*, Emanuel compared himself to the wheat before the devil figure.

Ley de Gracia of Calderón's *El día mayor*, another new figure, is particularly interesting from the stand-point of the technical difficulty it offered Calderón and how he resolved the problem. As mentioned above, Ley de Gracia took her turn in the procession of *leyes* appearing immediately after Ley Escrita but she did not appear with her corresponding figure, Emanuel. Until after Emanuel effected the Redemption in which grace and the supernatural life returned to man, Ley de Gracia could not assume the same role as did the other *leyes* without violating the doctrine of Redemption. When Ley de Gracia appears for the first time accompanied by Apostasía, she is an anomalous personage, a figure of the future and of hope and waiting. When Tiempo asks who she is, Ley de Gracia replies: "No sé quien soy/ quien seré sé" (p. 1644). When Tiempo becomes perplexed at Ley de Gracia's answer, "Enigma rara,/ ¿sin saber quien eres, sabes,/ quien serás?" (p. 1644) the grace figure answers, "Sí, porque el alma/ en fe de una promesa,/ que la mantiene en calma;/ alegre en lo que espera/ y triste en lo que tarda" (pp. 1644-45). After the coming of Emanuel and the Redemption, Ley de Gracia is no longer the figure of *esperanza* but of fulfillment as she assumes a normal role in the drama and in the parable as the last of the laborers to come into the fields "a la tarde" (p. 1658).

By dramatizing the three *leyes* who appear in company with their corresponding personages and by introducing the allegorical figures of Ingenio, Pensamiento, and Tiempo, Calderón found in his *El día mayor de los días* an opportunity to intersperse bits of philosophical and religious teachings. In his first *auto*, *La siembra del Señor*, Adán was asked to cultivate the ground and plant the seed. Judaísmo followed Adán and was entrusted with the reaping of the harvest. In his *El día mayor*, Ley Natural and Ley Escrita were to prepare the ground and plant the seed while Ley de Gracia after Emanuel's death was to reap the harvest. Besides the fact that natural and written law did prepare the way for Divine law and thus Calderón's dramatization in *El día mayor* proves to be doctrinally sound, the author continually stresses the importance of the *leyes* complementing each other and working together for the growth of the seed. Speaking specifically of the congruity of the natural and written laws, Tiempo says:

> Si, que una
> en Dos Preceptos fundada,
> como antes dije, subsiste;
> y aunque hasta Diez los alarga
> a otra el Decálogo, luego
> reduce los que dilata
> a los mismos Dos, de suerte
> que el tronco es uno y las ramas
> sólo en lo ceremonial
> del Levítico se apartan.
>
> (p. 1644)

Nor does Calderón permit his audience to think that any of the laws are obsolete and that their relevancy fades away with the ages. Tiempo speaking specifically of Ley Natural warns Ingenio:

> Te engañas,
> que la Ley Natural nunca
> pasó; con suma constancia
> subsiste en los dos Preceptos
> que a Dios sobre todo aman
> y al Prójimo como a sí.
>
> (p. 1640)

Ley Escrita expresses this same thought concerning the relevancy of the basic tenets inherited from natural law when it says to Ley Natural:

> Los dos Preceptos
> que de ti heredé me hacen
> tan tuya que el Tiempo no
> podrá nuestras-amistades
> romper.
>
> (p. 1653)

The bantering dialogue of the three characters, Ingenio, Pensamiento, and Tiempo as they comment on what they had seen and await the next scene in the salvation drama also affords Calderón some opportunity to philosophize. For example, Ingenio, who had accused Pensamiento of being a *loco* marvels at the soundness and depth of the latter's ideas and retorts: "Contra ésa/ hay la de que todos somos/ locos unos de otros" (p. 1638). Later Ingenio comments on the swiftness of thought when he asks Pensamiento, not Tiempo, to see who it is that comes upon the scene. Ingenio says to Tiempo: "Mejor es que vaya/ a saberlo el Pensamiento,/ que más veloz que tú anda" (p. 1640). More of Calderón's philosophic and instructional interjections appear as Ingenio asking Tiempo to enlighten him on the perplexing question says of history, into which they are about to regress in flashback: "Que las lecciones del Tiempo/ siempre doctas, siempre sabias/ han sido o por lo que enseñan/ o por lo que desengañan" (p. 1638). Instead of meddling with sin, Ingenio flees from Noche's waiting arms while giving the audience another piece of advice by telling the devil figure: "Antes,/ para vencerte, huiré de ellos/ que de la Culpa el combate,/ quien le vence más valiente,/ es quien le huye más cobarde" (p. 1656).

Before moving on to the next group of kingdom parables, that dealing with the Parable of the Vinedressers, there remains one last observation concerning Calderón's aesthetics found in his *El día mayor de los días*. Calderón knew that Christ taught through the parable by relating spiritual truths to everyday experiences and that the *auto sacramental* instructed in like manner by making the abstract concrete through drama and the stage. In his *El día mayor*, Calderón not only knowingly took a parable and upon it structured an *auto sacramental*, but he chose to capitalize upon the didactic principle upon which both the parable and the *auto sacramental* are based by constructing another drama within a drama. In other words, Ingenio of the parabolic *auto sacramental* discovered for himself the truths of the questions that puzzled him by witnessing the dramatic presentation of salvation history. That Calderón was aware of the value of experience learning and that he purposely chose the play within the play as the best way of enlightening Ingenio becomes clear in the words of Noche, who laments the efficaciousness of Tiempo's method of instructing Ingenio: "¿Qué luces son éstas,/ que el Ingenio las ignora,/ que el Pensamiento se lleva/ a que el Tiempo se las diga/ y el Tiempo a que las aprendan/ por parábolas que unan/ la lección con la experiencia?" (p. 1648). Ingenio himself admits that he has successfully learned through the salvation drama: "Pues el Trigo me ha dado/ Luz en entrambos lugares,/ con la experiencia de que/ visibles se me declaren" (p. 1655).

The Vinedressers

The Parable of the Vinedressers or of the Husbandmen can rightly be considered one of the truly tragic stories in all of literature. The parable describes the sad and sorry plight of a gentleman who diligently plants a vineyard, in the middle of which he constructs a wine press to process the fruits of his vineyard and a tall tower to guard it. Finding it necessary to go abroad because of compelling business, the owner leases his vineyard to some hired hands. Later when the harvest season draws near, he sends some servants as his emissaries to collect the fruits of the harvest. The husbandmen in charge promptly dismiss the servants, beating one, killing another and stoning the third. The lord of the vineyard, dismayed by the conduct of the hired hands and saddened by the injustice to his servants, sends his only son to the vineyard. The husbandmen promptly kill the owner's son. Finally, deeply grieved and angered by the death of his sole son, the lord of the vineyard punishes the vinedressers and entrusts the charge of his vineyard to others.[60]

Although the Parable of the Vinedressers is not accompanied in Scripture by an explanation of its meaning, the parable has been a favorite among scriptural scholars who have attempted to give it allegorical significance. As is the case with all the kingdom parables, although scholars have interpreted one or the other detail of the parable differently, nevertheless, they agree as to the over-all interpretation. God created the world and singled out the Jews as the first nation to aid in Christ's redeeming work. In the beginning, the Jews accepted the responsibility entrusted upon them and were loyal to God. However, they later rejected God's messengers and prophets and ultimately rejected his very son who was sent to fulfill the redemption plan. God punished the Jews for going against him and he turned to others — the Gentiles.[61]

As was the case in the parables of the Weeds and of the Laborers in the Vineyard, discussed above, there are three *autos sacramentales* based on the Parable of the Vinedressers, Mira de Amescua's *El heredero*, Lope de Vega's *El heredero del cielo*, and Calderón's *La viña del Señor*. Both Valbuena Prat and Hilborn agree that Calderón presented his *auto* on the Feast of the Corpus Christi in 1674.[62] As to Mira de Amescua's work and that of Lope, I can only ascertain their approximate dates. The former work appeared printed in 1655.[63] The latter work of Lope appeared in print in 1644, the same year in which Mira de Amescua died.[64] Because Lope's *auto* appeared eleven years before that of

---

[60] Math., 21:33-46. See also Mark, 12:1-12 and Luke, 20:9-19.

[61] For the allegorical interpretations of the parables see Maldonado, Vol. I, pp. 752-759.

[62] Valbuena Prat, *Obras*..., III, 1471, and Hilborn, 114.

[63] Mira de Amescua's *auto* first appeared in *Autos sacramentales con cuatro comedias nuevas y sus loas y entremeses* (Madrid: María de Quiñones, 1655). The edition used in this study is found in *Autos sacramentales y al nacimiento de Christo con loas y entremeses* (Madrid: Antonio Franco de Zafra, 1675), pp. 119-144.

[64] Lope's *auto* first appeared in *Fiestas del santissimo sacramento repartidas en doze autos sacramentales con sus loas y entremeses* (Madrid, 1644).

his contemporary does not mean, of course, that Lope wrote his drama before Mira de Amescua wrote his. In fact, although Valbuena does not pinpoint the precise nor even the approximate dates of either *auto*, he does assert that Mira de Amescua's must have preceded Lope's. Speaking of Mira de Amescua's sacramental work, Valbuena states: "Por su major sencillez, creo habrá precedido al mismo de Lope. Es posible que Calderón tuviera en cuenta los dos." [65]

Because the three sacramental plays on the Parable of the Vinedressers dramatize the allegory described above, I shall begin my study of this group of kingdom parable *autos* by presenting briefly Mira de Amescua's drama and by only pointing out some of the play's most salient features. I will then analyse in much greater detail the *autos* of Lope and of Calderón while accepting the challenge posed by Aicardo in the following statement:

> Sería utilísimo para la historia del arte dramático español estudiar las imitaciones que de Lope hizo Calderón; en una monografía así tendría su puesto un paralelo detallado entre *El Herededo y La viña*. [66]

In the same respect, a quotation by Valbuena also deserves attention, because it too affords the same enticing motivation to probe deeper into the two similar plays: "*La viña del Señor* sigue los pasos y situaciones de Lope; pero el drama se concentra, lo teatral se amplía y lo doctrinal se profundiza." [67] Keeping in mind both Aicardo's call for a detailed comparison of Lope's and Calderón's *autos* and Valbuena's critique that the Calderonian drama is more concentrated while the action itself is expanded, I will illustrate, first, the manner in which Calderón was better able than Lope to dramatize small incidents and entire scenes and, secondly, how the *maestro* of the *auto*, to a greater extent than Lope, incorporated the allegorical personages into the action of the play by expanding their dramatic role.

Quotations found in this study come from the *auto* found in the Academia edition, Vol. II, pp. 179-188.
 [65] Valbuena Prat, *Obras*..., p. 1472.
 [66] Aicardo, *Razón y Fe*, XXII, 322.
 [67] Valbuena Prat, *Obras*..., III, 1471.

In terms of drama and dramatic development, I would agree with Valbuena that Mira de Amescua's *El Heredero* ranks lowest of the three *autos* on the Parable of the Vinedressers.[68] In comparison with Lope and Calderón, Mira de Amescua introduces into his drama a bare minimum of allegorical figures, which reduces substantially his chances for good dramatic development. For example, the sole figure of Judaísmo in Mira de Amescua's drama becomes two personages in the *autos* of Lope and Calderón. To his allegorical representative of the Jewish nation, Pueblo Hebreo, Lope adds the Jewish religious leader, Sacerdocio. Calderón, in his drama, adds Sinagoga to the allegorical personage of Hebraísmo. By the addition of their respective allegorical figures of the Jewish religious leaders, both Lope and Calderón enhanced the drama of their play by creating a situation of conflict within the Jewish camp itself. For it is Sacerdocio and Sinagoga which in their respective plays contribute to the downfall of the Jewish nation by prodding her to reject the Heredero and to put Him to death.

The fact that only one prophet, John the Baptist, appears in Mira de Amescua's drama also greatly reflects the play's simplicity and lack of dramatic development. In the *autos* of Lope and Calderón, not only St. John the Baptist but Isaiah and Jeremiah procede the Son of God and come before the Jews and their leaders to ask their Lord's rightful share of the harvest. All three prophets are rejected by the Jews and are put to death.[69]

Besides Judaísmo and San Juan Bautista, there are other allegorical figures who, because of their lack of dramatic development, reflect the simplicity of Mira de Amescua's drama in comparison to the dramas of Lope and Calderón. For example, Mira de Amescua assigns the guarding of the vineyard to Custodio. While there is no comparable figure in Calderón because of the manner in which he handles his allegory, as it will be

---

[68] *Ibid.*

[69] There is a precedence for the appearance of the three prophets in the dramatization of the Parable of the Vinedressers with the very early Jesuit play of five acts, *Tragoedia Patris Familias de Vinea*. In the Jesuit play, besides Isaías, Jeremías, and San Juan Bautista, there is a fourth prophet, Zacharías. The Jesuit *comedia* is found in the *Códice de los jesuítas* (f° 47r-66r°). For a brief summary of the play see García Soriano, pp. 249-255.

seen, Lope gives allegorical significance to the basic Christian principle of the two precepts, love of God and love of neighbor, by portraying El Amor Divino and El Prójimo as the guardians of the precious harvest. Another of Mira de Amescua's allegorical abstractions, Envidia, finds comparable development in Lope's Idolatría but greater development and expansion in Calderón's two evil figures of Malicia and Lucero de la Noche.

One aspect of Mira de Amescua's drama deserves special mention because of the obvious importance relegated to it by the author in terms of length and because it remains the one distinctive feature of the *auto*. In his play, the principle characters of the Hijo, Custodio, Envidia, and Judaísmo spend a great deal of the *auto* engaged in a game of "El ave ciego," a type of "Guess who?" in which a blindfolded player must divine who it is that touches him. The game enables the dramatist to explicate by way of question and answer the nature of the players in terms of the play's allegory. For example, to Envidia's question, "¿Quién soy?" Hijo, blindfolded, replies, "un espíritu obstinado: /que con mi pueblo te uniste/ para perseguirme entrambos" (p. 137). To the "Guess who?" posed by Gentilidad, Hijo replies, in the following prediction of what is to happen in the drama, "El que ha de ser Mayorazgo/ de esta Viña: es el Jacob,/ y Maná es, que trocaron/ mis dos bendiciones" (p. 137). This game played by the personages also enables Mira de Amescua finally to make the transition into Christ's crucifixion, for Hijo, having guessed correctly the identity of all those who touched him, receives the victor's garland of flowers which Envidia promptly exchanges for a crown of thorns symbolic of the beginning of the passion. It is interesting to note that the "Guess who?" game of Mira's *auto* resembles the symbolic card game found in Mejía de la Cerda's *El juego del hombre* studied above, in that neither game contributes to the drama of the play, although the former better relates to the drama's established allegory.[70]

Having briefly commented on Mira de Amescua's *El heredero*, I begin a more detailed study of the Lopean and Calderonian *autos* on the Parable of the Vinedressers by comparing certain incidents and scenes which appear in both sacramental pieces but

---

[70] See above, pp. 92-93.

which find greater dramatic significance in Calderón's play. The first incident that illustrates Calderón's superior technique in augmenting the dramatic is found in the contrasting manner in which the lord of the vineyard leases his fields to the Jewish nation. In Lope's *El heredero del cielo,* before giving the Pueblo Hebreo the chore of caring for his vineyard, Labrador Celestial briefly recapitulates some of the past glories of Jewish history. With this brief resumé of Jewish history and with a strong admonition directed at Pueblo Hebreo and Sacerdocio to remain faithful to God as were Abraham, Saul and the other fathers of their tradition, Labrador Celestial entrusts the vineyard to the Jewish figures without any further reservations. In Calderón's *La viña del Señor,* El Padre de las Familias entrusts the care of his vineyards to the Jewish figure, Hebraísmo, but only after the two enter into a solemn contract. According to the terms of the contract between El Padre de las Familias and Hebraísmo, the lord of the vineyard gives the Hebrews the vineyards and promises to make their chores light and sweet ("suave el yugo, leve el peso" p. 1481). In turn, the Jews are to take diligent care of the vineyard and give back to the owner at harvest time "sólo el diezmo y la primicia" (p. 1482). Calderón further increases the dramatic power of this scene in which Hebraísmo and El Padre de las Familias agree to their contract. First, Calderón permits Hijo, the Second Person of the Trinity, to approve and ratify his Father's pact with the Jews: "Y yo,/ como inmediato heredero,/ mostrando que de mi padre/ la voluntad obedezco,/ aunque es patrimonio mío,/ en el contrato çonvengo" (p. 1482). Secondly, the dramatic impact of the contract is further intensified by the presence of the prophets Isaías, Jeremías and Lucero del Día who witness the contract. Finally, Calderón adds the last dramatic stroke to this all-important scene by portraying the Padre de Las Familias as finalizing the contract in a handshake with Hebraísmo who solemnly pledges fidelity to his word. Later in the *auto* when the Jews renege on their word, turn against the prophets, and finally end by murdering the landlord's son, Hebraísmo's actions become that much more treacherous in terms of conflict because of this earlier solemn contract elaborately dramatized.

A second incident found in both the Lopean and Calderonian *auto* also illustrates Calderón's refined dramatic sense. In Lope's

El heredero, El Labrador explains to his two faithful guardians, El Amor Divino and El Prójimo, that he must leave the vineyard, without giving any explanation as to why he must leave: "Yo me tengo de partir,/ Aunque siempre en ella estoy;/ Pero en efeto me voy,/ No tengo más que decir" (p. 179). This brief explanation, in which El Labrador really gives no reason for his departure from the vineyard, contrasts with that given by El Padre de las Familias in the Calderonian *auto* in which it is made quite clear why the creator of the vineyards must leave and why therefore he entrusts the care of his vineyards to the Jews. El Padre de las Familias explains to Hebraísmo: "Y es, que yo he de hacer ausencia/ de este valle; porque tengo/ que ajustar en otra parte/ la cuenta de unos talentos/ que he dejado, en confianza/ del que use bien o mal de ellos" (p. 1481). This brief explanation of the Padre de las Familias not only reveals why the Padre must leave the vineyards, but also affords an insight into the character of the Padre that is important to later action in the *auto*. It is obvious from the Padre's explanation that he is a conscientious business man who checks on those entrusted with his interests. In other words, early in his drama, Calderón makes it known that the Padre de las Familias is accustomed to taking stock of his trusts so that, later, when he sends his messengers to check up on Judaísmo and to collect his share of the harvest according to the terms of the contract, the Padre's actions are entirely plausible.

After the landlord entrusts his vineyard to the Jews and departs, the action of both Lope's and Calderón's *autos* focuses on the evil figures who try to gain entrance into the vineyard. The contrasting manner in which three evil figures are portrayed entering the vineyards embraces the third incident that reflects Calderón's greater dramatic awareness. It will be recalled that in Lope's two *autos* on the Lost Sheep, one of the most dramatic parts of both dramas is that in which the disguised evil figures try to enter the *cabaña* in order to seduce the Oveja.[71] The same is true with regard to Lope's sacramental drama on the Parable of the Weeds, where the most dramatic part is that in which Soberbia lulls Ignorancia to sleep with his heroic tale in order to

---

[71] See Chapter II, pp. 54-57.

gain access to the wheatfields.[72] In the *auto* presently under discussion, Lope completely neglects the dramatic value of the entrance scene. The wicked Idolatría, accompanied by *músicos*, easily enters the vineyard unchallenged by Amor Divino and Prójimo. In his *La viña del Señor*, Calderón dramatically portrays the evil figure's entrance into the vineyards. Before actually entering the vineyards, Malicia engages in a hand-to-hand struggle with Inocencia, the allegorical figure of grace and virtue. In the height of the battle between Malicia and Inocencia, the devil figure manages to steal Inocencia's clothing. Dressed in the new attire, Malicia runs off to the vineyards assured of being mistaken for Inocencia while the divested figure of grace shouts the warning: "¡Alerta, humana Milicia,/ que se viste la Malicia/ el traje de la Inocencia!" (1485). In Malicia's apparent triumph over Inocencia, Calderón takes great pains to preserve sound theology by making it clear to the audience in the words of Inocencia that Malicia's victory is only momentary, and that evil only exists and triumphs with God's permission, because only temptation and exposure to sin strengthen man:

> No moriré,
> bien que la eterna Justicia,
> no sin gran fin, dé licencia
> de padecer la Inocencia
> ultrajes de la Malicia,
> el día que significado,
> Dios en ese Padre está
> de Familias, y en él da
> a entender que del pecado
> se ausenta, y el Hombre siente
> en la lucha de los dos,
> que aunque no se ausenta Dios.
>
> (p. 1485)[73]

---

[72] See above, pp. 95-96.

[73] The importance of the devil as a dramatic figure and the difficulty Calderón faced in portraying the devil figures within the bounds of good drama and theology is the subject of A. A. Parker's "The Devil in the Drama of Calderón," in *Critical Essays on the Theater of Calderón*, ed. Bruce W. Wardropper (New York: The New York University Press, 1965), pp. 3-23.

In addition to the three incidents discussed thus far, nothing better demonstrates Calderón's superior dramatic skill than a comparison of the two dramas with respect to an episode found in both, in which the prophets come before the Jewish nation to take account of the fruits of the vineyard on behalf of the landlord. In Lope's *El Heredero*, the three prophets enter the scene in rapid succession. Beginning with Isaías, and then Jeremías and Lucero del Día, in that order, each appears only once in the drama. Each prophet visits the vineyard in order to ask Pueblo Hebreo and Sacerdocio for the fruit of the vines, but each is rejected promptly and put to death. In his dramatization of the prophets' episode, Calderón does not overwhelm his audience with a quick-fire parade of prophet figures never before seen in the play, but rather fits the coming of the three prophets smoothly into the action of the play and into what has preceded. When Isaías, Jeremías, and Lucero del Día appear, in their respective turns, the audience remembers them as being present as witnesses to the signing of the pact between Hebraísmo and Padre de las Familias. Whereas in Lope Pueblo Hebreo and Sinagoga did not recognize the prophets when they came to collect the fruits, because it was their first appearance, in every instance Calderón's Hebraísmo recalls seeing the prophet before in the heavenly court at the finalization of the pact. In Lope, each of the prophets asks for all of the vineyard's fruits, while in Calderón this is not the case. When the first of Calderón prophets, Isaías, enters upon the scene, he seeks only a part of the contract "la primicia" because "otro por los diezmos venga" (p. 1487). The second prophet, Jeremías asks for the tenth (diezmos) as Isaías had predicted. Calderón assigns to the third prophet, Lucero del Día, an entirely new function in the dramatic action of his *auto* that differs from the role of the other three prophets and from that given to St. John in Lope's drama as it will be observed shortly.

Whereas Lope neglected to develop the prophets' episode to the fullest, Calderón greatly expanded the scene in his *La viña del Señor*. In Lope, when the first of the prophets, Isaías, comes upon the scene, Pueblo Hebreo and Sacerdocio agree to dispose of Isaías, whom they have never met and whom they immediately kill without question. This entire scene takes on an air of dramatic artificiality. In the Calderonian *auto,* the scene with Isaías is intensely more dramatic and realistic. In the first place, Hebraísmo receives Isaías favorably for he remembers the prophet in the heavenly court and has no reason to dislike him, let alone kill him. One also discovers that Isaías, who seeks the *primicia,* requests permission to pass through the vineyard in order to determine the best of the vineyard's grapes. Isaías's request to inspect the vineyard affords Calderón an opportunity to develop the case against the prophet. While Isaías tours the fields, the vineyard's workers together with Sinagoga and the evil Lucero de la Noche team up to create an atmosphere of animosity that turns Hebraísmo against Isaías and terminates in the prophet's death. Having heard of Isaías's mission to the vineyard, the *zagales* or laborers were the first to complain to Hebraísmo: "¿Dónde la ganancia nuestra/ en beneficiar el fruto,/ para que otros por él vengan?" (p. 1488). However, Hebraísmo refuses to listen to the rebellious cries of his hired men and he orders them to return to work: "Así lo acepté, y conmigo/ no en demandas ni respuestas,/ os pongáis. Tras él, villanos, id" (p. 1488). The *zagales* having been silenced with the harsh scolding from Hebraísmo, Lucero de la Noche, one of the drama's devil figures, takes up the cry against Isaías by picking at Hebraísmo's pride and honor: "Porque si pensara que era/ rentero a quien yo venía/ a servir, nunca viniera;/ que no es bueno para dueño/ pundonor que se sujeta/ a que pueda un cobrador/ llamar tan recio a sus puertas" (p. 1488). With scarcely time enough to reply to Lucero de la Noche's mutinous outcry, Hebraísmo confronts still a third plea against Isaías, this time from his beloved wife, Sinagoga. In depicting Sinagoga's attempt to persuade her husband against Isaías, Calderón proves himself a master psychologist. Sinagoga begins her persuasive tactics by calling upon the female's most effective and age-old weapon against the male — tears: "Llorar con lágrimas tiernas/ que tenga un advenedizo/ razón de venir de ajena/ patria, a infamarte en la tuya" (p. 1488). Then drying her tears, Sinagoga appeals to her husband's pride, reminding him that he was chosen by the Padre de las Familias to be master of the vineyard and that he needs not give up the vineyard after all the work he has put into it. Only after being besieged by these incessant appeals from the workers, Lucero de la Noche and Sinagoga, does Hebraísmo succumb and order Isaías be put to death. However, Hebraísmo still reflects the doubt of his decision to murder Isaías and the anguish that torments his soul when he cries:

> De suerte vuestras razones
> el corazón me penetran,
> el espíritu me inflaman,
> y sentidos y potencias
> me perturban, que parecen
> dictadas de mi soberbia.
> ¿Qué Vesubio, que Volcán,
> qué Mongibelo, qué Etna,
> es el que en mí han revestido,
> que con su fuego me hiela
> y con su hielo me abrasa?
> (p. 1488-89)

With the death of Isaías, Sinagoga rejoices and expresses her gratitude to her husband, by preparing for him a big meal and a feast: "En muestra/ de mi hacimiento de gracias,/ para esta noche real cena/ te iré a prevenir, y a todo/ tu pueblo" (p. 1489). At the same time and also in the expression of gratitude, Malicia, another of the drama's devil figures, offers to provide the music for the party and promises much dancing and merriment. With the feast, Calderón carefully anticipates the coming of the other two prophets, especially that of St. John the Baptist and the Salome scene. Although, in his *El Heredero*, Lope also dramatized a feast, the festivities began much earlier in celebration of the marriage of Pueblo Hebreo with Idolatría. By the time the prophets, especially the last of them, St. John, appeared, the dramatic effectiveness of the feast as symbolic of Herod's royal feast was lost.

With regard to the scene's involving the remaining two prophets, Jeremías and Lucero del Día, when Jeremías enters and asks for the *diezmos*, Hebraísmo has already made up his mind to retain the vineyard and so quickly stones the prophet. However, when the last of the three prophets, Lucero del Día, enters the drama, Calderón once again is more successful as a dramatist than Lope. In fact, when Lucero del Día comes onto the stage in the Calderonian *auto*, the play reaches the heights of dramatic intensity. The festivities and merriment of Sinagoga's feast with its emphasis on the sensual has by now taken its toll on Hebraísmo, Sinagoga, Malicia, Lucero de la Noche, and the *zagales*. Hebraísmo so enjoys the festivities of the evening that he becomes exuberant and is the first to acknowledge: "Jamás los sentidos tuve / más bien divertidos" (p. 1491). Amid the merriment, and at the very point in which the *músicos* joyfully proclaim in a great chorus of song the same gleeful spirit expressed by Hebraísmo, one suddenly hears from off stage the somber moanings of Lucero del Día: "Penitencia, mortales, penitencia" (p. 1491). The contrasting moods conveyed by those celebrating the feast inside and the voice of Lucero outside are dramatically shocking. It is interesting to note that Calderón was well aware of the dramatic effect the use of the shocking contrast in moods would have on his audience. Upon hearing St. John's voice, Hebraísmo interrupts the feast shouting: "Parad y sabed qué voces/ tan contrarias de las nuestras/ a consonantes preguntas/ dan disonantes respuestas" (p. 1491).

When Lucero del Día comes in from the outside and enters the courtly feast, the allegorical figure of St. John tells Hebraísmo that he did not come "a cobrar sus rentas" but "a acusar sus ofensas" (p. 1491). With the coming of Lucero del Día, Calderón immediately initiates the famous Biblical scene of Herod — Salome and the dance of the seven veils. Lucero del Día accuses Hebraísmo of committing adultery, that is of being too much wedded to Sinagoga, instead of the old religion taking on the new Church of Christ. Wined and dined at the feast and amused by the dancing provided by Malicia, Hebraísmo promises Malicia anything she desires: "De manera/ me agrada, por festín tuyo,/ que nunca me hará molestia;/ y para mostrarte cuánto/ me divierte y me deleita,/ no habrá cosa que me pidas/ que yo no te la conceda" (p. 1492). Malicia consults the jealous Sinagoga, certainly implicated in Lucero del Día's accusation. Sinagoga asks for the head of St. John. In Lope's *auto*, San Juan alludes to the adultery theme but the reference is confusing. Certainly the adultery accusation found in Lope is not the direct cause of John's death as it is in Calderón's work, where the whole Herod-Salome scene is closely related to the play's dramatic action.

Besides being more efective than Lope in the dramatization of certain incidents and scenes found in the dramas of both authors,

Calderón incorporated his allegorical personages into his drama to a greater extent than did Lope. In fact, I have already pointed out in the discussion Calderón's ability to enhance the dramatic roles of his characters. For example, it was seen how the three prophets in the Calderonian *auto* not only appeared to collect the fruits of the vineyard but also how the same figures earlier witnessed the pact between the Padre de las Familias and Hebraísmo. With regard to the last of the prophets, Lucero del Día, I neglected to bring out clearly in the discussion above the diverse role of the St. John figure in Calderón's play. Not only does Lucero del Día interrupt the merriment of the court with his sombre call to penance but he also opens the play by calling together the laborers to the vineyard: "Jornaleros de la vida,/ que a providencias de Dios,/ pan de ángeles cogisteis/ sembrando pan de dolor./ ¡Venid a mi voz!" (p. 1474). In fact, the voice of Lucero del Día constantly rings out in the drama. After the contract, for example, Lucero del Día again goes around shouting the good news and thereby indicates to the audience in another manner the solemnity and importance of the contracted agreement dramatized on stage. Calderón greatly expands Lucero del Día's role in the play not only by portraying the prophet in the Herod-Salome scene but also by giving to him a function equivalent to St. John the Baptist's historical role as the heralder of good news and as the voice crying in the wilderness.

In addition to the three prophets, there are two other allegorical personages that come onto the scene only once in Lope's *El heredero* but that receive more extensive dramatic roles in Calderón's *La viña*. In Lope's sacramental drama on the Parable of the Vineyard, the Heredero appears for the first time on stage after St. John announces his coming on his way to be beheaded. The first dialogue between the newly arrived figure of the Son of Man and the figures of Pueblo Hebreo, Sacerdocio, and Idolatría demonstrates that Lope apparently had some difficulty in introducing Heredero within the allegory of his drama. On the one hand Heredero speaks of himself as espoused to the Church: "Con esta viña me casa [sic],/ Esta es mi hacienda y mi esposa" (p. 186); and on the other hand the Heredero is referred to in the same dialogue as a child: "Dejadle, amigos, que es niño" (p. 187). Lope confuses even more the analogies to Heredero when he begins to allegorize the crucifixion in which there appears neither the husband nor the child, but the middle-aged Christ. Heredero has the sole dramatic function of participating in the crucifixion in which the Christ figure utters the usual words such as "Padre y Señor, no se haga/ Mi voluntad, mas la tuya" (p. 187) and "Padre mío, Padre mío,/ ¿Por qué así me desamparas?" (p. 187).

Calderón's amplification of the dramatic role of the Heredero not only reflects his dramatic ability but also his theological awareness, particularly of the Trinity. It will be noted that, except for when Hijo assumes the role of the redeemer, the second person of the Trinity never leaves the side of his Padre, but rather the two function in unison throughout the play. The two God figures enter the drama together side by side. Hijo praises his Padre for his great glory and thanks him for having created the vineyard and for having entrusted its care to laborers. As it has been seen, the two God figures also appear together at the signing of the contract with Hebraísmo, where Hijo not only witnesses but ratifies his Padre's contract with the Jewish nation. The third time the two God figures enter the drama they again are together but this time the mood is not one of joy but of sadness. The scene happens to be one of the most intensely dramatic and emotional in the play. The Padre de las Familias has just learned of the death of his prophets and in a fit of anger stands ready to curse and destroy his creation. Hijo begs and pleads Man's salvation before his Padre and then in an act of supreme love and, in accordance with the theological function of the Second Person of the Trinity as Redeemer, offers to take upon himself Man's redemption and enter the vineyard as a common laborer (pp. 1493-94). When, at last, Calderón undertakes to dramatize the crucifixion, he does not encounter the same problems as did Lope because Hijo was already well familiar to the audience. In a calculated move to intensity the action of the drama, Calderón chose the Palm Sunday theme to introduce Hijo as the Savior. Unlike Lope's Pueblo Hebreo which immediately rejected the Heredero, Calderón's Hebraísmo at first accepts Christ as the Jews in fact did on Palm Sunday but then, stirred by Malicia and Lucero de la Noche who cry for crucifixion, Hebraísmo again concedes and puts Hijo to death as he had done with Isaías.

Like the allegorical figure of the *heredero*, a second personage, Pueblo Gentil, appearing only once in Lope's *auto*, receives greater development in the drama of Calderón. In the Lopean *auto*, the only appearance of the figure representing the Gentiles is so brief that, were the audience not familiar with the traditional interpretation of the Gospel parable in which the Gentiles are later entrusted with the vineyard, it would be at a loss to identify the allegorical figure. Never having seen Pueblo Gentil in any of the earlier scenes of Lope's play, one wonders how it is that the Gentile figure now receives the vineyard's care from the Heredero. In his *La viña*, not only by causing Gentilidad to take a more active part in the action of the *auto*, but also by portraying the contrasting attitudes of Gentilidad and Hebraísmo in scenes in which the two figures appear, Calderón made the drama's ending more plausible. Gentilidad first comes together with Hebraísmo in the *auto's* initial scenes. Both have heard Lucero's voice in the wilderness calling the laborers to the vineyard, and both are seeking the origin and meaning of the call. In order to search out more effectively the voice they seek, they agree to separate but make a solemn pact at Hebraísmo's suggestion that the one who finds the voice and discerns its meaning will return to inform the other: "En su alcance ir,/ discurriendo por diversas/ partes los dos el país;/ con pacto de que el que antes/ noticias halle, acudir/ al otro deba con ellas" (p. 1480). Later, when Gentilidad once again meets up with Hebraísmo in the desert, Gentilidad discovers that Hebraísmo had just signed a contract with the Padre de las Familias and that the Jewish nation never bothered to inform him of the voice's significance, as they had agreed. Although Gentilidad complains of Hebraísmo's disloyalty to his word, Gentilidad states that he holds grudges neither against Hebraísmo nor the co-signer of the pact, El Padre de las Familias, whom he both respects and fears; he says to Hebraísmo:

> Ni eso,
> ni cuanto en la gratitud
> del más alevoso pecho
> cabe, me coge de susto
> en ti, ni de ti me quejo,

> ¡oh gran Padre de Familias!,
> tampoco; porque suspenso,
> absorto y mudo, no sé
> qué reverencial respeto,
> qué interior cariño, qué
> ignorado amor, qué afecto
> no conocido, qué oculta
> veneración o qué miedo,
> por decirlo todo, es
> con el que te reverencio,
> que no me atrevo a la queja,
> embargada del silencio.
>
> (p. 1483)

Gentilidad's forgiveness, though reserved and filled with mixed emotions, contrasts greatly with Hebraísmo's nonchalant attitude. Hebraísmo considers the breaking of his word to Gentilidad and the signing of the agreement with the Padre de las Familias a slight matter and dismisses the whole ordeal by saying: "Como el natural derecho/ es que cada uno procure/ para sí lo mejor" (1483). Both attitudes presented side by side in one scene foreshadow the play's ending in which Hebraísmo, at first selected with the gift of the word, relinquishes it to Gentilidad. In case the audience misses the subtle prediction of the play's ending in Gentilidad's and Hebraísmo's contrasting attitudes, Calderón makes it clear in this same early scene what the play's final outcome will be. To the Padre's lament, "Desvalido el Gentilismo/ va de mí," Hijo consolingly replies, "Su sentimiento/ podrás en otra ocasión/ consolar" (1483). Further, after witnessing this scene in which Hebraísmo takes lightly the breaking of his word to Gentilidad, one cannot help but sense that the Hebrew figure will also later break his pact with Padre de las Familias which was made in the scene immediately preceding.

Although the other evil figures such as Pueblo Hebreo, Sacerdocio, and Idolatría, make more than one appearance in Lope's drama, there is greater expansion and development of comparable allegorical figures in the Calderonian *auto*. In Lope, Pueblo Hebreo is easily persuaded by Sacerdocio to reject the two principles of love and to keep selfishly the fruit of the vineyard. In fact, as it has been seen, there is no procrastination on the part of Pueblo Hebreo in killing the prophets and the Hijo, as Pueblo

Hebreo blindly does what Sacerdocio desires. In the Calderonian *auto*, Hebraísmo comprises one of the most complex and most dramatically refined figures in the play's repertoire of characters. I have already illustrated in my discussion the way in which Hebraísmo's matter-of-fact reaction to the breaking of his word with Gentilidad reflects Hebraísmo's character defect, all of which makes plausible the drama's ending, where Divine Justice metes out the true reward. However, the true complexity of Hebraísmo's character can best be observed in the humanity which Calderón attributes to the Jewish figure, especially in the three conflicts facing him in the latter stages of the drama. I have already considered the torment within Hebraísmo's soul as he sees himself falter in the face of the onslaught of pleas from the laborers, Lucero de la Noche and his beloved wife, and how he finally agrees to put Isaías to death.[74] Hebraísmo's second great moment of recognition, the decision to put Lucero del Día to death, has also been treated above. However, I wish to underscore the revelation of Hebraísmo's character and human weakness that the scene affords. Hebraísmo again outwardly expresses the struggle within as he reluctantly fulfills the promise that he had boastingly made to Sinagoga upon beholding Malicia's dance: "¡Oh justa pena/ del que ofrece o firma, antes/ de ver qué firme o qué ofrezca!/ Ya lo juré; a la prisión/ id y en un plato traedla" (p. 1492). The third time that the Jewish figure is seen in conflicting interests, Hebraísmo appears listening to the clamours of the *zagales* for the death of Hijo. Again, Hebraísmo's human frailty comes to light as he assumes the role of Pontius Pilate and proclaims in anguish to Lucero de la Noche: "Segunda vez de tus voces/ el espíritu inflamado,/ el corazón en el pecho/ se me está haciendo pedazos" (p. 1496).

Although in both Lope's *El heredero* and Calderón's *La viña* the figures representative of the Jewish religious leaders, Sacerdocio and Sinagoga, respectively, take an active part in the downfall of the Jewish nation, both authors have employed the religious figures differently in their respective dramas. In Lope's work, Sacerdocio alone convinces Pueblo Hebreo that he cannot love his enemy as the precepts command, and the Jewish priesthood

---

[74] See above, pp. 126-127.

convinces the people that they ought to rebel against the owner and keep the vineyard's fruits. In fact, in Lope's *auto*, Sacerdocio proves to be a more dynamic force in the drama than is the allegorical figure of the Jewish nation, since Pueblo Hebreo blindly follows Sacerdocio's dictates. In his *La viña*, Calderón poetically incorporates Sinagoga into the dramatic action of the play as Hebraísmo's wife. In spite of the fact that Sinagoga is the last personage to appear in the drama — she first enters in the middle of the play — her appearance is not shocking, for Hebraísmo has previously mentioned his wife in the play's action. Sinagoga is first mentioned at the signing of the contract early in the play, when Hebraísmo offers his wife as a sort of collateral and brags that Sinagoga possesses all the qualities necessary to realize the fulfillment of the contract. Because of his relationship by marriage to the richly endowed Sinagoga, Hebraísmo thinks that the Padre de las Familias should logically enter a contract with him: "Mi esposa,/ que es la Sinagoga, ofrezco/ que se obligue con su dote,/ caudal de infinito precio;/ pues arca de sus tesoros,/ el Arca del Testamento" (p. 1482). When Sinagoga assumes an active part in the drama with her entrance on stage, it has already been demonstrated how Calderón follows through with the wife image by depicting Sinagoga as she cries to get her way and connivingly picks at her husband's pride until he finally succumbs to her every whimper. Then she graciously rewards her spouse for granting her wishes by cooking his favorite meal and by providing wine and music with which to soothe him. Later, as it has been indicated, when Lucero del Día accuses Hebraísmo and Sinagoga of adultery, the wife becomes infuriated and pleads with Hebraísmo to save his pride and her honor: "¡Que esto consientas,/ sin hacer más sentimiento/ de tu injuria y de mi afrenta!" (p. 1491).

Since Sacerdocio single-handedly accounts for Pueblo Hebreo's fall, the devil figure, Ignorancia of Lope's drama has a very minor and undeveloped role. Idolatría simply enters the vineyard without any opposition as Pueblo Hebreo and Sacerdocio have already driven away the two precepts of love, Amor Divino and Prójimo, who were guarding the vineyard. Later in Lope's play Idolatría marries Pueblo Hebreo and all celebrate the *fiesta* which leads into the scene with the prophets. Malicia and Lucero de la Noche play a major part in Calderón's drama. As is the case with many of the Calderonian autos, the two devil figures make their appearance in the very opening of the play, as they are the first to hear Lucero del Día's voice calling the laborers to the vineyard.[75] Unlike Lope's Idolatría, the two evil figures in Calderón's work play an active part in Hebraísmo's temptations. Indirectly, they participate in tempting the Jewish figure by creating havoc among the *zagales* and the Jewish people, who in turn molest and torment a Hebraísmo plagued with doubts. Of course, both Malicia and Lucero de la Noche also directly enter the play's action, as, for example, when Malicia struggles with Inocencia or when Lucero de la Noche directly incites Hebraísmo's passions and doubt with regard to killing Isaías and the other prophets.[76]

There remains one allegorical figure found in Calderón's *auto* that has no real parallel in Lope's work. Although in a sense Inocencia is the vineyard's custodian in Calderón's *La viña*, her dramatic role is much greater than that of Amor Divino and Prójimo, who watch the vineyards in Lope's work and who never again enter the drama after having been driven away in the play's early moments. Calderón, whose ability to incorporate theology into good drama remains supreme among *auto* writers, gives Inocencia a unique dramatic function. Inocencia, who represents virtue and grace, is never depicted on the side of evil but is always seen in company with the good. Inocencia first presents herself in the desert scene in which Hebraísmo and Gentilidad are searching out Lucero del Día's mysterious call to work in the vineyard. In this first appearance, Inocencia sides with no one but observes the two questors. She then singles out Hebraísmo and favors the Jewish nation as having been the first to find the voice, saying "Y yo sacaré de aquí/ que habló primero la voz/ al hebreo que al gentil" (p. 1480). Grace makes it clear that she favors the Hebrews first, and Inocencia then remains in the company of Hebraísmo and is constantly seen with the Jewish figure until finally, as it was shown above, Malicia is permitted

---

[75] In the majority of his *autos*, Calderón begins his dramas with the devil figure, "who imagines and evokes the dramatic action." See A. A. Parker, *The Allegorical Drama of Calderón*, p. 90.

[76] See above, pp. 125-127.

momentarily to get the better of Inocencia.[77] Malicia, by clothing herself in Inocencia's garb, symbolically indicates that evil is about to replace innocence in the Jewish nation. Significantly, from the time Malicia disguised as Inocencia enters the vineyard, the grace figure never enters the action of the play until the very end when Hijo dies on the cross. At the very instant Hijo expires on the cross made from the "viga de lagar," — representing an effort to symbolically portray the theological significance of man's redemption and the opening of the gates of heaven — Inocencia appears as she had left the stage struggling with Malicia. This time Inocencia overcomes Malicia and putting on the cloak of innocence says: "¡Albricias, que ya ha quedado/ la Malicia descubierta,/ pues yo mi traje restauro!" (p. 1497). In the *auto's* final stages just before the Padre de las Familias takes the vineyard away from Hebraísmo and renders it to Gentilidad, Inocencia completely disassociates herself from Hebraísmo and goes to Gentilidad, whom the grace figure now addresses: "El hebreo hizo al contrario,/ que luego las olvidó;/ por eso contra él me valgo/ de ti a glorioso fin" (pp. 1497-98).

Before moving on to the next group of kingdom parable *autos* and leaving the Lopean and Calderonian *autos* on the Parable of the Vinedressers, I make one last observation concerning Calderón's *La viña* and the author's aesthetic awareness. Although Calderón allegorized his drama in his sacramental plays, he nevertheless was concerned with preserving verisimilitude in the portrayal of his characters. At least this is the case with regard to the two figures, Inocencia and Malicia. When Inocencia first appears in the desert with Hebraísmo and Gentilidad, who are seeking the meaning of the mysterious voice, the grace figure speaks of the need she has to appear simple in dress and speech in conformity with the allegorical personage she represents: "Porque como fuí/ sencilla virtud, conformen/ el hablar con el vestir" (p. 1480). Later, when Malicia assumes Inocencia's dress and enters the vineyard to accompany Hebraísmo, she reminds herself that she must act in accordance with the simple dress she has acquired: "Ya que su disfraz tomé,/ su sencillez fingiré" (p. 1485). Shortly thereafter, when Malicia first meets Sinagoga, the Jewish religious

---

[77] See above, pp. 123-124.

leader asks Malicia to introduce herself. Malicia replies in the language of the *campesino,* "Mi locuencia/ ¿no la ha dicho que yo só la Nocencia?" (p. 1486).

The Great Supper

In terms of the number of *autos sacramentales* written on a single parable, the Parable of the Great Supper, or Wedding Feast, is the most popular among the authors. As Luke presents the account in his Gospel, the parable tells of a certain man who gives a great supper.[78] The man sends his servants to those who have been invited to announce that preparations are complete and that the banquet is ready. However, those who were asked and had initially accepted the invitation now refuse to come because they are preoccupied with personal matters. One of those originally invited purchased a farm and goes off to examine his new investment. Another refuses to come because he has just bought five oxen and wants to try them. A third guest has just married and refuses to leave his young bride. Upon hearing that those originally invited refuse to honor his invitation, the man giving the supper becomes angry and orders his servants, "Go out quickly into the streets and lanes of the city, and bring in here the poor, and the crippled, and the blind, and the lame" (v. 21).

In his Gospel, Matthew tells basically the same story as Luke but adds some elements to Luke's account.[79] In Matthew's Gospel, the man giving the feast is a king and the occasion for the festivities is the marriage of the king's son. Matthew also states that those who had refused the invitation after having accepted beat the king's servants, "treated them shamefully, and killed them" (v. 60). At the very end of the parable, Matthew appends another incident to the account as told by Luke when he tells of a man who came to the wedding feast improperly dressed and who was ejected by the host from the feast and condemned to the "darkness outside, where there will be the weeping and the gnashing of teeth" (vv. 11-14).

---

[78] Luke, 14: 15-24.
[79] Math., 22: 1-14.

Because of Matthew's addenda, scriptural scholars have stressed the close relationship of the Parable of the Great Supper, or Wedding Feast, to the Parable of the Vinedressers, the subject of the last group of *autos* discussed above.[80] The king has been traditionally viewed as allegorically representing God and the king's son as Jesus Christ. The son's marriage is Jesus' incarnation, whereby he takes on man's human nature. The servants who announce the "marriage" are the prophets rejected and killed by the Jews, who were first called. The wedding feast has been seen traditionally as representing the heavenly kingdom, from which all are excluded who are not properly disposed, like the man without the proper garments.[81] Matthew's account with the additions, together with their traditional allegorical significance, greatly influenced the *auto* writers in their dramatization of this Gospel parable, for only one *auto* on the Great Supper parable to be discussed here does not specifically state the purpose of the feast as the marriage of the king's son, and only one other does not allude to the incident of the guest improperly dressed.

Three of the seven sacramental dramas on the Parable of the Great Supper belong to the sixteenth century.[82] The anonymous *Egloga al santísimo sacramento sobre la parábola evangélica Math. 22 y Luc. 14* is believed to be among the earliest of the dramas on the Parable of the Great Supper.[83] Alenda says of the anonymous *Egloga al santísimo sacramento* that it was written in "el segundo tercio del siglo XVI."[84] Another early *auto* from the sixteenth century, Juan de Timoneda's *Obra llamada los desposorios de Cristo*, was first printed in Timoneda's *Ternarios sacramentales* of 1575.[85] In a note to his edition of Timoneda's work, Pe-

---

[80] Fonck, 363.
[81] Juan de Maldonado, I, 760-768.
[82] Also belonging to the latter part of the sixteenth century, the five act drama, *Comoedia Habita Hispali in Festo Corporis Christi*, is based on the Great Supper Parable and is found in the *Códice de los jesuítas* (Biblioteca de la Real Academia de Historia; Colección de Cortés, No. 383).
[83] The *auto* appears in manuscript found in the *Cuaderno de Sancho Rayón* (Biblioteca Menéndez Pelayo, Santander; 24 fº, numbers 1-24). Quotations found in this study come from the manuscript.
[84] Alenda y Mira, *Boletín de la Real Academia Española*, IX, 402.
[85] Timoneda's *auto* also appears in Pedroso's edition, pp. 102-112. Quotations found in this study come from this edition.

droso expresses the idea that the *auto* could not have been written before 1571 because of a passage which appears in the play and which refers to the battle of Lepanto. He concludes that the *auto* was printed in 1575 and that "habiendo ocurrido en 1571 la batalla de Lepanto, queda circunscrita a los tres años intermedios la fecha en que seguramente fue escrito y representado este auto." [86] The third early *auto* on the Great Supper Parable has the title, *Parabola Coenae*. [87] Speaking of the *Parabola Coenae*, Crawford maintains that the play was written and performed in the Jesuit College at Salamanca after 1557 and further asserts that the play's probable author was Padre Juan Bonifacio. [88]

Three *autos sacramentales* on the Parable of the Great Supper were composed by Calderón in the seventeenth century. Valbuena Prat and Hilborn agree that Calderón wrote his *Llamados y escogidos* between 1648 and 1649. [89] Approximately the same time as his *Llamados y escogidos*, Calderón wrote a second *auto* based on the Great Supper, *La segunda esposa y triunfar muriendo*. [90] This second of the Calderonian dramas on the Gospel parable of the Great Supper commemorates Philip IV's marriage to Mariana of Austria, which took place on November 8, 1648. [91] Calderón composed a third *auto sacramental* on the same Great Supper Parable, *El nuevo hospicio de los pobres*. According to Valbuena Prat this third *auto* by Calderón commemorates another historical event, the founding of the "Hospicio por la Congregación del dulce Nombre de María, en una casa particular de la calle de Santa Isabel." [92] Valbuena Prat's theory, which is based on internal

---

[86] Pedroso, p. 108, n. 1.
[87] The *auto* is found in Pedroso, pp. 122-132. Quotations found in this study come from this edition.
[88] Crawford, p. 158.
[89] Valbuena Prat, *Obras*..., III, 1471, and Hilborn, 114. Quotations found in this study come from Valbuena Prat's edition, pp. 449-468.
[90] In the prologue to his edition of Calderonian *autos* (*Obras*..., III, 27), Valbuena Prat explains that Calderón's *auto* actually is known by three titles, *La segunda esposa, Triunfar muriendo*, and *La nueva esposa*. Quotations from the *auto* found in this study come from Valbuena's edition, pp. 423-447.
[91] Valbuena Prat, *Obras*..., III, 423. Hilborn (p. 114) agrees with Valbuena's date.
[92] Valbuena Prat, *Obras*..., III, 1179. Quotations found in this study come from Valbuena's edition, pp. 1179-1207.

evidence from the *auto* itself and which posits the idea that *El nuevo hospicio de los pobres* celebrates the founding of the house of charity, allows him to establish the *auto's* date at 1668, the year in which the *Hospicio* was founded. According to Valbuena Prat, the previously known date of *El nuevo hospicio de los pobres*, 1675, is that of the *auto's* second presentation. If Valbuena Prat's theory proves to be correct, then the date of 1675 that Hilborn gives to Calderón's *El nuevo hospicio* is in effect the date of the *auto's* second presentation.[93]

Much confusion surrounds the identity of another *auto sacramental* on the Parable of the Great Supper, *El convite general*. Alenda lists two sacramental plays with the title of *El convite general*, one by Calderón and another by José Villalpando.[94] Although Alenda lists Calderón's *El convite general* separately in his catalogue, he agrees with La Barrera and others who believe that Calderón's play, first mentioned by Vera Tassis in his list of Calderonian *autos*, is really Calderón's *Llamados y escogidos* and that the two *autos* are synonymous.[95] Concerning the second *El convite general* written by José Villalpando, Alenda writes: "Cítalo en su Catálogo La Barrera, y dice que está formado con trozos de varios autos de Calderón."[96] Considering what Alenda and others have said concerning the two *autos*, one concludes that Calderón's *El convite general* is really the alternate title for the *Llamados y escogidos* found in the readily available edition of Valbuena. Using the bibliographical data afforded by the cataloguers, I sent for the Villalpando manuscript.[97] However, the manuscript that I received from the Biblioteca Nacional was not an *auto* by Villalpando but one by Calderón with the title, *El convite general*. Furthermore, the *auto* now in my possession is not identical to Calderón's *Llamados y escogidos* nor to any one of his previously known plays on the Great Supper Parable.

---

[93] Hilborn, 114.

[94] Alenda y Mira, *Boletín de la Real Academia Española*, III, 676.

[95] Alenda y Mira, *Boletín de la Real Academia Española*, III, 676. See also La Barrera, pp. 479 and 594; Julián Paz, Vol. I, p. 121.

[96] Alenda y Mira, *Boletín de la Real Academia Española*, III, 676.

[97] The manuscript is found at the Biblioteca Nacional in Madrid (45 ho², del siglo xviii, perg. (0); No. 16. 282²).

The present treatment of the *autos* on the Parable of the Great Supper will consist of three phases. First, the dramatic structure of the sixteenth-century *autos* will be examined. The second phase will have the threefold objective of showing how Calderón's *Llamados y escogidos*, though patterned after the sixteenth-century *autos*, is, nevertheless, better drama than its predecessors; how Calderón's *La segunda esposa y triunfar muriendo* is uniquely different from any of the early *autos* on the Great Supper Parable because of the purpose for which it was written; and finally, how Calderón's third *auto*, *El nuevo hospicio de los pobres*, stands out as the perfection of the author's earlier attempts, especially of his *Llamados y escogidos*. The third and final phase of this section of the kingdom parable *auto* on the Great Supper will deal with the *auto*, *El convite general*, and show that the *auto* extant in the Biblioteca Nacional greatly resembles Calderón's *El nuevo hospicio de los pobres*, with a few traces of influence from his earlier *La segunda esposa y triunfar muriendo*.

Of the three *autos sacramentales* on the Great Supper Parable written in the latter part of the sixteenth century, the anonymous *Egloga al santísimo sacramento sobre la parábola evangélica Math. 22 y Luc. 14*, following closely the Gospel account, is the simplest in terms of dramatic development. In the initial scene, the king conversing with his four servants, Calisteno, Aretino, Aretinoquio, and Pluteo, tells them that he wishes his son to marry "de buena gana/ con naturaleza humana," and that they should go and summon those invited to the wedding. Leaving the king's court, the four emissaries first meet Philargirio, Acribeo, and Edismeno, who, one by one, excuse themselves from the feast. Philargirio has just bought a farm and has to inspect his purchase. Acribeo has recently acquired five pairs of oxen and has to feed them. Edismeno also finds reason to excuse himself from the banquet, stating:

> Y como holgaré, señores,
> de cumplir esta embajada.
> Pero dejar mis amores,
> mis deleytes y favores
> parece cosa crusada.
> Tengo una mujer hermosa,

> galana, apuesta y graciosa
> y no la puedo dejar.
>
> (fol. 4)

Having been informed of those who refused the invitation, the king orders his servants, "Id por aquesta ciudad/ con diligencia y buscad/ pobres, cojos, viejos, ciegos,/ y traedlos a mis ruegos/ y a todos decid, entrad." At the banquet filled with social outcasts, the king discovers a man improperly clothed and has him ejected from the feast. The anonymous author associates this entire scene with the Sacrament, the banquet representing the Eucharistic meal of which no one may partake who is in the state of serious sin. [98]

The anonymous author of the *Egloga al santísimo sacramento* presents little more than a dramatic dialogue in his representation of the Gospel parable. First, though the king speaks of his son's marriage to human nature, neither Christ nor human nature appear as acting figures in the play. Nor does the author dramatize the potentially dramatic scene of the man who is evicted from the banquet. In the wedding scene, the king becomes angry at one of the guests who he sees is not wearing the proper attire, but once again the guest figure never enters the drama as one of the acting personages. The scene in which the poor man, the blind man, the lame man, etc., dispose themselves to accept the wedding invitation presents a third instance in which the writer of the *Egloga al santísimo sacramento* might have heightened the drama of his play, but did not. The dramatic ineffectiveness of his scene in the *Egloga al santísimo sacramento* in which those accepting the general invitation to the wedding feast readily change their garments can best be observed by comparing it with the same scene in the *Parabola Coenae*.

The *Parabola Coenae*, the second anonymous *auto* on the Parable of the Great Super, follows closely the Gospel account as does the *Egloga al santísimo sacramento*, but is better drama than the latter. First, not only does the Padre speak of his son's forthcoming marriage but Christ and human nature have an active

---

[98] In order to be properly disposed to receive the Eucharist, the recipient must be free from grievous sin and in the state of grace. See Morrow, pp. 312-313.

role in the drama in the allegorical figures of Esposo and Esposa, respectively. In a beautiful love scene which recall those in the Lopean *autos*, Esposo and Esposa pledge fidelity to each other and then discuss the meaning of their common human nature and the result of Divine love epitomized in the Esposo's crucifixion so dreaded by the Esposa. Second, unlike the *Egloga al santísimo sacramento*, where the king only mentions the man without the proper garments condemned to darkness, in the *Parabola Coenae* the condemned man appears on stage in the person of the Pecador. Although the Pecador's dramatic role is limited to a brief lamentation of his tragic fate, the actual appearance of the allegorical figure enhances the drama. Immediately after the Pecador's lamentation, the author further intensifies the *auto's* drama by ending this brief scene with a chorus of Demonios hailing their victory over the condemned Pecador. That those accepting the invitation are actually cured of their physical and spiritual infirmities by the Padre so as to be properly disposed to enter the banquet reflects still another dramatic element found in the *Parabola Coenae* but absent in the *Egloga al santísimo sacramento*. In a scene containing many references to Christ's miracles related in the New Testament, Padre, at the plea of his servant, Amor, cures the lame, the blind, the deaf, and the dumb of their physical defects. After being freed from their infirmities, all put on the clothes of humility and charity and enter the nuptial celebration.

Besides the three instances discussed above illustrating how the *Parabola Coenae* better dramatizes the Gospel parable than does the *Egloga al santísimo sacramento*, the names given to the various personages of the former *auto* contain more allegorical and symbolic significance than those of the latter. For example, instead of the four figures, Calesteno, Aretino, Aretinoquio, and Pluteo of the *Egloga al santísimo sacramento*, it is the two figures, Amor and Celo, who act as the Padre's messengers in the *Parabola Coenae* and who spread the good news of the banquet of love to men. In place of Philargirio, Acribeo, and Edismeno who decline the invitation in the *Egloga al santísimo sacramento*, in *Parabola Coenae*, Soberbia is the name of the figure who brags about the quality of his newly acquired land, Avariento the figure who must work to full capacity and utmost productivity, and Lujurioso the figure who refuses to give up his conjugal pleasures.

Special attention should be drawn to one of the most interesting and distinctive scenes found in both the *Egloga al santísimo sacramento* and the *Parabola Coenae*. The scene in which the *cojo*, the *ciego*, and the other needy members of society first enter the drama of the respective *autos* reflects the characteristic realism of these two early sacramental plays. In the *Egloga al santísimo sacramento*, not only do the figures expose the social problems of the epoch by lamenting in common language their poverty and their afflictions, thus presenting a sort of *cuadro de costumbres*, but also such picturesque details as the *ciego* entering the scene riding upon the shoulders of the *cojo* all contribute to the realistic tone of the *auto*. In this same scene in the *Egloga al santísimo sacramento*, there appear two women pilgrims en route to the shrine of Santiago. The presence of the two female figures adds a burlesque touch to the *auto*, for upon meeting the women, the Ciego asks his crippled friend if the two girls are cute and if they have clothes on:

> CIEGO. ¿Quiénes son ésas que cantaban?
> COJO. Son romericas que han venido.
> CIEGO. Dime, Marcos, ¿son hermosas?
> COJO. Calla, ya ciego, [te] he pedido.
> CIEGO. Dime, ¿qué traen vestidos?
> COJO. ¿Para qué son esas cosas
> que me has dicho, pequeñuelo?
> CIEGO. ¿No puedes callar?, cojuelo.
> ¿Quieres que te eche en un borrico?
> (fol. 6)

The introduction of the two *romericas* into the play marks a distinct departure from the Gospel story, nowhere in which is there mention of any women characters. This innovation brings to mind a similar addition of a female character, the quarrelsome mother of the anonymous *Hijo pródigo* of the Rouanet edition.

This scene of the social outcasts in the *Parabola Coenae* reflects the same note of realism as that of the parallel situation in the *Egloga al santísimo sacramento*. However, the scene in the former *auto* is more distinctive in that it transpires rapidly and is written in prose unlike the rest of the play, which is in verse. This true-to-life scene written in prose provides the audience with a comic relief and is sometimes considered as a short *entremés* called "La gallofa." [99]

The most distinguishing characteristic of Juan Timoneda's *Los desposorios de Cristo*, the third sixteenth century *auto* on the Great Supper Parable, is that Timoneda's *auto* does not dramatize the refusal of the king's invitation by the ungrateful guests nor the subsequent acceptance by the socially deprived. In fact, not only are these two scenes, which are found in the *Egloga al santísimo sacramento* and in the *Parabola Coenae*, totally missing in Timoneda's *Los desposorios* but also none of the personages such as Soberbia, *el cojo*, etc. ever appear in the play. Conveying the first part of the Parable's story more in dialogue than in drama, Timoneda passed over the early incidents of the great Supper Parable and instead emphasized the banquet scene itself as the focal point of his dramatization. In Timoneda's *auto*, the lengthy banquet scene becomes a vast allegory of Christ's passion and Eucharistic sacrifice. Each of the various courses served at the banquet symbolically represents an aspect of Christ's passion, such as the whips with which he was beaten and the wreath of thorns with which he was crowned. Timoneda's dramatization of the passion through the figurative courses of the banquet recalls the other dramatic techniques employed by the *auto* writers to dramatize the passion on stage: for example, the card game in Mejía de la Cerda's *El juego del hombre*, and the "Guess who?" in Mira de Amescua's *El heredero*. [100] This tendency of Timoneda to overlook some of the parable's more potentially dramatic scenes has been pointed out in the discussion of his *La oveja perdida* in which the author failed to dramatize the *oveja's* temptation and subsequent fall. [101]

If Valbuena Prat and H. Hilborn correctly set the date of Calderón's *Los llamados y escogidos* as 1648, then this Calderonian *auto* on the Great Supper represents one of Calderón's first attempts to dramatize a Gospel account. Even in this initial attempt

---

[99] "La voz *gallofa* con que, según la Academia, era conocido en un principio el mendrugo de pan dado de limosna á los peregrinos que iban á Santiago de Galicia, sirvió luego para designar la vida libre y holgazana de los que pordiosean, pudiendo subsistir de otro modo" (Pedroso, p. 126, n. 3).

[100] See above, pp. 92-93 and p. 121.

[101] See above, p. 53.

to present a Gospel parable, one can easily observe how Calderón characteristically developed, in his drama, the same salvation-history theme of Jewish rejection and Christ's saving redemption always present in the other kingdom parables. In fact many of the allegorical figures found in *Los llamados y escogidos* are already familiar and are found in almost all of the other kingdom parables written by Calderón. Instead of Acribeo, Philargirio, and Edismeno of the earlier *Egloga al santísimo sacramento* and the allegorical Soberbio, Avariento, and Lujurioso of the *Parabola Coenae*, in the *Llamados y escogidos*, Gentilidad and Sinagoga turn down the Rey's invitation to the Príncipe's marriage to the Esposa. The royal invitation to the wedding feast is delivered by the king's prophets Daniel and Isaías, who are harshly treated, especially by Sinagoga. As the Calderonian drama unfolds, Gentilidad reconsiders the king's offer, ends his vacillation, and agrees to accept the invitation to the banquet, while Sinagoga becomes even more hostile and is doomed to the role of the *desterrado*.

In developing his play of the Great Supper within the allegorical framework of the salvation-history theme, Calderón achieved a greater degree of drama than did the three writers of the sixteenth-century *autos* on the same parable. In the previous anonymous *autos*, those who rejected the king's invitation did so for the three reasons specified in the biblical account. One declined to come to the banquet because he had just bought a farm, another because of his oxen, and a third because of his new wife. In Calderón's *Llamados y escogidos*, the introduction of the two figures, Verdad and Mentira, greatly heightens the dramatic conflict of this part of the Gospel parable. Verdad tries to convince the vacillating Gentilidad and the hostile Sinagoga to accept the invitation extended by Daniel and Isaías on behalf of the Rey. Mentira propounds the opposite views and tries to convince the two religious figures to disregard the invitation on the grounds that it is false and misleading. Gentilidad and Sinagoga must decide on their own account which of the two opposing figures of good and evil they will believe. The decision to accept the invitation or to decline it creates a situation of mental tension. Sinagoga and Gentilidad reflect their confusion in the dialogue, all of which leads to greater conflict, an essential part of drama.

The introduction of Mentira and Verdad also allows Calderón an opportunity to present another scene that is in itself intensely dramatic. Verdad and Mentira, alone on stage, engage in a hand-to-hand struggle in which Mentira steals the cape worn by Verdad and clothes herself with it. Verdad's cape helps Mentira deceive Sinagoga and Gentilidad, Calderón thereby portraying the manner in which evil disguised as good deceives man. In dramatizing this same scene, Calderón was aware of the theological dangers inherent in depicting evil as conquering good, and he takes great care to tell the audience that Mentira's overthrow of Verdad is only temporary and that Verdad permitted Mentira to win for the moment. This care of Calderón to leave the audience with the right idea concerning Mentira's win over Verdad is reflected in their dialogue at the end of the scene:

> VERDAD. Fuerza esta vez me faltó.
> MENTIRA. Si en tierra esta vez estás,
> ¿para que te opones más?
> VERDAD. Para que tú atropellarme
> podrás hoy y retirarme,
> mas vencer no podrás.
> (p. 459)

This entire scene in which the allegorical figures of good and evil engage in a face-to-face struggle from which the evil personage triumphs temporarily recalls a similar scene in one of the Calderonian *autos* studied earlier in this chapter, *La viña del señor*.[102]

In the three sixteenth-century *autos* on the Great Supper Parable, the respective authors failed to capitalize upon the full dramatic potentiality of the scene concerning the man who attended the feast improperly dressed. It will be remembered that in the *Egloga al santísimo sacramento*, the Rey only mentions seeing a guest improperly dressed and orders him thrown out of the banquet, and that the man never takes an active part in the drama. In the *Parabola Coenae*, the *pecador* remains only long enough in the play to utter a brief lament before he is seized by the chorus of demons who hurry him away to the depths of the eternal abyss. In Timoneda's *Desposorios de Cristo*, the *soldado's* role

---

[102] See above, pp. 123-124.

is almost as brief as that of the *pecador* in the *Parabola Coenae*, although he does appear a little before the wedding feast in a brief scene in which he brags of how he will gain entrance into the banquet even though he lacks the proper clothes. However, in his *Llamados y escogidos*, Calderón cleverly incorporates this same scene of the improperly disposed guest into the salvation-history theme established in his drama. Mentira, who had earlier functioned as the devil figure tempting Sinagoga and Gentilidad, in this scene assumes a second dramatic function, for it is she who assumes the Judas role by bargaining with Sinagoga and finally agreeing to steal the mysterious bread from the banquet for thirty pieces of silver. The *auto's* entire last scene of the banquet supper, with the mysterious bread possessing miraculous qualities and the reference to the thirty pieces of silver, clearly relates to the last Supper, with its Eucharistic bread which the betrayer Judas was unworthy of receiving.

Calderón's second dramatization of the Great Supper Parable, *La segunda esposa y triunfar muriendo*, written around the same time as his earlier *Llamados y escogidos*, represents an entirely unique approach to the Gospel account. Calderón wrote the *auto* in honor of Philip IV's second marriage to Doña Mariana of Austria and therefore the author felt obliged to somehow relate the Gospel account to the historical event taking place in some meaningful allegory. Calderón naturally chose the parabolic wedding celebration but he also altered the allegorical significance of the marriage itself. It was noted that in the earlier *autos* the authors chose to interpret the marriage found in the Gospel parable as being the matrimonial bond between Christ and human nature. In his *La segunda esposa*, Calderón chose to interpret the marriage as allegorically representing the marriage of God to his Church, the second spouse, the first wife being the Jewish religion. At least twice in his drama, Calderón justifies this interpretation of the marriage in the parable. One of the seven sacraments and loyal liege of the Rey, Matrimonio, tells the Rey that a second marriage would be desirable since the Rey's first wife, Sinagoga, was disloyal:

> Viendo, que tu suma Ciencia
> esta Familia eminente

del ejemplar de tu Mente
pasa a práctica experiencia,
usando de tu licencia
dicen, que ya que la hermosa
Sinanoga, que dichosa
(tu primera Esposa fué)
yace, será justo que
elijas Segunda Esposa.

(p. 429)

In another scene later in the play, Calderón again makes reference to his interpretation of the marriage in the parable and points out that St. Gregory himself, one of the Church fathers, gave alternative meanings for the marriage in the Gospel parable on the Great Supper. In this scene, Pecado, Muerte, and another allegorical figure simply called Otro, are reading to each other from the Scriptures and ecclesiastical writings:

PECADO. Escucha pues.
(Lee)
"Convida el Rey a sus bodas
príncipes y emperadores,
potentados y señores,
y luego a las gentes todas,
desde el Rey al peregrino,
que a nadie excepta y admite
los pobres a su convite."
OTRO. (Lee) "Estas bodas, que previno
el Rey, ser dos imagina:
una, la Naturaleza
Humana; otra, la Pureza
de la Iglesia, Fe Divina;
así, creer es notorio,
que tuvo en su Unión Piadosa
Primera y Segunda Esposa."
MUERTE. Y ¿quién dice eso?
PECADO. Gregorio.

(p. 434)

Based on the alternative interpretation of the "marriage" in the Gospel parable, that which views the marriage as a union between God and His Church, Calderón's whole drama consists of an allegorical portrayal of man's journey through life. The seven sacraments, the king's servants and handmaidens of his wife, the Church, aid man in his struggles with life's two destructive forces, sin (Pecado) and death (Muerte), the former snuffing out man's spiritual strength, the latter his physical prowess. In the drama, Hombre, having begun his pilgrimage of life in the midst of original sin, is cleansed by the life-giving waters of Bautismo. Having been purged by Bautismo, Hombre receives the added assurance of Confirmación, which signifies man's passage from childhood into adulthood. No longer a child, Hombre becomes aware of the pleasures of the world and like the Prodigal Son goes off to enjoy them. At this stage in Hombre's life, the third sacrament, Penitencia, enters the drama and offers solace to the penitent Hombre, whose life is being choked out by frivolity. Another allegorical figure, *Comunión*, follows Penitencia and is brought to Hombre by Orden Sacerdotal. When Orden Sacerdotal utters the sacred words of consecration, "esto es mi Sangre y Cuerpo mío," which call down God himself, the Rey enters and Calderón begins to allegorize the crucifixion and redemption scenes. The significance of one of the three titles of the play *Triunfar muriendo*, comes from the fact that with Christ's death man's mortal enemies, Pecado and Muerte, are overcome. In fact at one point in the *auto*, the Rey himself states: "¿Quién haya visto,/ que cuando el triunfar muriendo,/ la Vida a la Muerte quito,/ la vida al Hombre restauro?" (p. 443). Finally in the *auto*'s denouement, the resurrected Rey is seen coming upon the scene in the company of his Esposa and her seven sacraments and all are riding in a ship symbolic of the Church. The seven sacraments pledge their fidelity of service to the Segunda Esposa, and Hombre, now accompanying the sacred group, praises the Rey for his goodness.

In his marvelous allegorical representation of man's pilgrimage through life, Calderón always maintained the basic principles of his orthodox beliefs. For example, when the allegorical figures of the sacraments come to Hombre in the various stages of his life, never once do the sacraments impose themselves upon man against his free will. At the beginning of the play, Hombre in the state of original sin stands up against Pecado and Muerte and makes a profession of faith (Fe pido/ para creer tus Misterios" [p. 437]); only then do Bautismo and Confirmación free Hombre from the fetters of Pecado.[103] Later when Hombre goes out into the world, he becomes disillusioned with its deceits and again seeks spiritual aid. Only then does Penitencia, followed by her companion sacrament, Comunión, come to rescue Hombre once again from the evil powers. The same is true for the remaining sacraments. Each one enters the drama only after Hombre himself seeks help against Pecado and Muerte.

Another example of how Calderón adhered to the basic tenets of his orthodox faith can be found in the skillful manner in which he handles the difficult problem of dramatizing the various sacraments in relation to the two evil figures of Pecado and Muerte. For example, after Bautismo and Confirmación have freed Hombre from the grasp of Pecado, only Muerte escapes the effect of the two sacraments and continues to stalk Hombre, for both Bautismo and Confirmación admit they have no power against physical and corporal death, which is inevitable to mortal man. Later, when Hombre, having reached adulthood, goes off into the sinful world, Bautismo and Confirmación remain in the background, peering through their fingers, helpless to prevent Hombre from once again befriending Pecado. The two sacraments console themselves with the thought that they are nevertheless indelibly imprinted upon man's soul, in spite of the fact that man sins. When Hombre, now in the company of Pecado, asks Bautismo whether or not the effect of the two sacraments he has received has been lost because of his friendship with Pecado, Bautismo replies: "No,/ que el carácter que te dimos,/ fijo se queda en el alma" (pp. 438-39).[104] How Calderón preserved Catholic dogma while masterfully dramatizing the sacraments in relation to the two evil figures can be seen in one of the *auto*'s later scenes, when Hombre, now aged, becomes severely afflicted with all types of physical and spiritual

---

[103] Although the sacraments of Penance and the Eucharist are usually administered sometime after Baptism and before Confirmation, because in the past the Bishop frequently had great difficulty in visiting the various parishes under his jurisdiction, the Church regularly permitted Confirmation to be given immediately after Baptism in spite of the tender age of the recipient. This custom still holds true today in remote areas where the Church is still in her missionary stages. See Morrow, p. 274.

[104] Baptism, Confirmation, and Holy Orders are the only three of the seven sacraments that are believed to imprint an indelible character on the soul of the recipient. See Morrow, p. 267.

infirmities heaped upon him by Muerte and Pecado. Once again Hombre seeks help and is aided by the Viaticum and the Sacrament of the Sick, which give him renewed grace and temporarily restore some of his physical health.[105]

Before proceeding to Calderón's third sacramental drama on the Great Supper Parable, it would be well to point out another interesting scene in Calderón's *La segunda esposa* that takes place early in the *auto* immediately before the first appearance of Hombre. The entire scene allegorizes the Annunciation, in which the Angel Gabriel announces to Mary that she has been chosen by God to be the mother of Jesus. In the *auto*, Matrimonio makes known to Esposa the Rey's desire to marry her and asks her consent. Paraphrasing the Virgin Mary's words found in Scripture and repeated in the prayer known in Roman Catholic tradition as the "Angelus," Esposa answers Matrimonio:

> Si liberal y piadoso
> tu Rey, viendo mi humildad,
> quiere con la Majestad
> de ser todo Poderoso,
> hacerme Grande, sus dones
> a tanto me ensalzarán
> que beata me dirán
> todas las generaciones;
> y así, atenta mi humildad,
> sólo dirá con temor.
>
> (p. 435)

After uttering these initial words from the "Angelus," Esposa utters together with the chorus the famous words quoted directly from the "Angelus" prayer:

> "Esclava soy del Señor,
> cúmplase su Voluntad."
>
> (p. 435)[106]

---

[105] "Viaticum" is the name given to the Eucharist received in the last rites of the Church. The sacrament of the Anointing of the Sick is commonly believed to contribute to the physical betterment of the recipient as well as to his spiritual welfare. See Morrow, pp. 342-43.

[106] With these words of Mary, Jesus became incarnate and was conceived in the womb of the Virgin. See Morrow, pp. 68-69.

This same scene, besides continuing the direct and implied references to the "Angelus," has parts of another prayer to the Virgin popular in the Roman Catholic Church which also helps to convey the significance of the scene as allegorizing the Annunciation and Incarnation. Such direct phrases carefully arranged in order throughout the scene as, "Dios te Salve, Reina," "Madre de Misericordia," "Vida y Dulzura," "Esperanza nuestra," "Los que en este Valle estamos/ llorando," "Desterrados Hijos de Eva," "Señora, Abogada nuestra," "Esos misericordiosos/ ojos a nosotros vuelve," all come from the prayer to Mary, "Salve Regina." The references to these two popular Marian prayers of the "Angelus" and the "Salve Regina" give this part of the Calderón *auto* a distinctly popular tone, all of which adds credence to the idea that the people of Calderón's day understood the allegory of the *auto sacramental*.[107]

In 1668, the prolific author of *autos sacramentales* composed his third allegorical play on the Great Supper Parable, *El nuevo hospicio de los pobres*. It will be remembered that, according to Valbuena Prat, Calderón wrote this third *auto* in commemoration of the founding of a house of charity by one of the religious orders. Although Calderón's desire to write an *auto* suitable for the occasion had some bearing on his choice of the Great Supper Parable, particularly because of the scene in which the poor, the blind, the lame, and others in need receive the invitation to feast at the banquet, basically *El nuevo hospicio* represents a perfecting of the author's earlier *Llamados y escogidos*.

In his *El nuevo hospicio*, Calderón introduces the allegorical personage, Sabiduría. Sabiduría not only augments the dramatic potentiality of the play by making available another acting character, but the figure also allows Calderón to obtain structural balance in that Sabiduría, representing the third person of the Trinity, complements the first and second persons, represented

---

[107] The "Angelus" is still commonly said by Roman Catholics three times a day, morning, noon, and night. Often the bells of a church will ring signaling the "Angelus." The "Salve Regina," until the recent innovations of the Vatican II Council, had always been said after each of the masses. For a study of how Calderón used the liturgy in his *autos* see Margaret Pauline Young, *The Liturgical Element in the Autos Sacramentales of Calderón* (Unpublished Dissertation; Boston University, 1947).

by Rey and Príncipe, respectively. Calderón could not have successfully developed the three God figures in proper relationship to one another had he not fully understood the complex theological problem of the Trinity itself. That the author of *El nuevo hospicio* fully intended to complete the Trinity with the addition of Sabiduría and that he wanted to express the full mystery of how the three persons of God proceeded one from the other is made clear in the play when Rey says to Sabiduría:

> Un Hijo tengo, tan Hijo
> mío en todo, que la idea
> en mi cariño, sin duda,
> continuamente le engendra.
> Tanto en él me complací,
> y él en mí, que la Unión nuestra
> produce un Amor de entrambos,
> que nos hace de manera
> tan Uno a los Tres, que somos
> en la igualdad de la Ciencia,
> del Poder y del Amor,
> Tres personas, y una esencia.
>
> (p. 1186) [108]

As has already been observed in this study, often when Calderón rewrote in later years some of the themes he had used in his earlier *autos*, he saw the importance of achieving greater structural balance and symmetry.[109] In his *El nuevo hospicio*, Calderón once again set up the structural pattern of four.[110] To the two figures representing the Jews and the Gentiles found in *Llamados y escogidos*, Calderón introduces in his *El nuevo hospicio* four entirely new figures who serve as the messengers an-

---

[108] The true mystery of the Trinity of how the three Persons proceeded One from the Other is known as "intelligible immanation." Calderón's presentation of the mystery in very exact terms reveals the author's great knowledge of the profundities of his faith. It is interesting to note that, in his early years as an *auto* writer (before 1660), Calderón did not seem to grasp the full significance of the Trinity, or at least he was unable to dramatize it effectively in his *autos sacramentales*. See and compare Calderón's early edition of his *La vida es sueño*, the *auto*, and his *refundición* of the same *auto* in 1673. The early manuscript of *La vida es sueño* is printed in Valbuena's edition, Vol. III, pp. 1864-1875.

[109] See above, pp. 110-117.

[110] See above, pp. 98-102.

nouncing the wedding invitation. The four allegorical figures represent the three theological virtues of Faith, Hope, and Charity plus the virtue of Mercy. Significantly it is Sabiduría who dispenses the virtues to the four corners of the earth.[111] Fe visits the faithless lands of Africa, where Ateísmo gloriously reigns. Caridad announces the invitation in América, the land of Idolatría, who blinds the hearts and minds of the people with her splendor and riches. The third theological virtue, Esperanza, goes to Asia, which is ruled by Hebraísmo, who still waits and hopes for the coming of the Messiah. The last of the virtues, Misericordia, hurries off to Europe, which is under the control of Apostasía. In Calderón's *El nuevo hospicio*, Ateísmo Hebraísmo, Idolatría, and Apostasía represent those of the Gospel parable who refuse the invitation to the wedding feast.

In *Llamados y escogidos*, Príncipe gets angry upon hearing that his father's invitation to the wedding was refused, and he orders Verdad to invite those who walk the roads and byways. However, in the *Llamados y escogidos*, the audience never sees Verdad invite those in the roads and byways as it does in the "la gallofa" scene of the anonymous *Parabola Coenae* and in a similar scene of the *Egloga al santísimo sacramento*. By developing and dramatizing in *El nuevo hospicio* this important incident of the Gospel parable, which Calderón only mentioned in his *Llamados y escogidos*, the author again succeeded in perfecting his earlier *auto*. In fact, in his *El nuevo hospicio*, Calderón had a particular interest in dramatizing that part of the Gospel parable in which the lame, the blind, the poor, and other needy persons appear. It is precisely this incident in the parable that best relates to the historical event that he was attempting to commemorate: namely, the founding of the house of charity. It is also of interest to observe that with the introduction of the four allegorical personages, Apetito, Pereza, Lascivia, and Avaricia, Calderón continued to structure his drama around the symmetrical pattern initiated with the four virtues and the four religion figures. Apetito (*de villano ciego*) wanders about blindly searching and groping for gratification and fulfillment of his endless desires. Pereza (*de*

---

[111] The third person of the Trinity is traditionally viewed as the dispenser of the spiritual gifts and virtues to man. See Morrow, pp. 90-93.

leproso llagado) lies paralyzed, covered with the wounds of leprosy, rotting from inactivity. Lascivia (*de pobre mendigo*) begs constant satisfaction that ends in total frustration and exhaustion. Avaricia (*de hidrópico galán*) suffers from a type of cancerous growth in that the more she has, the more she desires.[112] In *El nuevo hospicio*, the four virtues sent out by Sabiduría and rejected by the four religion figures now invite the four suffering figures, who willingly accept the invitation but who must first be cured of their "infirmities."

The scene in which the four virtues lead the four suffering figures to the Príncipe constitutes another addition to the *El nuevo hospicio* not found in the *Llamados y escogidos* and related to the historical event being commemorated in the sacramental play. By performing a series of miracles, well-known through the New Testament, Príncipe cures each of the suffering figures. The blind Apetito led by Fe approaches the Príncipe and receives sight when Príncipe applies earth to his eyes and says: "Pues para ver, su ver vió,/ contigo he de enviarle, Fe,/ (ya que enviado declara/ quien dice Siloé) a la clara/ Laguna de Siloé,/ vea el mundo en su cara" (p. 1200).[113] To the leprous paralytic, Pereza, guided by Caridad, Príncipe commands: "Toma tu lecho y camina" (p. 1201).[114] Príncipe also heals Avaricia and Lascivia, brought to him by Misericordia, by showing the former figure that her riches and worldly possessions will turn to dust and by demonstrating to the latter figure how vain it is to lust for "delicias y placeres,/ juegos, galas y mujeres" (p. 1201). In dramatizing the cure of Lascivia, there are obvious allusions to the *hijo pródigo* who lost his youth and fortune before realizing his mistake and repenting (p. 1202). It will be recalled that this entire scene of the cures and miracles found in Calderón's *El nuevo hospicio*, is also found in a less dramatized form in the *Parabola Coenae*, the most dramatically developed of the three sixteenth-century *autos*.

---

[112] The *Diccionario de la lengua española* of the Real Academia Española gives a figurative meaning for *hidrópico*: "insaciable" or "sediento con exceso."

[113] The account of the man born blind is found in John, 9:2-41.

[114] The cure performed on the leper and the paralytic can be found in John, 5:1-18. See also Luke, 5:12-26.

Although in *Llamados y escogidos* Esposa represents human nature in an allegory signifying Christ's "marriage" to human nature at the moment of his Incarnation, in *El nuevo hospicio*, Calderón gives to the figure of human nature an even greater allegorical and dramatic meaning. In his *El nuevo hospicio*, Sunamitis is the name Calderón gives to *naturaleza humana*, the wife of the Príncipe. What Calderón had in mind in choosing the name "Sunamitis" and its allegorical implications can best be seen in the words of one of the drama's personages. Rey explains to Sabiduría why he selected Sunamitis as the future wife of his son, Príncipe, and what significance the name itself possesses:

> Determino darle Estado,
> y para que resplandezca
> en la elección de la Esposa
> más mi amorosa clemencia,
> ha de ser la Sunamitis,
> que aunque en la versión hebrea
> se interpreta, la que Duerme;
> también mudada una letra,
> que por Sunamitis, diga
> Sulamitis, se interpreta,
> la Perfecta; con que a un tiempo
> conviene en entrambas señas;
> en Naturaleza Humana,
> pues en achaques envuelta
> yace, bien como dormida,
> que es no estar viva, ni muerta;
> pues muerta para la Gracia,
> vive capaz de tenerla,
> el día que con mi Hijo
> se despose; de manera,
> que de sus joyas dotada,
> vendrá a quedar tan perfecta,
> que a las dos luces que dije,
> la Naturaleza, y ella,
> no habrá quien dude, que son
> por hoy una cosa mesma.
>
> (p. 1186)

Having defined in Rey's words to Sabiduría the dual nature of Sunamitis as being asleep yet possessing the potentiality of becoming perfect, Calderón masterfully undertakes to convey dramatically the twofold significance of Sunamitis. When Sunamitis makes her first appearance on stage, she is seen in company with Avaricia, Lascivia, Apetito, and Pereza, who reflect the worst of human nature. She is seen weeping over the sad state of humanity which she represents and she yearns to be relieved of her misery. In this first scene in which Sunamitis appears, Calderón represents her as human nature unfulfilled, sleeping, "Que no está viva ni muerta." In the very next scene, which enacts the Angel Gabriel's visit to Mary and which Calderón borrowed almost word for word from *La segunda esposa*, Sunamitis agrees to marry the Príncipe. Sunamitis no sooner gives her consent to the marriage than Príncipe makes his first appearance on stage and immediately tells her that it is he who by becoming man gives to human nature its greatest fulfillment and perfection:

> Bien mi amorosa Pasión
> estuvo con suspensión
> a ver, qué respuesta das;
> porque ese mérito más
> tenga tu resignación.
> Y ya, hermosa Sunamitis,
> que envuelta en mortales ansias,
> dormida explicó la noche,
> a que una letra mudada,
> entre Celestes Anuncios,
> Perfecta te explica el Alba.
>
> (p. 1197)

Having dealt with the three early sixteenth-century *autos sacramentales* and with Calderón's three seventeenth-century plays, in the remainder of this section on the Great Supper Parable *autos* I shall consider the problematic *El convite general*. It will be recalled from the discussion above that there are two *autos sacramentales* listed in the catalogues with the title *El convite general*, one written by Calderón and supposedly identical to his *Llamados y escogidos*, the other attributed to José Villalpando, consisting of fragments borrowed from Calderonian *autos*.[115] The manuscript which I received from the Biblioteca Nacional in Madrid and which I thought was an *auto* by José Villalpando

---

[115] See above, p. 140.

is not Villalpando's play but one written by Calderón de la Barca that is different from Calderón's *Llamados y escogidos* studied above.

Instead of being identical to *Llamados y escogidos*, the manuscript of *El convite general* borrows from all three of the Calderonian *autos* on the Great Supper Parable and especially from *El nuevo hospicio*. For example, the four religion figures, Hebraísmo, Ateísmo, Idolatría, and Apostasía, appear in the manuscript of the *El convite general* just as in the *El nuevo hospicio*. In the scenes in which the religion figures appear, entire passages are taken *verbatim* from corresponding scenes of *El nuevo hospicio*. Such is the case in one of the early scenes of *El convite general*, in which Apostasía, Ateísmo, and Idolatría question Hebraísmo as to the meaning of the voice announcing the invitation.[116] The "Judas" scene, in which Hebraísmo contracts Apostasía to enter the wedding feast for thirty pieces of silver and, in fact, the entire last part of the manuscript *El convite general* come almost entirely word for word from *El nuevo hospicio*, with only slight occasional variations.[117]

Besides the undeniable influence of *El nuevo hospicio* in the manuscript, there exist in it also some traces of Calderón's *La segunda esposa*. Such influence is particularly evident in one rather lengthy scene in *El convite general*, in which Hombre attempting to walk the straight and narrow path wrestles with Albedrío, who has become attracted to the worldly pleasures set before him. Hombre finally gives in and enjoys the earthly goods but later, like the Prodigal Son of the Gospel story, seeks repentance and salvation. This whole passage from *El convite general* recalls a similar scene in *La segunda esposa* in which Calderón depicts the allegorical journey of man's struggle with the world and his salvation through Redemption and the Sacraments.

To be sure, there are several elements in the manuscript, *El convite general*, not present in the other Calderonian *autos* on the Parable of the Great Supper. The two evil figures, Rencor and Sombra, who open the play with a long tirade against God and Creation, have no equal in any of the other Calderonian

---

[116] In Valbuena Prat's *Obras...*, Vol. III, pp. 1189-1190.
[117] *Ibid.*, pp. 1202-1207.

autos studied in this section. Another new personage, Fama, announces the invitation to the wedding feast, and the four apostles, San Pedro, San Diego, San Juan, and San Andrés are those who receive the invitation after the four religion figures decline to go to the feast.[118] The substitution of the four apostles for the blind man, the beggar, the leper and the man with dropsy who accept the Lord's invitation constitutes the most noteworthy alteration in *El convite general*.

Missing from *El convite general* but present in the three Calderonian *autos* discussed above, is the *esposa* figure. In fact, unlike the three preceding Calderonian *autos*, in *El convite general* the purpose of the banquet is not a wedding — for there is no mention of a nuptial feast — but rather all are summoned by the King to "el convite de la Gracia."

If, in fact, the manuscript of *El convite general* which comes from the Biblioteca Nacional and which differs from the *Llamados y escogidos* was written by Calderón, then the question arises when did Calderón compose the former *auto*. Certainly, the manuscript seems to have been written before the more perfected *El nuevo hospicio de los pobres* composed in 1668. By presenting all three of the God figures, thus completing the Trinity, and by including the scenes in which the four virtues invite first the four religion figures and then the four suffering personages, Calderón achieved greater symmetry and structural balance in his *El nuevo hospicio* than in his *El convite general*, in which the sole figure, Fama, calls the four religions and then the four apostles to the feast. Calderón continually strove in the rewriting of his dramas to achieve structural balance and symmetry, which he succeeded in attaining only in his later efforts, after 1660.[119] *El convite general* was probably written around the same time or perhaps after *Llamados y escogidos*, which, in terms of structural balance, has only two of the four religion figures and entirely omits the "gallofa" scene. It may be concluded that

---

[118] The allegorical figure of Fama is not entirely new to the Calderonian *auto* and is found in Calderón's *Quien hallará mujer fuerte*. See Valbuena, *Obras...*, Vol. III, pp. 656-681. The four apostles appear in another Calderonian *auto*, *El Maestrazgo del Toisón*, found in Valbuena's edition of the Calderonian *autos*, Vol. III, pp. 889-913.

[119] See above, pp. 110-117.

the manuscript, *El convite general*, in all probability represents an intermediate attempt by Calderón to dramatize the Great Supper Parable and, if that is so, was composed after *Llamados y escogidos* but before *El nuevo hospicio de los pobres*. The manuscript's dates may be fixed at around 1650-1660.

The Treasure and the Pearl

While the Parable of the Great Supper may rightly be considered one of the most popular of the Gospel parables among the *auto* writers, this chapter on the kingdom parable *autos* will conclude with a consideration of the two parables of the Treasure and of the Pearl, for which there are only two sacramental plays. The evangelist Matthew describes the two closely related parables in his Gospel immediately after the explanation of the Parable of the Weeds. The account relating the two parables qualifies as one of the shortest in the New Testament:

> The kingdom of heaven is like a treasure hidden in a field; he who finds it hides it, and in his joy goes and sells all that he has and buys that field.
>
> Again, the kingdom of heaven is like a merchant in search of fine pearls. When he finds a single pearl of great price, he goes and sells all that he has and buys it. [120]

According to Valbuena Prat, Calderón wrote his *El tesoro escondido* on the first of Matthew's two brief parables, in 1679.[121] Calderón's *El tesoro escondido* typifies a great many of the author's plays on the kingdom parable *autos*. In Calderón's play on the Hidden Treasure, one encounters such familiar figures as Gentilismo, Idolatría, Hebraísmo, and Sinagoga, all of whom have appeared time and again in the Calderonian *autos* studied above. In *El tesoro escondido*, Gentilismo leaves Idolatría and goes in search of the distant land containing the priceless hidden treasure. Hebraísmo and Sinagoga possess the Holy Land which contains the hidden treasure but as they are unable to recognize

---

[120] Matthew, 13:44-46.
[121] Valbuena Prat, *Obras*..., III, 1661. Hilborn (p. 114) assigns the play an earlier date: 1662.

its true worth, they willingly sell the sacred soil with its hidden treasure to Gentilismo. In this manner, Calderón once again portrays the Jewish rejection of the Messiah and Christianity which Gentilismo readily adopts. The play ends with these words of Inspiración to all those who followed the star and found the sought-after treasure:

> En Fe de la buena Estrella,
> el *Tesoro* celestial
> que perdió la Sinagoga
> halló la Gentilidad.
> (p. 1688) [122]

Although Idolatría and Gentilismo have appeared together several times in the Calderonian *auto*, for the first time in *El tesoro escondido*, the relationship of the two allegorical figures is quite different. In his *auto* on the hidden treasure, Calderón presents Idolatría as the wife of Gentilismo. In his portrayal of the two figures as spouses, Calderón proves to be a master of feminine psychology just as he had been in the depiction of Sinagoga as the wife of Hebraísmo in *La viña del Señor*.[123] In the beginning of *El tesoro escondido*, although Gentilismo loves his wife, Idolatría, and admires her beauty, and although he pays tribute to her many gods, Gentilismo yearns to leave her and go in search of the far-off land containing the hidden treasure. Idolatría, becoming jealous and not wanting her husband to stray from her, attempts to persuade him to remain at home. Failing to convince Gentilismo with verbal arguments, Idolatría resorts to magic, calling upon the gods to conjure up the presence of Hebraísmo and Sinagoga, who hopefully would dispel the idea of the hidden treasure from Gentilismo's mind. Instead, the conversation with the two Jewish figures, who themselves are aware of some hidden treasure but are unable to comprehend its meaning, makes Gentilismo more determined than ever to seek out the treasure. Gentilismo soon leaves his home and his wife and finds the land of the Jews. Later, when Gentilismo returns to his

---

[122] Quotations found in this study come from Valbuena, *Obras*..., Vol. III, pp. 1661-1688.

[123] See above, pp. 133-134.

native land to gather his wealth in order to buy the land that he believed contained the precious treasure, Idolatría once again tries to dissuade her husband by lamenting her sorry plight and by reminding him of her faithful love:

> Ingrato dueño mío,
> a quien los ritos de mis dioses fío,
> ya que, soñado bien, de mí te alejas,
> donde quiera que estés oye mis quejas;
> sabrás cuán verdadero
> es el constante amor con que oír espero
> en desenojo de aflicciones tantas,
> que me diga tu voz.
>
> (p. 1677)

Gentilismo then tries to console Idolatría by reminding her that he seeks the valued land not to be a disloyal or unfaithful husband but in order to present her with the precious treasure:

> De que si logro el intento
> de hacer esta heredad mía,
> es para hacerte a ti dueño
> de su Infinito Tesoro.
>
> (p. 1678)

Having done what she could by magic and by tears to persuade her persistent husband to give up his adventure of the hidden treasure, Idolatría rebels against him and swears to get revenge by undermining his plan to form a contract with Hebraísmo and Sinagoga:

> Mas no me doy por vencida,
> que yo tras ella y tras ellos
> iré a estorbar el contrato,
> segura de que el hebreo
> allá me admita, bien como
> ingrato, obstinado y ciego
> tantas veces me admitió
> en la Mansión del Desierto;
> conque espero que, vengado
> vuestro honor y mi desprecio,
> vuelvan tristes los que ahora
> alegres van repitiendo.
>
> (p. 1682)

The desperate and enraged wife goes after her husband and follows him to the land of the Jews, but she arrives too late to stop the contract between the three parties. Finally at the play's end, bitter and on the brink of despair, Idolatría stubbornly refuses to accept the treasure offered to her by Gentilismo.

It will be recalled that, as Calderón's *El tesoro escondido* begins, Gentilismo is obsessed with the idea of finding the hidden treasure. Gentilismo originally learns of the existence of the hidden treasure while reading a passage from the prophet Balaán. It is also interesting to note that when Idolatría conjures up the magical scene in which Hebraísmo and Sinagoga appear, the two Jewish figures are seen reading from the Jewish prophet Isaiah about the coming Messiah and the hidden treasure. These early scenes, in which the *auto*'s major characters concern themselves with a problem from Scripture or other sacred readings, the solution of which becomes the focal point of the drama's plot, recall the early scene in *El día mayor de los días*, where Calderón presents another problematic passage to be resolved by the play's dramatic development.[124]

Calderón's ability to integrate into the dramatization of the Gospel parable various incidents taken from other parts of Scripture, a characteristic found in the Calderonian *autos* already studied, also becomes very evident in his *El tesoro escondido*. When Gentilismo first beheld the land of the Jews he experienced a warm inward joy. Convinced that he had discovered the land with the hidden treasure, he hastened home and summoned the three wise men of his native land, Sabá, Tarsis, and Arabia, in order that they, being rich, might contribute their wealth in the purchase of the desired land. It is at this point in his *El tesoro escondido* that Calderón begins to weave into his dramatic presentation of the Gospel parable the story of the Epiphany. At first, the wise men refuse to turn over the security of their abundant wealth for the uncertainty of a supposed treasure. Their reluctance is reflected in the words of the elder Arabia:

> Dejadme a mí hablar primero,
> que las canas siempre tienen

---

[124] See above, pp. 112-113.

ganado este privilegio.
¿Cómo quieres, Gentilismo,
que nosotros te entreguemos
nuestros propios bienes para
ir a buscar los ajenos?

(p. 1680)

However, the reluctance of the three *magos* diminishes as they behold far off in the heavens the bright shining star of Inspiración allegorically representing Grace, the spiritual light of man. The three wise men set out at the side of Gentilismo for the land of the hidden treasure with all their wealth but, upon arriving in the land of the Jews, they consult Hebraísmo and Sinagoga, who become disturbed at the possibility of a treasure hidden in their very own territory. The whole scene allegorizes the wise men's approaching Herod and his concern at the birth of a new king.

It would be well to point out still another characteristic which is found in most of the Calderonian *autos* treated above, and which also presents itself in his *El tesoro escondido*. Through the words of his figurative personages, Calderón often expresses in his sacramental dramas his aesthetic ideas on the function of allegory and his sacramental representation. This characteristic of Calderón of presenting in the dialogue of his plays his aesthetic tenets is found particularly in the *El tesoro escondido* when Sinagoga explains to Hebraísmo how the invisible attributes of God are made intelligible only through the visible, and how allegory helps make the invisible, visible, when the meaning behind the allegory is understood:

Como es tan incomprehensible
Dios, que en su Inmenso Poder
lo Invisible ha menester
valerse de lo Visible,
para que el Entendimiento
objeto Visible tenga
y de lo Invisible venga
en algún conocimiento.
... ...
Que Atributos de Bondad
a su Infinita Virtud,
sean por similitud,
pero no por propiedad.

> La retórica energía
> allá en sus tropos penetra,
> que un sentido es de la letra
> y otra de la alegoría,
> cuando explicarte pretende
> con lo que se contradice,
> pues siendo uno lo que dice
> es otro lo que se entiende.
>
> (p. 1671)

Just as Calderón's *El tesoro escondido* represents the sole example of a sacramental drama written on the Parable of the Treasure so also Lope's *La margarita preciosa* remains as the only *auto sacramental* that I found on the Parable of the Pearls.[125] Flecniakoska sets the date of Lope's *auto* at 1616.[126] Lope's *auto* could not have existed before Cervantes's *Quijote* since there can be found in Lope's work a direct reference to Sancho Panza.[127]

La margarita preciosa begins in much the same manner as did many of Lope's other dramas discussed above, with the evil personages — in this case the three sources of sin, Mundo, Carne, and Demonio — boasting of their power to destroy man's spirituality. In trying to outdo each other by boasting of their innate ability to surpass one another in ruining man, each of the three malicious figures singles out incidents and passages from Scripture that best describe them and their awesome power over frail humanity. For example, Demonio singles out among other works what the Book of Apocalypse says about his powers: "El Apocalipsis dice/ Que soy el que el mundo engaño:/ Grande me llama en engaño/ Y en el mal que a tantos hice" (p. 580). Mundo points to the writings of St. James saying: "Diego dice que mi amigo/ Es enemigo de Dios" (p. 580). The third evil figure, Carne, not only quotes the Church fathers to show her devastating effect on man, but she also makes reference to biblical

---

[125] In the *Códice de los jesuítas*, there exists a full length play on the Pearl, *Comoedia Quae Inscribitur Margarita* (F° 81 r° - 99v°).
[126] Flecniakoska, *Bulletin Hispanique*, LXVI, 44.
[127] For the reference to the *Quijote*, see the Academia edition, *Obras de Lope de Vega*, Vol. II, p. 585. Quotations of Lope's *auto* appearing in this study are taken from the Academia edition, Vol. II, pp. 579-588.

figures who have met destruction by placing too much trust in her:

> Y ansí Jerónimo dijo
> Que ninguno se fiase
> De mí, ni se descuidase
> Contra mi rigor prolijo.
> Porque ninguno, advertid,
> Es más fuerte que Sansón,
> Más sabio que Salomón
> Y más justo que David.
> (p. 580)

After the initial scene in which the wicked elements brag of the evil force they possess and after they pledge themselves to man's destruction, Mercader appears accompanied by the three figurative personages, Alma, Voluntad, and Entendimiento. The major figures representing man, his soul, and the two intellectual faculties of reason and of will, engage in various discussions designed to identify themselves to the audience. For example, Mercader makes it clear that man is a composite of body and soul, the former composed of earth, the latter made to the image of the Creator:

> Tierra soy, yo lo confieso;
> Pero soy, Alma, aquel vaso
> En que Dios depositó
> Ese licor soberano.
> Pero puesto que le hizo
> Del limo y grosero barro,
> Tiene de excelencia y precio
> Ser hechura de su mano.
> Que cuando un noble escultor
> Hace un modelo, el trabajo
> Y estudio todo está en él;
> Y aunque la joya alabamos,
> Todo el arte del platero
> estuvo al principio, dando
> Formas á la informe cera.
> (pp. 581-582) [128]

---

[128] For an explanation of the viewpoint of how man is made in the image and likeness of God, see Morrow, pp. 42-43.

Later still speaking of the properties of the body and soul, Mercader talks of the reunion of the body with the soul after death. Mercader addresses himself to Alma saying:

> Tú has de ir al cielo, hasta cuando
> Aqueste cuerpo que miras
> Vuelva á vestir renovado
> De estos miembros que tu riges,
> Como lo dijo Job santo;
> Porque soy el que tú dices,
> Y soy la divina mano.
> (p. 582) [129]

In this dialogue of Mercader, Alma, and the two faculties, Lope's belief in the primacy of the intellect over that of the will is seen when Voluntad dressed "en hábito de villano" admits to Mercader: "Su razón sirvo y no hablo" (p. 582). Later, Entendimiento confirms his supremacy over Voluntad when he warns her to restrain herself with regard to pleasures and to follow man's intellect, which capably perceives the deception of worldly pleasure:

> Apetito intelectivo,
> Voluntad, te has de llamar;
> Que aquí no has-de ejecutar
> Lo que tienes sensitivo;
> Que en esto el hombre conviene
> Con los rudos animales,
> Y aquí a cosas celestiales
> El intelectivo tiene.
> (p. 583)

After this first part of Lope's *La margarita preciosa*, in which the major dramatic figures identify themselves in an engaging dialogue, the *auto* is relatively simple in terms of allegorical and dramatic development. Mercader goes in search of the precious jewel for his wife Alma. Each of the three evil figures, Mundo, Carne, and Demonio, come on stage one by one in an attempt to sell their deceitful wares to the Mercader. In every case,

---

[129] This doctrine of the resurrection of the body is contained in the Creed. See Morrow, pp. 170-171.

Voluntad is the first to be attracted to the pleasures offered by the devil figures but is restrained by Entendimiento who, together with Desengaño, causes Voluntad to reflect upon the vanity of worldly possessions. Desengaño exposes the true worth of the devil's deceitful merchandise. Mundo's ark, supposedly full of honors and riches, turns out to be a chest filled with dust and smoke. Demonio's book reportedly steeped with worldly pleasures and Carne's licentious *affaires d'amour* are also exposed by Desengaño as worthless trinkets in a vain and self-centered world. As the *auto* draws to a close, the man Mercader finally meets up with Mercader de la Gloria, who at long last offers to man the priceless pearl — *la margarita preciosa*. That Lope interpreted the *margarita preciosa* as allegorically representing the Church and the celestial paradise may be seen in Desengaño's call to man in one of the drama's final scenes:

> Ven conmigo; que aquí vive
> El Mercader de la Gloria,
> Que yo sé que sólo tiene
> La Margarita preciosa.
> ¡Ah de la iglesia! ¡Ah del cielo!
> (p. 588)

Chapter IV

GENERAL OBSERVATIONS AND CONCLUSIONS

In an attempt to arrive at the essence of the *auto sacramental* and the Gospel parable, literary analysts and biblical exegetes, respectively, have presented varying points of view and different approaches through the ages. Although the *auto* dramatists themselves, especially Calderón, and later the literary critics of the eighteenth and early nineteenth centuries, were cognizant of the allegorical qualities of the *auto sacramental*, González Pedroso, perhaps in an effort to ameliorate the attitude of his Neoclassicist contemporaries, chose to emphasize the historical elements of the *auto sacramental* when he proposed the first formal definition of the sacramental play in his edition of the *autos sacramentales*. Pedroso's view of the *auto sacramental* as a one-act drama presented on the feast of Corpus Christi and dealing with the Eucharist influenced the thinking of literary Hispanists for more than a half a century, until, in 1924, Angel Valbuena Prat challenged the many inadequacies of Pedroso's definition. Although Valbuena's definition did little to clarify the theme of the *auto*, he turned attention away from the historical aspect of the *auto* and focused attention on its literary side, especially its allegorical qualities. Nineteen years later, in 1943, Alexander A. Parker also focused attention on the *auto*'s literary aspects and insisted upon its allegorical nature. Parker also shed light on the problem of the theme when he distinguished between the *auto*'s plot, which may vary from play to play, and its underlying theme, which is always the Eucharist the core of all dogma. Subsequent studies by Bruce Wardropper and Jean-Louis Flecniakoska on the sacramental drama in Spain supplement the work of Valbuena and Parker and further substantiate the *auto*'s allegorical nature.

This same evolving process to arrive at the essence of the New Testament parable may be found in the attempts of the biblical exegetes. Beginning with the evangelists themselves and continuing later with the Church fathers, particularly Origen and those of the Alexandrian school, the Gospel parable was always viewed as an allegory containing some profound religious or moral truth. The practice of interpreting the allegory by associating each element in the parable with some figurative meaning continued unabated in exegesis until the late nineteenth century. In 1899, Adolf Jülicher was among the first to resist the allegorical mode of scriptural interpretation by insisting that scholars should attempt to discover the true meaning of Scripture through the study of language and the historical facts which surrounded Jesus, the parables' author. Jülicher's theories found many sympathizers among scriptural scholars such as Joachim Jeremias, A. T. Cadoux, and others who came to be known as "form critics." Although most biblical students today accept Jülicher's idea that the parables are not hidden allegories but similes and analogies, nevertheless they qualify Jülicher's definition by allowing for some allegorical elements in the parables, especially those parables treating of God's kingdom to come on earth or the one to come in eternity.

Both the *auto sacramental* and the Gospel parable functioned as instruments of instruction. Whether the *auto* was employed primarily as a weapon in a direct attack against the heresies of the Church or whether it was used simply to strengthen the faith of the on-lookers, no one doubts that the *auto sacramental* of the sixteenth and seventeenth centuries instructed the people in religion and morals. Furthermore, all the scholars who have studied the matter concur in stating that, however incomprehensible the allegory may prove to be to today's reader or audience, it was completely intelligible to the contemporaries of the times. Similarly, drawing from the occurrences of daily living, Jesus composed the parables in order that he might better instruct his listeners in certain religious and moral truths. The only question that arises with regard to the didactic value of the parable concerns the puzzling passage in Mark (4: 11-13) implying that certain listeners are excluded from the parable's meaning. This disconcerting passage has received sundry explanations from the exegetes, most of whom uphold the parable's didactic end by explaining the passage as a reflection of God's justice or mercy or by denying that Christ ever spoke the passage, which they attribute to the evangelist himself. Because of their figurative nature and didactic purpose, the artistic worth of the *autos sacramentales* and the Gospel parable has been continually questioned.

On the one hand, for the capable dramatist, the Gospel parable was ready material, first, because the allegorical mode of scriptural interpretation still prevailed in sixteenth and seventeenth century Spain; second, because the people were acquainted with the age-old interpretations handed down from the Church fathers and popularized from the pulpits, through literature, and by other media of the day; and third, because, as is the case particularly with the kingdom parables, the setting afforded by the parable itself of the vineyards, the wheatfields, and the wedding banquet permitted easy association with the Eucharist. On the other hand, for the unskilled dramatist, the fixed parable stories with their traditional allegories became an insurmountable obstacle which fettered his poet's imagination and caused him to present little more than dramatized readings by abstract personages. The degree to which the playwright took advantage of the dramatic situations afforded by the Gospel parable and its allegory, and also the degree to which he was able to develop and expand the roles of the dramatic figures is the extent to which he succeeded in making the parable come alive in drama.

Dramatic Situation

Milton Marx in his study on drama writes: "The essence of drama is conflict."[1] The same critic then goes on to say:

> The playwright must keep the idea of conflict continually before the audience. In fact, the dramatic method of telling a story is to set it forth in a series of dramatic

---

[1] Marx, 21.

situations, one following another in the order best calculated to hold the interest.[2]

Every parable affords the *auto* writer some obvious dramatic situations. Some of the playwrights, more than others, were able to seize upon these dramatic opportunities found in the Gospel parable and its allegory and convert them into good dramatic scenes. For example, from among the non-kingdom parables, the most potentially dramatic situation is undoubtedly that in which the Prodigal runs off and squanders his inheritance. Lope and Valdivielso in their respective *autos* depict at great length the Prodigal's downfall — his encounter with the figures of Gambling and Lust and his eventual marriage to Pleasure, — while the earlier Rouanet *auto* presents the two bawds who only talk of taking the Prodigal's money and exploiting his desires for wine and women at a banquet which is never dramatized. A similar dramatic opportunity exists in the Lost Sheep Parable, in which the lamb strays from the flock and is ravished by wolves. In his two *autos* on the Lost Sheep, Lope makes this part of the Gospel parable the focal point of his entire drama, as he dramatizes in his *El pastor lobo y la cabaña celestial* the abduction scene and in his *La oveja perdida* a scene similar to the Prodigal's downfall. On the other hand, Timoneda and the anonymous author of the Villagarcía *autos* overlooked the inherent dramatic possibilities of the temptation scene when the Oveja obligingly follows Apetito's first invitation to sin. The Good Samaritan Parable gave Valdivielso a similar dramatic situation for he depicts the Peregrino's downfall in much the same way that he depicts the Pródigo's fall in his *Auto del hijo pródigo*.

An obvious dramatic situation also presented itself to the *auto* writer in most of the kingdom parables where evil attempts to enter the wheatfields, the vineyards, and the supper banquet and mingle with good. In Lope's dramatization of the Parable of the Weeds, *La siega*, Ignorancia resists Soberbia's and Envidia's attempt to enter the wheatfields until Soberbia lulls her to sleep with a long heroic tale. Interestingly enough, in his *El heredero del cielo*, Lope passes up a similarly potentially dramatic situation

---

[2] *Ibid.*, pp. 22-23.

from the Parable of the Vinedressers when he permits the two evil figures in the drama to walk unchallenged into the vineyards left unguarded by Amor Divino and Prójimo, who had fled earlier from their posts of guarding the vineyards. In his *La viña del Señor* on this same Parable of the Vinedressers, Calderón portrays a hand-to-hand struggle between the evil figure, Malicia, and the good figure in charge of watching the vineyards, Inocencia. This face-to-face encounter of an evil and a good figure appears in a similar situation also in Calderón's *Llamados y escogidos*. Finally, it is Calderón who best seizes upon the dramatic situation of the man without a wedding garment, afforded by the Great Supper Parable, by portraying in both his *Llamados y escogidos* and *El nuevo hospicio de los pobres* the respective evil figures who sneak into the banquet to spy for thirty pieces of silver. In the earlier *autos*, the same scene is just mentioned in the dialogue, as in *Egloga al santísimo sacramento*, or clumsily introduced into the play, as in Timoneda's *Los desposorios de Cristo* or the anonymous *Parabola Coenae*.

Some *auto* playwrights went far beyond merely presenting the most obviously dramatic scenes in the parables and they sought to represent other aspects of the parable as well in an effort to achieve more drama. In at least four instances in his *El heredero del cielo*, Lope achieves less drama in his portrayal of the Parable of the Vinedressers than does Calderón in his *La viña del Señor*, even though the two dramatists approach the Gospel parable in the same manner and employ almost identical dramatic figures. In one such instance, already mentioned, Lope permits the evil figures to enter the vineyards unchallenged, while, in the parallel scene, Calderón depicts Malicia struggling with Inocencia. A second instance sees Lope's Padre de las Familias taking leave of the vineyards without explaining why, while in Calderón the same personage carefully explains his custom of checking his accounts, just as he would later send his messengers and then his own son to inspect the harvest of the vineyards. The way in which Lope and Calderón dramatize the leasing of the vineyards illustrates another example of the varying abilities of the two authors to search out other dramatic elements of the parable's story. Lope depicts the Padre de las Familias simply turning over the vineyards to the Jewish figures with barely a word of admonishment to tend the vineyards carefully, while Calderón dramatizes in a powerfully dramatic scene how the Padre de las Familias and Hebraísmo enter into a solemn contract which is witnessed by all the play's figures. Finally, the manner in which Lope introduces the prophet figures in rapid succession into his drama and the way in which they are immediately put to death by the hostile Jews contrasts sharply with Calderón's portrayal of the prophet figures, in which each of them appears singularly and in which they are well received by Hebraísmo until the audience actually witnesses Sinagoga and the other figures dramatically turn Hebraísmo against them. In another of Lope's plays, *La siega*, the Sembrador is never seen planting the good seed as in Calderón's corresponding *auto*, in which Sembrador is seen in a boat preaching the Word of God, which is the figurative interpretation for the seed.

The *auto* playwrights themselves seemed to be aware of the importance of dramatizing as many elements and incidents in the parable as they possibly could, for always in their rewriting of a parabolic theme in a later *auto* they would incorporate new scenes from the parable's story that they had overlooked or had not developed in their first efforts. Lope, who had abruptly ended his *El pastor lobo y la cabaña celestial* after the Oveja's downfall, in his *La oveja perdida* tries to expand, however unsuccessfully, the last part of the parable story by portraying the Oveja's repentance and forgiveness. On two occasions when he rewrote one of his earlier *autos* on a parabolic theme, Calderón also sought to dramatize some incident of the story that he had previously neglected or merely mentioned in dialogue. In his *El nuevo hospicio de los pobres*, he includes and fully dramatizes the "gallofa" scene and the subsequent scene of the cures. In the recasting of *Tu prójimo como a ti*, he shows on stage how Hombre receives his gifts when he introduces into the beginning of the reworked play the "prodigal scene" which is absent from the first writing where he only mentions in dialogue the fact that Hombre possesses certain senses and intellectual faculties given to him by his Creator.

Development and Role of the Dramatic Figures

Allegory begins only when the quality is set in motion. Abstractions cannot act except metaphorically.... Since it is only by action that abstractions become allegorical at all, there must be action if the work in which they appear is to exist in allegory.[3]

The expansion and the development of the dramatic role of the allegorical figures determines to a great degree the amount of action and dramatic conflict the *auto* playwrights achieved in presenting the Gospel parable. In the *auto* parables discussed in the present study, there are four stages discernible in the development and expansion of the allegorical figures.

1. *Simple Presentation and Relatively Minor Involvement of the Dramatic Figures.* The first stage is particularly true in the early sixteenth century *autos sacramentales* found in the *Códice de los jesuítas* where the dramatic personages are really not allegorical except on a few occassions and where their dramatic involvement is relatively simple, for the figures usually appear in the play where they are mentioned in the Gospel story. For example, in the Prodigal Son *auto* of the Rouanet edition, the Prodigal's father is seen twice in the play, at the beginning and at the end, just exactly as in the parable. Similarly, other figures of the Rouanet *auto* such as the swineherd and the Prodigal's older brother appear only once, as they do in the parable, the swineherds extending employment to the destitute Prodigal, and the older brother coveting the attention given to his Prodigal brother by their father. In the same Rouanet *auto*, although the author introduces a minimum of new personages not present in the parable story, such as the quarrelling mother, the two plotting bawds, and the Portuguese dog vender, the Prodigal's mother appears only in the initial scenes of the play, while the two prostitutes and the cheating dog seller are seen only once during the dramatization of the Prodigal's spree. This simplicity in the role of the dramatic figures is reflected to an even greater extent in two other sacramental pieces found in the *Códice de los jesuítas*, the *Parabola Samaritani* and the *Egloga al santísimo sacramento*, both of which consist of little more than dramatic readings in which the personages receive concrete names and in which the characters appear precisely where one acquainted with the parable stories would expect them to

---

[3] Ellen Douglass Leyburn, *Satiric Allegory: Mirror of Man* (New Haven: Yale University Press, 1956), pp. 4-5.

appear. Although the anonymous Villagarcía *auto* on the Lost Sheep Parable contains the allegorical figure, Apetito, who makes but a brief appearance, the *Parabola Coenae* contains the only other truly allegorical figures found in the early parable *autos* in the figures of Amor and Celo, who are the Rey's servants, and Soberbia, Avariento, and Lujurioso, who refuse the Rey's invitation. Of all the *autos* in the *Códice de los jesuítas*, the latter mentioned *Parabola Coenae* stands out as one of the best not only because it possesses the greatest number of allegorical personages but because these personages receive the greatest dramatic development as evidenced, especially, by the portrayal of the "cure scene" immediately following the "gallofa" scene.

2. *Greater Development and Integration of Dramatic Figures.* This second stage in the development and role of the dramatic characters is found particularly in the parable *autos* of Lope and Valdivielso and is characterized by the expansion of the simple figures contained in the early dramatizations of the *Códice de los jesuítas*, by a greater integration of the parable's minor figures, and by the introduction of the "conscience" figure. Both Lope and Valdivielso took the two bawds and the dog vender of the Rouanet *auto* on the Prodigal and expanded them into a whole host of allegorical figures such as Juventud, Juego, Placer, etc. In his dramatic adaptation of the Lost Sheep Parable, Lope took the sole figure of evil, Apetito, appearing in the Villagarcía *auto* and multiplied it by three, so that the number of evil figures corresponds with that of the good. The Oveja, never seen in the Villagarcía *auto* as a dramatic figure on stage, becomes in Lope's two *autos* the protagonist of the plays.

In their respective *autos* on the Prodigal Son, Lope and Valdivielso introduce the parable's minor figures of the swineherds and the Prodigal's older brother not once, as in the Rouanet edition, but twice. The appearance of the two swineherds in an earlier scene, in which they discuss the need to hire additional hands, lends credibility to the play's later scene, in which they actually give the job to the Prodigal. The early appearance of the Prodigal's older brother in the two plays also makes the drama more plausible, for in it he affords a glimpse into his selfish and envious character in what represents a simple attempt by the author at character delineation.

The introduction into the sacramental plays of the "conscience" figure is still another example of the greater expansion and development of the allegorical figures in this second stage. Such figures as Valdivielso's Inspiración (*Auto del hijo pródigo*) and Verdad (*El peregrino*), and Lope's Memoria (*La oveja perdida*) and Desengaño (*La margarita preciosa*) remain at the side of their respective protagonists and constantly remind them, as they face the temptations of the evil figures, that good alone is worthwhile and that evil is destructive and ultimately leads to unhappiness. The continual presence of good and evil in every dramatic scene and the necessity of making the choice between the two causes stress and tension in the protagonists, all of which effectively heightens the dramatic action of the play.

3. *Multiple Integration and Charactization of Dramatic Figures.* In this third stage of character development, the figures assume several dramatic roles and there is greater character delineation of the allegorical figures. The point may best be illustrated by referring to a comparison made in this study of the dramatic roles of the allegorical figures in Calderón's *La viña del Señor* and Lope's *El heredero del cielo*. While in Lope Isaiah, Jeremiah, and John the Baptist appear only once in their role as the messengers, in Calderón the same prophet figures not only assume the role as the messengers but they also take on the additional roles of witnesses to the contract between God and the Jewish nation in the beginning of the play and of triumphant saints in the play's finale. In addition, John the Baptist of Calderón's *auto* takes on still another important dramatic function as the voice in the wilderness, as he is seen calling the Jewish figure to repentance in the Salome scene and also calling the laborers to the vineyards in the drama's initial scenes. Heredero, another figure of the two plays, functions in a multiple role in Calderón's *auto*, as he is depicted, not only as the Great Prophet and Redeemer as in Lope's play, but also as a Son figure to the Father when he confers with the latter as to the feasibility of the contract and when he appeases his angry Father wrought with bitterness over the death of his messengers. By attributing to his allegorical personages multiple dramatic roles, Calderón was able to integrate his figures into the early scenes of the drama. In fact, it is a distinguishing mark of all the Calderonian *autos* treated in this study to present in the

first few scenes all of the figures who are to take any part in the drama.

The more frequent the appearance of the dramatic figures in the play, the greater the opportunity there is for the dramatist to depict the character of the various figures. Furthermore, the greater the character delineation, the more plausible the parable's dramatization becomes. The Parables of the Weeds and the Vinedressers allow for the Jews to lose the charge of the vineyard and for the Gentiles to assume it. In his two *autos* on the parables, *La siega* and *El heredero del cielo*, respectively, Lope characterizes to some extent the role of the Jewish figures in that they do take an active part in the drama, are chiefly responsible for the death of the Christ figure, and thus deserve the punishment meted out to them. However Lope's character portrayal of the Gentile figure in his plays is usually extremely weak, as evidenced, for example, in his *deux ex machina* appearance of the Hebrew Nation in *El heredero*. On the other hand, Calderón takes extreme care in the parallel *autos* on the two parables to develop the characters of both the Jewish and Gentile figures so as to make what happens to the two figures at the drama's end entirely reasonable and expected. In *La semilla y la cizaña*, Hebraísmo obstinately refuses to listen to Sembrador's sermon, while Gentilidad pays close attention even though he does not fully understand its content; Hebraísmo is quick to condemn the Sembrador and tries to turn the other religious figures against him, while Gentilidad exerts every effort to be patient and will have no part of the rebellion against the Sembrador. In his *La viña del Señor*, Calderón goes to even greater lengths to characterize the two figures as he presents a violent contrast in attitudes. When the two figures meet in the desert, Gentilidad sincerely proposes to cooperate in finding the significance of the voice in the wilderness, and the two then agree in gentlemanly fashion to consult one another on their findings. Hebraísmo reneges on his word and thinks nothing of it while Gentilidad, angered at Hebraísmo's insincerity and at his signing of the pact with the Padre de las Familias, nevertheless is willing to overlook Hebraísmo's insincerity and even admits his awe and admiration for the Padre de las Familias.

Calderón's fine portrayal of the wives in two of his *autos* also demonstrates the extent of integration and characterization found in this third stage in the development of the dramatic figures. In *La viña del Señor*, Sinagoga frets and cries to have her way as she tries to persuade her husband, Hebraísmo, to put the prophet figures to death; and when all else fails, she appeals to his masculine pride by reminding him that he has an exclusive right to all the fruits of the vineyards. When she gets her way, she rewards him by cooking an elaborate meal. When the question of adultery enters the drama, she again appeals to her husband in a sense of outrage to have the accuser put to death. Calderón also effectively portrays Idolatría as the wife of Gentilismo in his *El tesoro escondido* as Idolatría uses tears, an appeal to masculine pride, and even sorcery to get her way.

4. *Multiple Allegorical Dimensions of the Dramatic Figures.* This fourth stage in the development of the role of the dramatic figures is apparent only in Calderón whose figures sometime take on multiple allegorical dimensions. In Calderón's play-within-a-play, *El día mayor de los días*, the figure of the Padre de las Familias assumes a complex allegorical role when, on the one hand, he functions as the landlord of the vineyards in the dramatization of the parable story and, on the other hand, he represents the figure of time, who transcends the barrier of the *chronos* and takes the two allegorical figures, Pensamiento and Ingenio, back through the epochs for the dramatization of man's salvation. Another figure who assumes multiple allegorical roles is Hebraísmo of *La viña del Señor*, as he not only functions as the Jewish Nation and the husband of Sinagoga but also as Herod, when in a brief scene he is forced to keep his word and behead John the Baptist in fulfillment of a promise to Malicia, and as Pontius Pilate when in another scene he washes his hands of the Heredero's death. At the same time in the brief Salome scene of this same *auto*, Malicia clearly takes on the role of Salome herself while Sinagoga plays Salome's mother, who asks for John's head through her daughter. Other instances are found in other plays in which Calderón gives his already allegorical figures a brief new metaphorical dimension. In the *Llamados y escogidos* and in the problematic *El convite general*, Mentira assumes the Judas role in a scene toward the end of the play as she bargains with Hebraísmo for thirty pieces of silver to enter the banquet as a spy. This same Mentira figure

upon entering the banquet then assumes the figurative role of the man without the wedding garments found in the parable account.

The representation of the Annunciation scene found in some of Calderón's parable *autos* could not have been possible had Calderón not given his already existing figures another allegorical dimension. In *La segunda esposa y triunfar muriendo*, Matrimonio, normally functioning as the Sacrament of Matrimony, assumes in the Annunciation scene the role of the Angel Gabriel, and Esposa, normally seen as the Príncipe's wife symbolic of the 'Church, functions in the scene as Mary. In *Nuevo hospicio de los pobres*, a similar Annunciation scene takes place in which Sunamitis plays Mary's role and Fortaleza, that of the Angel .Gabriel. In adding a new allegorical dimension to his already allegorical figures, Calderón always respects the original metaphorical nature of his figures, in that there always exists some intrinsic association between the original and assumed allegorical roles. The bad figure never assumes a good figure role and vice versa. Hebraísmo, not Gentilidad, is Herod and Pontius Pilate, not only because these historical men are traditionally associated with the "bad side," but also because Hebraísmo himself is portrayed as a vacillating figure who is easily persuaded, just as Herod and Pontius Pilate are most remembered for acting against their better judgement. Mentira never assumes the allegorical dimension of the good personage, but instead is Judas. The Padre de las Familias, who represents God also acts as Tiempo, who takes the figures back into history, because only God is timeless. One notes also the logic in the choice of such figures as Sunamitis and Fortaleza in the Annunciation scene, for Sunamitis represents human nature which became wedded to the San of God precisely at the moment of Mary's acceptance of God's will. Sabiduría sent Fortaleza as the Angel Gabriel, because Sunamitis, like Mary at the Annunciation, needs to take courage.

In adding new allegorical dimension to his figures Calderón chooses brief roles that are well-known and taken usually from Scripture. Often he paraphrases the passages in Scripture and uses them as the dialogue of his personages, thus clearly conveying to the audience the precise moment in which the personages are assuming a new allegorical dimension. In the Annunciation scene, Calderón signals the transition in the allegorical roles by employing familiar Marian prayers such as the "Salve Regina," the "Angelus," and the "Magnificat."

It is interesting to note that Calderón also gives a multiple allegorical dimension to things and concepts. A perfect example from his *La semilla y la cizaña* would be the spoils of the plagues being turned into the instruments of the passion: the rocks into the stones; the thistles and thorns into the crown of thorns; the mildewed tufts into the blindfold; the straw into the sceptre. Another example from the same *auto* of a thing acquiring a multiple allegorical significance is the *nave*, which in the beginning of the *auto* is associated with "ave" referring to the Virgin bearing the Word, then in the middle of the *auto* becoming a pulpit-ship from which Sembrador preaches to the crowd on the seashore, and finally in the *auto*'s end symbolically representing the Church militant. The most commonly occurring example of the multiple allegorical dimension applied to concepts can be found in the *trigo-pan, semilla-palabra* concepts at the very basis of *La semilla y la cizaña, La siembra del Señor,* and *El mayor día de los días.*

Early Jesuit Autos

Among the early, relatively undeveloped sacramental plays on the parables contained in the *Códice de los jesuítas*, the many realistic elements, sometimes bordering on the burlesque and even crude, stand out as the most distinctive characteristic of this group. In the *Auto del hijo pródigo*, the prodigal's mother argues with her husband over the discipline and rearing of children; the two bawds discuss what they will do with the money after they prostitute themselves; the Portuguese dog seller guarantees the economical maintenance of his dogs when he promises that the animals will eat their own excrement. In another early *auto* the *Egloga al santísimo sacramento*, a lame beggar comes onto the stage riding on a blind man's shoulders. In the same scene, the appearance of two pilgrim girls causes the blind man to question his crippled companion concerning the beauty of the two women, and he asks if the girls are wearing clothes. In the *Parabola Coenae* in a similar scene, a blind man, a lame man, a poor man, and another beggar criticize society's failure to adequately provide for them. This entire prose scene in the *Parabola Coenae* serves as a burlesque interlude in the dramatization of the more serious parable story and is distinctive enough to be known by its own title, "La gallofa." In a long scene appearing at the end of the *Parabola Samaritani*, the Good Samaritan enters into a discussion with the inn keeper on Church laws, especially on the rules and regulations governing the proper disposition for the reception of the Eucharist, the entire discussion revealling some of the fetishes and superstitions of the day surrounding the reception of this Sacrament.

Juan de Timoneda

In terms of dramatic development, Timoneda's sacramental dramas are little better than those found in the *Códice de los jesuitas*. The most distinctive characteristic of the two Timoneda *autos*, *La oveja perdida* and *Los desposorios de Cristo*, is that in both plays Timoneda overlooks the most potentially dramatic part of the Gospel parables and instead develops other scenes of a more religious and didactic nature. It has already been seen how Timoneda failed to dramatize the Oveja's downfall, for the Oveja never even appears in his drama. Instead, Timoneda choses to spend most of his play depicting how Christ established his Church upon the rock of Peter and how the Church would serve as a refuge for the sheep ravaged by the wolves. In his *Los desposorios de Cristo*, Timoneda again passes up the dramatic opportunities afforded him by the Parable of the Great Supper as he fails to portray, as did even the earlier Jesuit *Parabola Coenae* and *Egloga al santísimo sacramento*, the three refusals of the king's invitation and the "gallofa" scene. Instead, Timoneda dwells upon the banquet scene and in it artifically allegorizes the passion and crucifixion through the medium of the various courses offered in the meal, which symbolize different aspects of Christ's suffering. Timoneda's banquet courses symbolic of the passion recall other devices seen in other parable *autos* which metaphorically present the passion, such as Mejía de la Cerda's card game in *El juego del hombre* and Mira de Amescua's "Guess who?" in *El heredero*.

José Valdivielso

Valdivielso's two *autos* discussed in this study deal with the two non-kingdom parables of the Prodigal Son and the Good

Samaritan. Valdivielso was able to see the relation of the repentance theme of the two parables, and he developed both of his sacramental plays similarly. The protagonists' meeting with their respective parent figures in an attempt to acquire their inheritance, their journey through life and their encounter with evil and their subsequent disillusionment with the world, and their attempt to find help and aid in repentance and forgiveness reflect the similarity of the two Valdivielso *autos*. The presence and the role of the conscience figures, Inspiración and Verdad, in the respective plays also illustrate the similarity in the development of the two *autos*. The one characteristic note of Valdivielso's two parable *autos* can be found in the development of every phase of the parables' story, from the initial scenes of youthful rebellion, through disillusionment and recantation, to the all important final scenes of forgiveness and rejoicing culminated by the thanksgiving meal, which easily lends itself in both *autos* to an association with the Eucharist theme.

Lope de Vega

One of the most salient characteristics of almost every one of the six Lopean *autos* appearing in this study is the underlying presence of the love motif, with its themes of honor and *pundonor*, that is found in most of his *comedias*. The point has already been made in these general observations that Lope took advantage of the temptation scenes afforded by the various parables and that he delighted, for example, in portraying the Pródigo's downfall, the Oveja's abduction or her giving in to Apetito's temptations, the evil figures' efforts to enter into the vineyards and the wheatfields. Actually, these temptation scenes are closely related to the love motif of honor, fidelity, and *pundonor* in the manner in which Lope portrays the scenes: the Pródigo's marriage to the lust figure, Placer; the Cordera's love for and fidelity to the Cordero and her abduction by Pastor Lobo; Esposa's pledge of fidelity to the Señor de la Heredad while the two evil figures unsuccessfully try to abduct her from the *cabaña celestial*. The last mentioned incident particularly illustrates how Lope actually goes out of his way to introduce the love motif, for the scene in which Soberbia and Envidia try to enter the *cabaña celestial* to abduct the reposing Esposa is really tangential to the dramatization of the parable's story, as the evil figures need only be interested in gaining entrance into the vineyard and not into the *cabaña celestial*. After the brief unnecessary scene of the attempted abduction in *La siega*, Lope again returns to the parabolic theme, as the figures then lull the guard of the vineyard to sleep.

In centering his efforts upon the temptation scenes, Lope often forgot or deliberately chose not to dramatize the other aspect of the Gospel story. After depicting in an elaborate manner the Prodigal's downfall, the *auto* quickly ends. Similarly in *El pastor lobo y la cabaña celestial*, the return of the Cordera is only briefly depicted. The finales of *La siega* and *El heredero del cielo* are equally disappointing in their abruptness and inadequate development. Lope's failure to maintain a consistent and total allegory in his sacramental dramatizations has prompted critics like Sanzoles to see in him a fault of fragmentation, an inability to develop a completely unified and coherent allegory.

By failing to fully dramatize every aspect of the Gospel parable's ending, Lope often missed the full force of the parable's message with its moral and religious teaching, which almost always comes in the story's final moments. For example, in the parables of the Prodigal and of the Lost Sheep, the importance of repentance and forgiveness, the main theme of the parables, does not come until after the Prodigal and the Lost Sheep return to the father's house and the good shepherd's flock, respectively.

In some of the parable *autos*, Lope had trouble reconciling theology with drama. In the *El pastor lobo y la cabaña celestial*, Cordera, who represents man's soul, has no choice in Lope's drama, for she is taken by Lobo against her free will. The problem of reconciling theology with drama is also seen in *La siega*, where the Jews are those in the parable bound and thrown into the fires, Lope's portrayal thus conveying the idea that the Jews are solely responsible for the deicide and that they are deserving as a nation of the fires of hell. That Lope must have been somewhat concerned with the problem of sound theology in good drama, at least in later years, is evident in the rewriting of his *auto* on the Lost Sheep Parable, *La oveja perdida*, where he restructures the plot of his *El pastor lobo y la cabaña celestial* so as to omit the abduction scene entirely and thus to avoid the problem of violating the important doctrine of free will. In his rewriting of the parable, the Oveja now choses of her own accord to follow the evil figures. However, in recasting his drama on the Lost Sheep Parable to avoid the theological problem of the free will, Lope actually wrote a more loosely structured drama, as is evidenced by the play's confusing mixture of metaphors and its rambling final scenes.

Calderón de la Barca

In nine of the eleven Calderonian *autos sacramentales* that have been treated in the present study, Calderón not only dramatizes the basic parable story as contained in the evangelists' account, but he also develops as an underlying theme the salvation-history story by structuring his plays around a set group of allegorical figures that best represent the various stages and periods of man's religious history. In four of his parable *autos*, *La semilla y la cizaña*, *El nuevo hospicio de los pobres*, *Llamados y escogidos* and *El convite general*, the dramatization of the parable is centered about religious figures representing the religious expression of the various corners of the earth. Two of Calderón's *autos* which revolve around the four religion figures show a remarkable degree of symmetry and balance in their structure and allegory. In *La semilla y la cizaña*, the four religion figures always act in association with the four continents and the four plagues to form a structured pattern consisting of four combinations of three personages: Asia-Judaísmo-Cierzo, Africa-Paganismo-Ira, América-Idolatría-Cizaña, Europa-Gentilidad-Niebla. A similar symmetrical pattern of allegorical figures is found in *El nuevo hospicio de los pobres*, where the four religion figures again appear in a trio with their respective figures of virtues and vices: Hebraísmo-Esperanza-Avaricia, Ateísmo-Fe-Apetito, Idolatría-Caridad-Pereza, Apostasía-Misericordia-Lascivia. In the problematic *El convite general*, the central figures of the four religions still permit the development of the underlying salvation-history theme. However there does not exist the same degree of symmetry in the allegorical personages as in the two plays just mentioned. The fourth *auto*, *Llamados y escogidos*, contains only two of the religion figures and is an early, less perfect attempt to dramatize the Parable of the Great Supper within the framework of the salvation-history story.[4]

Instead of the four religion figures, Calderón employs the three law figures to obtain the same result of dramatizing the parable story within the over-all context of the salvation-history theme. In *El día mayor de los días*, Calderón achieves the same symmetrical perfection with the three law figures as he had done on two occasions with the four religion figures. The three law figures appear in combination with the corresponding prophet and religion figures: Ley Natural-Adán-Idolatría, Ley Escrita-Moisés-Judaísmo, Ley de Gracia-Emanuel-Apostasía. A similar situation revolving around the three law figures is seen in the two versions of *Tu prójimo como a ti* only with less symmetrical perfection in the patterned appearances of the figures. This time the law figures are represented in the allegorical personages of the priest, the Levite, and the Good Samaritan, who appear in corresponding relation to the figures of light and evil. Because there are only three law figures but four light and four evil figures in the play, Calderón combines two light figures and two evil figures in the following pattern of corresponding personages: Levita-Noche-Culpa, Sacerdote-Lucero *and* Alba-Lascivia, Samaritano-Sol-Mundo *and* Demonio. Another Calderonian *auto*, *La siembra del Señor*, depicts only two of the law figures represented in the personages of the two prophets, Adán and Emanuel, while at the same time three of the corresponding religion figures appear. This lack of symmetry in the *auto*'s structure suggests that the play is an early attempt to dramatize the Parable of the Laborers in the Vineyard.[5]

In addition to the four religion and three law figures, Calderón constructed his *La viña del Señor* around the four prophet figures which, again, resulted in the dramatization of the parable's story with the presence of the underlying religious history of mankind. The appearance of Isaiah, Jeremiah, John the Baptist, and the Heredero, the Christ figure, who present themselves before the Jewish and Gentile figures at intervals in the play, conveys the idea of the passage of time in the various stages of man's salvation.

---

[4] See the end of the present Chapter for a discussion of the play's dates, pp. 191-193.
[5] *Ibid.*

In the nine *autos sacramentales* in which Calderón developed the salvation-history theme along with the dramatization of the Gospel parables, the parable's allegorical interpretation found in the popular exegesis of his day provided for the presence of the religion, law, and prophet figures. However, in one of his *autos* on the Great Supper Parable, *La segunda esposa y triunfar muriendo,* beneath the parable's dramatization there is the underlying theme, not of the salvation-history story, but rather that of the *peregrino* theme of man, the traveler trodding life's journey, beset with temptations and pitfalls and having to choose between the good and bad roads (*dos caminos*). The *peregrino* motif appears in almost all of the non-kingdom parable *autos,* especially those on the Prodigal Son and the Lost Sheep, whose allegorical exegesis centers about a diary of the soul and its struggle to return to its Creator. The *peregrino* motif was commonly employed by the early *auto* writers in their sacramental dramatizations and it was Lope and other dramatists that were acustomed to structuring their plays around the theme of the traveler who had difficulty in adapting their dramas to the broader salvation-history theme. For example, whereas Calderón employs the prophets to cause the movement of the ages by introducing them at different intervals throughout the drama, Lope in his *El heredero del cielo* fails to effect the passage of time with the prophets because he presents them successively toward the play's end. Mejía de la Cerda in his dramatization of the Parable of the Weeds does little more than dramatize the parable within the *peregrino* motif, as Hombre must choose between Verdad's counsel to follow the bad road and the Gusto's temptations to seek worldly pleasures.

In spite of the fact that Calderón adhered to a structured pattern revolving around certain central figures upon which he constructed his dramas and in spite of the fact that he covers the entire span of salvation history within a single dramatic act, he achieved in his representations a dramatic dynamism, a certain fluidity, which enabled him to present the Gospel parable, not in a series of *cuadros* or unrelated scenes, but in a succession of dramatic events, one flowing from the other in a continuum until the *auto*'s end. The reasons for Calderón's success in achieving this dramatic dynamism within his well-structured drama are multiple and have already been mentioned in these concluding remarks: the use of religion, law, and prophet figures to effect the movement of the ages; the high degree of dramatic involvement of his allegorical figures, which assume complex dramatic roles; the multiple allegorical dimensions given to these same dramatic figures, as well as to things and concepts; the use of familiar passages from Scripture such as those referring to miracles and events in the life of Christ recorded in the New Testament to permit the audience a frame of reference whereby they may know what part of man's salvation history is being represented.

Calderón never lost sight of the didactic purpose of the *auto sacramental*, and he constantly strove to make the parable *autos* both good drama and sound theology. However, in creating dramas of such symmetrically structured and highly complex allegory as that found in *La semilla y la cizaña*, *El nuevo hospicio de los pobres*, and *El día mayor de los días*, Calderón necessarily imposed upon himself some difficulties with regard to the theological aspects of his plays. His ability to cope with these problems without sacrificing theology for drama manifest his great versatility as an *auto* playwright. For example, when the Gospel Parable of the Weeds calls for the separation of the wheat from the weeds, the latter to be burnt, Calderón simply departs from the parable's ending and depicts Judaísmo as being driven from the fields as a *desterrado*, for to picture Judaísmo as condemned to the fires would be to run the risk of condemning the Jews as a nation for eternity. In *La viña del Señor* and *Llamados y escogidos*, when the drama of the scene so demands, Calderón depicts the respective grace figures, Inocencia and Verdad, fighting hand-to-hand with the evil figures, Malicia and Mentira, respectively. In the ensuing struggle, in order to permit the evil figures to gain entrance into the company of the good, Calderón allows the former to triumph and even to steal the capes of their respective grace figures, but he constantly emphasizes in the dialogue of his personages that evil here triumphs over good only momentarily and that God sometimes uses evil for a good end.

Other aspects of Calderón's handling of the grace figures in two of his *autos* also reflect his awareness of the problems involved in the dramatization of this difficult figure. In *La viña del Señor*, Inocencia never appears on the side of the good. When she first appears in the play, she is seen in the desert with Hebraísmo and Gentilidad, but she befriends neither of them for neither one has yet entered into a contract with the Padre de las Familias. After the contract, she is seen with Hebraísmo and remains with him until it is obvious that Hebraísmo has become friends with Malicia. Inocencia then remains out of the action of the play until the final scenes, after the death of the Heredero, when she goes over to the side of Gentilidad, who has been recently entrusted with the vineyards.

The problem of dramatizing the grace figure in conformity with its theological sense is even more acute in *El día mayor de los días*, where the rigidity of the symmetrical pattern with the three law figures must be maintained. In the play, Ley de Gracia, in order to maintain the structural balance of having the law figures appear successively on stage early in the drama, takes her turn after Ley Escrita, but since she cannot assume her full role until after the appearance of her corresponding prophet figure, Emanuel, she appears as an anomalous personage, a figure of the future, waiting and hoping. Only after Emanuel effects the redemption does Ley de Gracia become a figure of fulfillment.

If at times the demands of a rigid structure, with its highly complex allegory, imposed certain technical problems with regard to the reconciliation of drama and theology, more often Calderón's depth in theological knowledge enabled him to dramatize theology on stage and made him a more accomplished writer of the *auto sacramental*. This is particularly true of his ability to dramatize the Trinity, especially in his later years, by presenting all three of the God persons, instead of one or two, and by delineating the dramatic role of the respective God persons so as to make them conform with their role in the Trinity, as defined by theology. Such is the case with *El nuevo hospicio de los pobres* written in the author's later years, where the two God figures of the earlier *Llamados y escogidos* become three, each functioning harmoniously in the capacity of his role in the Trinity: Padre—creator, Príncipe—redeemer, Sabiduría—the dispenser of the gifts. Calderón's later realization of the harmonious nature of the three laws also resulted in better drama. In *El día mayor de los días* and in the second version of *Tu prójimo como a ti*, the laws not only dramatize their complementary nature by functioning harmoniusly in the drama, but also express it continuously in their dialogue.

The perfection of the structure, the complexity of the allegory, the profundity of the theology that appear in most of Calderón's parable *autos* are the result of his ideas as to what drama should be, and, more specifically, as to what the *auto sacramental* should be. Especially in his later *autos*, bits of the author's aesthetic tenets are buried in the dialogue of his created figures. In his *La semilla y la cizaña*, for example, Calderón expresses his belief that symmetry and balance must be maintained, and thus it is proper that the earth be divided into four parts to coincide with the four plagues. He continues to say in the same *auto* that the four to four relationship of his dramatic characters of evil and good must be present because the odds in the conflict to be dramatized must be fair and even. In his *La viña del Señor*, Calderón makes known through his dramatic personages his concern for congruity and verisimilitude in character, dress, and speech, for Inocencia says she must be simple in dress and speech because of the simplicity she represents. And Malicia in the same play, when she wears the cloak of Inocencia, constantly reminds herself that she must put away her crude and harsh mannerisms and act in accordance with the dress she has assumed. In another play, *El día mayor de los días*, Calderón explains that metaphor and allegory need not concern themselves with time and anachronisms because allegory transcends time. Again with regard to allegory, Calderón makes known his thoughts concerning its didactic function, when in his *El tesoro escondido* he speaks of the invisible made visible, and then goes on in his *El día mayor de los días* to clearly demonstrate his point on the pedogological nature of allegory by presenting a play within a play.

I should like to conclude these general remarks on the Calderonian parable *autos* by taking up the matter of dates in the two sacramental plays, *La semilla y la cizaña* and *La siembra del Señor*. These are the only two parable *autos* in which there is a considerable disparity in the dates given by Valbuena Prat, who attributes the two plays to Calderón's early career as an *auto* writer, and those given by Harry Hilborn, who sees both of the *autos* written in the last decade of the author's life. Valbuena sets the date of *La semilla y la cizaña* at 1651, while Hilborn assigns to the play the year 1678.[6] Valbuena also sets the date of the *La siembra del Señor* at 1655, while Hilborn says the play was written between 1673-75.[7] The one fact that comes to light from the general observations of this concluding chapter is that the most perfectly structured parable *autos*, the ones that exhibit the greatest degree of allegorical complexity, and those that contain the greatest expression of aesthetic awareness are those written by Calderón in the last ten to twelve years of his life. There can be no question that Calderón's *La semilla y la cizaña* is one of those *autos* belonging to the latter part of the author's career and that Hilborn's later date of 1678 is more accurate than Valbuena's earlier one. The perfect structure of *La semilla y la cizaña* based on the four religion figures accompanied by the corresponding four figures of the *mayorales* and the plagues and all in perfect symmetry with the four seeds of the Gospel parable, the intricacy of its allegory revolving around the concepts of *trigo-pan, semilla-palabra*, its reflection of an aesthetic creed concerning the symmetry in drama and equality in conflict are signs that the *auto* belongs with *El día mayor de los días* and the second version of *Tu prójimo como a ti*, whose perfection in these areas is equally remarkable and whose dates have been fixed by both Valbuena and Hilborn to the last decade of Calderón's life.

With regard to Calderón's *La siembra del Señor*, it is one of the two plays written by its author on the Parable of the Laborers in the Vineyards. In structure, I have indicated that it is inferior in its dramatic development and allegory to the more perfect *El día mayor de los días*, which is structured around the three law figures and their corresponding religion and prophet figures and which contains the added complexity of a play within a play. In terms of symmetry, although the three religion figures appear, *La siembra del Señor* has only two of the three prophet figures who also function as the law figures. This lack of symmetry and development in the dramatization of the *La siembra del Señor*, when compared to the more perfect *El día mayor de*

---

[6] See discussion of the play's dates, Chapter III of the present study, pp. 90-91.
[7] *Ibid.*, p. 108.

los días on the same Gospel parable, makes me believe that the latter *auto* represents a rewriting of the former. Furthermore, although *La siembra del Señor* may have been written about the same time as *El día mayor de los días* and still represent a second effort by the author, I believe that *La siembra del Señor* belongs to the early years of Calderón and that Valbuena's date of 1655 is probably accurate, certainly more precise than Hilborn's later dates of 1673-75. The type of unperfected structure and allegory present in the *La siembra del Señor* resembles those present in *Llamados y escogidos*, another early *auto* whose dates Valbuena and Hilborn both set at 1648-49. Calderón perfected in his later years the early *La siembra del Señor* with the play *El día mayor de los días* just as he had perfected in his later years *Llamados y escogidos* with his play *El nuevo hospicio de los pobres*.[8]

---

[8] Alexander A. Parker in his article, "The Chronology of Calderón's *Autos Sacramentales* from 1647" [*Hispanic Review*, XXXVII (1969), 165-188], attempts to confirm the dates of Calderón's *autos* which were written before 1647. In the chronological table that appears at the end of his study, Parker agrees with Valbuena on 1651 as the date for *La semilla y la cizaña*. In a footnote, Parker claims that Hilborn "resurrected" the doubt about the dating of *La semilla y la cizaña* because Hilborn "made no mention of Valbuena's earlier study" (n. 6, p. 165). With regard to *La siembra del Señor*, the *auto* is not found in Parker's chronological table. Thus it appears that he would agree on an early date for the play, sometime before 1647.

LIST OF REFERENCES

Manuscripts

Comoedia Habita Hispali in Festo Corporis Christi, Códice de los jesuítas. Colección de Cortés. Madrid: Biblioteca de la Real Academia de la Historia. No. 383, F° 152-168.

Comoedia Que Inscribitur Margarita, Códice de los jesuítas. Colección de Cortés, in *Incipit Liber Tragaediarum*. Madrid: Biblioteca de la Real Academia de la Historia. No 384, F° 81-99.

[Cordero, Jacinto.] *Rico Avariento*. Madrid: Biblioteca Nacional. No. 15. 266.

Egloga al santísimo sacramento sobre la parábola evangélica Math. 22 y Luc. 14. Cuaderno de Sancho Rayón. Santander: Biblioteca Menéndez Pelayo. F° 1-24.

Parabola Samaritani, Códice de los jesuítas. Colección de Cortés, in *Incipit Liber Tragaediarum*. Madrid: Biblioteca de la Real Academia de la Historia. No. 384, F° 119-128.

Ramón, Alonso. *Auto del hijo pródigo*. Madrid: Biblioteca Nacional. No. 15. 312, 16 F°, 4°, del s. xvii.

Rojas Zorrilla, Francisco. *El rico avariento*. Madrid: Biblioteca Nacional. No. 15. 150, 22 hojas, 40°, del s. xvii.

Tragoedia Patris Familias de Vinea, Códice de los jesuítas. Colección de Cortés, in *Incipit Liber Tragaediarum*. Madrid: Biblioteca de la Real Academia de la Historia. No. 384, F° 47-66.

[Villalpando, José.] *El convite general*. Madrid: Biblioteca Nacional. No. 16. 282², 45 ho. del s. xvii, perg. (O).

Books and Articles

Aicardo, José María. "Autos anteriores a Lope de Vega." *Razón y Fe*, V (1903), 312-326; VI (1903), 20-33, 201-214, 446-458; VII (1903), 163-176.

———. "Autos sacramentales de Lope de Vega." *Razón y Fe*, XIX (1907), 459-470; XX (1908), 277-288; XXI (1908), 31-42, 443-453; XXII (1909), 319; XXIII (1909), 289-300.

Alenda y Mira, Jenaro. "Catálogos de autos sacramentales historiales y alegóricos por don Jenaro Alenda." *Boletín de la Real Academia Española*, III (1916), 226-239, 336-391, 576-590, 668-684; IV (1917), 224-241, 356-376, 494-516, 643-663; V (1918), 97-112, 214-222, 365-383, 492-505, 668-678;

VI (1919), 440-454, 755-773; VII (1920), 496-512, 663-674; VIII (1921), 94-108, 264-278; IX (1922), 271-284, 387-403, 488-499, 666-682; X (1923), 224-239.
Alonso, Dámaso, and Bousoño, Carlos. *Seis calas en la expresión literaria española*. Madrid: Editorial Gredos, 1963.
Autos sacramentales con cuatro comedias nuevas y sus loas y entremeses. Madrid: María de Quiñones, 1655.
Autos sacramentales y al nacimiento de Christo con loas y entremeses. Madrid: Antonio Franco de Zafra, 1675.
Barrera y Leirado, Cayetano Alberto de La. *Catálogo bibliográfico y biográfico del teatro antiguo español desde sus orígenes hasta mediados del siglo XVIII*. Madrid: M. Rivadeneyra, 1860.
Barry, Colman. "The Literary and Artistic Beauty of Christ's Parables." *Catholic Biblical Quarterly*, X (1948), 376-383.
Bartrina Gassiot, Sebastián. *La Biblia y Calderón* (Contenido bíblico en "El gran teatro del mundo"). Barcelona: Editorial Ifiba, 1957.
Bataillon, Marcel. "Essai d'explication de l'auto sacramental." *Bulletin Hispanique*, XLII, No. 3 (1940), 193-212.
Bonilla y San Martín, Adolfo. *Las Bacantes o del origen del teatro*. Madrid: Rivadeneyra, 1921.
Brenan, Gerald. *The Literature of the Spanish People*. Cambridge: The University Press, 1951.
Cadoux, A. T. *Parables of Jesus: Their Art and Use*. London: James Clarke and Co., 1931.
Calderón de la Barca, Pedro. *Obras completas*, ed., Angel Valbuena Prat. 3 vols. Madrid: Ediciones de Aguilar, S. A., 1952.
Cayuela, Arturo M. "Los autos sacramentales de Lope de Vega, reflejo de la cultura religiosa del poeta y su tiempo." *Razón y Fe*, CVIII (1935), 168-190, 330-349.
Cossío, José M. "Racionalismo del arte dramático de Calderón." *Cruz y Raya*, XXI (1934), 37-76.
Cotarelo y Mori, Emilio. *Ensayo sobre la vida y obra de Don Pedro Calderón de la Barca*. Madrid, 1924.
―――. "Mira de Amescua y su teatro." *Boletín de la Real Academia Española*, XVII (1930), 467-505, 611-658; XVIII (1931), 7-90.
Crawford, J. P. Wickersham. *The Spanish Drama before Lope de Vega*. Philadelphia, 1922.
Denzer, George A. *The Parables of the Kingdom: A Presentation and Defense of the Absolute Mercy Theory of the Kingdom Parables with a Review and Criticism of Modern Catholic Opinion*. Washington, D.C.: The Catholic University of America Press, 1945.
Diccionario de la lengua española. Real Academia Española. 16 ed. Madrid: Talleres de Publicaciones Herrerias, 1941.
Dodd, Charles H. *The Parables of the Kingdom*. New York: Scribners' Sons, 1961.
Entwistle, William J. "Calderón et le théâtre symbolique." *Bulletin Hispanique*. LII (1950), 41-54.
―――. "La controversia en los autos de Calderón." *Nueva Revista de Filología Hispánica*, II (July-September, 1948), 223-238.
―――. "Controversy in the Dramas of Calderon." *Romanische Forschungen*, LX (1947), 631-646.

Flecniakoska, Jean-Louis. *La Formation de l'auto religieux en Espagne avant Calderon, 1550-1635.* Montpellier: Imprimerie Paul Déran, 1961.

———. "Les rôles de Satan dans les *autos* de Lope de Vega." *Bulletin Hispanique,* LXVI (1964), 30-44.

Fonck, Leopold. *The Parables of the Gospel,* trans. E. Leahy. Ratisbon: Frederick Pustet and Co., 1915.

Frutos, Eugenio. *La filosofía de Calderón en sus autos sacramentales.* Zaragoza: Institución "Fernando el Católico" de la Excma. Diputación Provincial, 1952.

García Soriano, Justo. "El teatro de Colegio en España: Noticia y examen de algunas de sus obras." *Boletín de la Real Academia Española,* XIV (1927), 235-277, 374-411, 535-565, 620-650; XV (1928), 62-93, 145-187, 396-446, 651-669; XVI (1929), 80-106, 223-243.

———. *El teatro universitario y humanístico en España.* Toledo, 1945.

González Pedroso, Eduardo (ed.). *Los autos sacramentales desde su origen hasta fines del siglo XVII. Biblioteca de Autores Españoles.* LVIII. Madrid: Ediciones Atlas, 1952.

González Ruiz, Nicolás (ed.). *Piezas maestras del teatro teológico español.* 2 vols. Biblioteca de Autores Cristianos. Madrid: La Editorial Católica, S. A., 1953.

———. "El auto sacramental, martillo y espada." *Teatro,* No. 5 (March, 1953), 47-48.

Grant, Robert M. *The Bible in the Church.* New York: MacMillan Co., 1954.

Hanson, Richard P. C. *Allegory and Event: A Study of the Sources and Significance of Origen's Interpretation of Scripture.* Richmond. Virginia: John Knox Press, 1959.

Hilborn, Harry W. *A Chronology of Calderon's Plays.* Toronto: The University of Toronto, 1938.

Honig, Edwin. *Dark Conceit: The Making of Allegory.* New York: Oxford University Press, 1966.

Hunter, Archer M. *Interpreting the Parables.* London: SCM Press Ltd., 1960.

Jeremias, Joachim. *Die Gleichnisse Jesu.* Zurich, 1954.

———. *The Parables of Jesus,* trans. S. H. Hooke. New York: Charles Scribner's Sons, 1962.

Jones, Geraiant Vaughan. *The Art and Truth of the Parables: A Study of Their Literary Form and Modern Interpretation.* London: S. P. C. K., 1964.

Jülicher, Adolf. *Die Gleichnisreden Jesu.* 2 vols. Tubingen, 1899.

Knox, Ronald. *The Mystery of the Kingdom.* London, 1937.

Leavitt, Sturgis. "Humor in the *Autos* of Calderon." *Hispania,* XXXIX (1956), 137-144.

Leyburn, Ellen Douglass. *Satiric Allegory: Mirror of Man.* New Haven: Yale University Press, 1956.

Luzán Claramunt de Suelves y Guerra, Ignacio. *La poética o reglas de la poesía general y de sus principales especies.* 1737.

Maldonado, Juan de. *Comentarios a los cuatro evangelios.* 3 vols. Biblioteca de Autores Cristianos. Madrid: La Editorial Católica, S. A., 1954-1956.

Mariscal de Gante, Jaime. *Los autos sacramentales desde sus orígenes hasta mediados del siglo XVIII.* Madrid: Renacimiento, 1911.

Martín Gamero, Antonio (ed.). *Cancionero de Sebastián de Horozco.* Sociedad de Bibliófilos Andaluces, Vol. VII. Sevilla: Imprenta de Rafael Tarasco y Lassa, 1874.
Marx, Milton. *The Enjoyment of Drama.* New York: Appleton-Century Crofts, Inc., 1961.
McGarry, Sister Francis de Sales. *The Allegorical and Metaphorical Language in the "Autos Sacramentales" of Calderón.* Washington, D. C.: The Catholic University of America, 1937.
Medel del Castillo Francisco. *Indice general alfabético de todos los títulos de comedias que se han escrito por varios autores antiguos y modernos y de los autos sacramentales y alegóricos así de D. Pedro Calderón de la Barca como de otros autores clásicos.* Madrid: Imprenta de Alfonso de Mora, 1735. (Reprinted by John M. Hill in *Revue Hispanique*, LXXV [1929], 144-369).
Mejía de la Cerda, Luis. *Auto sacramental del juego del hombre*, ed. Louis Imbert. *Romanic Review*, VI (July-September, 1915), 239-282.
Menéndez Pelayo, Marcelino. *Calderón y su teatro.* Buenos Aires: Emecé Editores, S. A., 1912.
———. *Estudios sobre el teatro de Lope de Vega*, ed. A. Bonilla y San Martín, 6 vols. Madrid: Librería General de Victoriano Suárez, 1919.
Mérimée, Henri. *L'Art dramatique à Valencia.* Paris: Imprimerie et Librairie Edouard Privat, 1913.
Mickelsen, A. Berkeley. *Interpreting the Bible.* Grand Rapids, Michigan: Eerdman's, 1963.
Mira de Amescua, Antonio. *Teatro*, ed. Ángel Valbuena Prat. 2 vols. Clásicos Castellanos. Madrid: Espasa-Calpe, S. A., 1943.
Miranda, Luis. *La comedia pródiga.* Sevilla, 1554; reprinted. Sevilla, 1869.
Monroy, Juan Antonio. *La Biblia en el Quijote.* Madrid: Editorial V. Suárez, 1963.
Moratín, Nicolás Fernández de. *Desengaño al teatro español.* 1763.
Morgan, G. C. *The Parables of the Kingdom.* New York: Fleming H. Revel Company, 1907.
Morley, S. G., Bruerton, C. *Cronología de las comedias de Lope de Vega.* Madrid: Editorial Gredos, 1968.
Morrow, Louis Laravoire. *My Catholic Faith.* Kenosha, Wisconsin: My Mission House, 1963.
Moschner, Franz M. *The Kingdom of Heaven in the Parables.* St. Louis: B. Herder, 1960.
Navidad y Corpus Christi festejados por los mejores ingenios de España en diez y seis autos a lo divino diez y seis loas y diez y seis entremeses. Madrid: José Fernández de Beundia, 1664.
Olmedo, Félix G. "Un nuevo *Ternario* de Juan de Timoneda." *Razón y Fe*, XLVII (1917), 277-296, 485-497; XLVIII (1917), 219-227, 489-496.
Parker, Alexander A. *The Allegorical Drama of Calderon.* Oxford: The Dolphin Book Co. Ltd., 1943.
———. "The Chronology of Calderón's *Autos Sacramentales* from 1647." *Hispanic Review*, XXXVII (1969), 165-188.
Paz, Julián. *Catálogo de las piezas de teatro que se conservan en el Departamento de Manuscritos de la Biblioteca Nacional.* 2 vols. Madrid: Blass, S. A., 1934-1935.

Pfandl, Ludwig. *Cultura y costumbres del pueblo español de los siglos XVI y XVII: Introducción al siglo de oro*, trans. P. Félix García. Barcelona: Editorial Araluce, 1929.
Post, Chandler A. *Medieval Spanish Allegory*. Cambridge: Harvard University Press, 1915.
Puente, Luis de La. *Meditaciones de los misterios de nuestra santa fe*. 2 vols. 10th edition. Madrid: Editorial Apostolado de la Prensa, S. A., 1953.
Restori, Antonio. *Degli "Autos" di Lope de Vega Carpio*. Parma: R. Pellegrini Editore, 1898.
Révah, I. S. *Deux Autos Méconnus de Gil Vicente*. Lisbonne: Agrégé de l'Université, 1948.
Rodríguez-Puértolas, Julio. "La transposición de la realidad en los autos sacramentales de Lope de Vega." *Bulletin Hispanique*, LXXII (1970), 96-112.
Rouanet, Leo (ed.). *Colección de autos, farsas, y coloquios del siglo XVI*. 4 vols. Madrid: Biblioteca Hispánica, 1901.
Sanvisens, Alejandro (ed.). *Autos sacramentales eucarísticos*. Barcelona: Editorial Cervantes, 1952.
Sanzoles, Modesto de. "La alegoría como constante estilística de Lope de Vega en los autos sacramentales." *Revista de Literatura*, XVI (1959), 90-133.
Smalley, Beryl. *The Study of the Bible in the Middle Ages*. Notre Dame, Indiana: University of Notre Dame Press, 1964.
Sorrento, Luigi. "I *Trionfi* del Petrarca *a lo divino* e l'allegoria religiosa negli *autos*," in *Estudios eruditos in memoriam de Adolfo Bonilla y San Martín (1875-1926)*, II, 397-435. Madrid: Imprenta Jaime Rates, 1930.
The Holy Bible. New York: Benziger Brothers, Inc., 1961.
Thomas, Lucien-Paul. "François Bertaut et les conceptions dramatiques de Calderón." *Revue de Litterature Comparée*, IV (1924), 199-221.
———. "Les jeux de scéne et l'architecture des idées dans le théâtre allegorique de Calderón," in *Homenaje a Menéndez Pelayo*, II, 501-530.
Ticknor, George. *History of Spanish Literature*. 3 vols. London: John Murray, 1855.
Timoneda, Juan de. *Auto sacramental de la oveja perdida*, ed. García Boiza. Salamanca: M. Pérez Criado, 1921.
———. *Ternario sacramental*. Valencia: Casa de Juan Navarro, 1575.
Valbuena Prat, Ángel. "Los autos calderonianos en el ambiente teológico español." *Clavileño*, No. 15 (May-June, 1952), 33-35.
———. "Los autos sacramentales de Calderón: Clasificación y análisis." *Revue Hispanique*, LXI (1924), 1-302.
Valdivielso, José. *Doze autos sacramentales y dos comedias divinas por el maestro Joseph de Valdivielso*. Toledo: Juan Ruiz, 1622.
Vega Carpio, Lope Félix de. *El peregrino en su patria*. Sevilla: Imprenta de Clemente Hidalgo, 1604.
———. *Obras de Lope de Vega publicadas por la Real Academia Española*, ed. Marcelino Menéndez Pelayo. 15 vols. Madrid: Sucesores de Rivadeneyra, 1890-1902.
Wardropper, Bruce W. (ed.). *Critical Essays on the Theater of Calderon*. New York: The New York University Press, 1965.
———. *Introducción al teatro religioso del siglo de oro: Evolución del auto sacramental, 1500-1648*. Madrid: Revista de Occidente, 1958.

Wardropper, Bruce W. "Menéndez Pelayo on Calderón." *Criticism*, VII (1965), No. 4, 363-372.
——. "The Search for a Dramatic Formula for the 'Auto Sacramental'." *PMLA*, LXV (1950), 1196-1211.
Wilson, Edmund M. "The Four Elements in the Imagery of Calderon." *Modern Language Review*, XXXI (1936), 34-47.
Young, Margaret Pauline. *The Liturgical Element in the Autos Sacramentales of Calderón*. Unpublished Dissertation. Boston University, 1947.
Zabaleta, Juan de. *El día de fiesta por la tarde*, ed. George Lewis Doty. Jena: Gesellschaft für romanische Literatur, 1938.

INDEX

A tu prójimo como a ti. See *Tu prójimo como a ti.*
Aicardo, José María, 36n, 37, 38, 39, 43, 61n, 119n.
Alenda y Mira, Jenaro, 10, 36, 37, 40, 77, 138, 140.
Alexandrian school, parable interpretation of, 20, 33, 34, 35, 171.
Alonso, Dámaso, 102n.
Antiochene school, parable interpretation of, 20.
Aquinas, Thomas, 17.
Aucto del hijo pródigo, 36n, 37, 38-40, 42, 43, 44, 46, 47, 48, 49, 53, 144, 173, 176, 177, 182.
Augustine of Hippo, St., 20.
Auto de Alejandría, 77.
Auto de la oveja perdida, 51, 52-55, 58, 173, 177.
Auto del hijo pródigo. See Ramón, Alonso.
Auto del hijo pródigo (Valdivielso), 36, 37, 38, *44-48*, 49, 50, 55, 59, 67, 68, 173, 177, 178, 184.
Auto del rico avariento de Dn. Francisco de Rojas, 76, *77-83*.
auto sacramental, historical nature of, 13-15; allegorical nature of, 15-18; didactic purpose of, 22-24, 26-27; defensive purpose of, 27-28, 87-88; artistic value of, 29-31; anti-Semitism in, 88, 97-98.

Barrera y Leirado, Cayetano Alberto de La, 10, 36, 37, 76, 77, 140.
Barry, Colman, 31n.
Bartina, Gossiot Sebastián, 34.
Bataillon, Marcel, 28n.

Bonifacio, Juan, 139.
Bonilla y San Martín, Adolfo, 30n.
Bousoño, Carlos, 102n.
Brenan, Gerald, 29n.
Bruerton, Courtney, 90.
buen gusto, 29. See also Neoclassicists.

Cadoux, A. T., 20, 30, 171.
Calderón de la Barca, Pedro, 9, 10, 16, 17, 23, 28, 34, 38, 63, *186-193*. See also *El convite general*, *El día mayor de los días*, *El nuevo hospicio de los pobres*, *El tesoro escondido*, *La segunda esposa y triunfar muriendo*, *La semilla y la cizaña*, *La siembra del Señor*, *La viña del Señor*, *Tu prójimo como a ti.*
Calvin, John, 33.
Cayuela, Arturo M., 23n.
Cervantes, Miguel de, 14.
Chrysostom, John, 20.
Clement, St., 20.
Códice de los jesuitas, 51n, 63, 64, 120n, 138n, 166n, 176, 177, 182, 183. See also Jesuit *autos*.
Colección de Cortés. See *Códice de los jesuitas*.
Comedia famosa del rico avariento y vida y muerte de San Lázaro, 77n.
Comoedia Habita Hispali in Festo Corporis Christi, 138n.
Comoedia Quae Inscribitur Margarita, 166n.
Cordero, Jacinto, 76.
Cossío, José M., 112n.

Cotarelo y Mori, Emilio, 52n, 77, 90, 91.
Crawford, J. P. Wickersham, 35n, 109, 139.
Cuaderno de Sancho Rayón, 138n.

Denzer, George A., 21, 25n, 87.
Dodd, Charles H., 20-21, 26, 29n, 32n, 33.
Doze autos sacramentales, 36, 37.
dramatic figures, development and role of, 175-182; in early *autos*, 176-177; in Valdivielso, 177-178; in Lope de Vega, 177-180; in Calderón de la Barca, 177-182.
dramatic situations, of *autos*, 172-175.

Egloga al santísimo sacramento sobre la parábola evangélica Math. 22 y Luc. 14, 138, *141-145*, 146, 155, 174, 176, 182, 183.
El convite general, 140, 141, *158-161*, 180, 186.
El cubo de la Almudena, 90, 91, 103n.
El día mayor de los días, 73n, 100n, 108, 109, *110-117*, 164, 180, 182, 187, 189, 190, 191, 192, 193.
El hijo pródigo (Lope de Vega), 36, 37, 38, *40-44*, 46, 47, 48, 49, 59, 60.
El hijo pródigo. See Vidal Salvador, Manuel.
El heredero, 118, 119, *120-121*, 145, 183.
El heredero del cielo, 118, 119, *121-137*, 173, 174, 178-179, 185, 188.
El juego del hombre, 89, 90, *92-93*, 145, 183.
El Maestrazgo del Toisón, 160n.
El nuevo hospicio de los pobres, 139, 140, 141, *153-158*, 159, 160, 161, 174, 175, 181, 186, 189, 190, 193.
El pastor lobo y la cabaña celestial, 52, *55-58*, 61, 62, 94, 95, 96, 173, 175, 184, 185.
El peregrino, 63, 64, *65-68*, 69, 173, 178, 184.
El premio de limosna y rico de Alejandría. See Godínez, Felipe.
El rico avariento, 75, *77-83*.
El tesoro escondido, *161-166*, 180, 191.
Encina, Juan del, 50.

Entwistle, William J., 23, 28.
Erasmus, 34.

Flecniakoska, Jean-Louis, 9, 10, 15, 16, 17, 26, 27, 34, 35, 39, 40, 51n, 52n, 55n, 88n, 90, 166, 170.
Fonck, Leopold, 25n, 27n, 32n.
"form critics," See Parable.
Frutos, Eugenio, 112n.

García Soriano, Justo, 10, 51, 120n.
Godínez, Felipe, 76.
Good Samaritan, Parable of, 31, *62-73*. See also *El peregrino*, *Tu prójimo como a ti*, *Parabola Samaritani*.
Good Shepherd, Parable of, 19n, 54n, 63.
González Pedroso, Eduardo, 13-14, 37n, 51, 52, 56n, 63n, 89n, 138.
González Ruiz, Nicolás, 15n, 27, 29, 50n, 89n.
Grant, Robert M., 33n, 34n.
Great Supper, Parable of, 32, 86, 87, *137-161*. See also *Egloga al santísimo sacramento sobre la parábola evangélica Math 22 y Luc. 14*, *El convite general*, *El nuevo hospicio de los pobres*, *La segunda esposa y triunfar muriendo*, *Llamados y escogidos*, *Obra llamada los desposorios de Cristo*, *Parábola Coenae*.

Hanson, Richard P. C., 19n.
"hardening theory." See Parable.
Hastings, 86, 87.
Hilborn, Harry W., 90, 91, 108, 118, 139, 140, 145, 191, 192, 193.
Honig, Edwin, 26n.
Horozco, Sebastián de, 108, 109.
Hunter, Archer M., 20n, 22, 34n.
Husbandman, Parable of. See Vinedressers, Parable of.

Imbert, Louis, 89, 93.
Incipit Libert Tragaediarum. See *Códice de los jesuitas*.
Irenaeus, 20.

Jeremias, Joachim, 19, 21n, 26, 27n, 30, 85, 86.

Jesuit *autos*, characteristics of, *182-183*. See also *Auto del hijo pródigo* (Ramón, Alonso), *Egloga al santísimo sacramento, Parabola Coenae, Parabola Samaritani*.
Jones, Geraiant, Vaughan, 20n, 22, 29n, 31, 86, 87n.
Jülicher, Adolph, 20, 25, 26n, 33, 86, 171.

kingdom parables, definition of, 32; allegorical tradition of, 84-88; See also Great Supper, Laborers in the Vineyard, Treasure and the Pearl, Vinedressers, Weeds.
Knox, Ronald, 32n.

La comedia pródiga. See Miranda, Luis.
"La gallofa" scene, *144-145*, 160, 177, 183. See also *Parabola Coenae*.
La margarita preciosa, 166-169, 178.
La nave del mercader, 91, 103n.
La nueva esposa. See *La segunda esposa y triunfar muriendo*.
La oveja perdida, 52, *58-62*, 94, 175, 177, 178, 184, 185, 186.
La segunda esposa. See *La segunda esposa y triunfar muriendo*.
La segunda esposa y triunfar muriendo, 139, 141, *148-153*, 158, 159, 181, 188.
La semilla y la cizaña, 89, *98-107*, 108, 109, 110, 179, 182, 186, 189; date of, 90-91, 191-193.
La siega, 89, 90, *93-98*, 103, 107, 173, 175, 179, 185.
La siembra del Señor, 73n, 100n, 108, *110-117*, 182, 187; date of, 108, 191-193.
La vida es sueño, 154n.
La viña del Señor, 70n, 118, 119, *121-137*, 147, 162, 174, 178, 179, 180, 187, 189, 191.
Laborers in the Vineyard, Parable of, 86, 87, 100n, *108-117*. See also *El día mayor de los días, La siembra del Señor, Representación de la parábola de Sant Mateo a los veinte capítulos de su sagrado evangelio*.

Las espigas de Ruth, 23.
Leavitt, Sturgis, 112n.
Leyburn, Ellen Douglass, 176.
Llamados y escogidos, 139, 140, 141, *145-148*, 154, 155, 156, 157, 158, 160, 161, 174, 180, 186, 189, 190, 193.
Loa entre un villano y una labradora, 27.
Lost Coin, Parable of, 50n.
Lost Sheep, Parable of, *49-62*. See also *Auto de la oveja perdida, El pastor lobo y la cabaña celestial, La oveja perdida, Oveja perdida*.
Luther, Martin, 33, 108.
Luzán, Ignacio, 17-18.

"*Magnificat*," in the *auto*, 72, 182.
Maldonado, Juan de, 34n, 45-46, 47n, 74, 118n, 138n.
Mariscal de Gante, Jaime, 35, 54n, 95.
Marriage Feast, Parable of. See Great Supper, Parable of.
Marx, Milton, 102, 172-173.
mâshal, 27.
McGarry, Sister Francis de Sales, 110n.
Medel del Castillo, Francisco, 10, 52n.
Mejía de la Cerda, Luis, 89, 90. See also *El juego del hombre*.
Menéndez Pelayo, Marcelino, 18, 29-30, 31, 37, 38, 52n, 59n, 90, 93, 95.
Mérimée, Henri, 14n.
Mickelsen, A. Berkeley, 22n, 24n.
Mira de Amescua, Antonio, 76, 77. See also *El heredero*.
Miranda, Luis, 38.
Monroy, Juan Antonio, 34n.
Moratín, Nicolás Fernández de, 18, 31.
Morgan, G. C., 32n.
Morley, Sylvanus Griswold, 90.
Morrow, Louis Laravoire, 105n, 106n, 142n, 151n, 152, 155n, 167n, 168n.
Moschner, Franz M. 32n.

Navidad y Corpus Christi festejados por los mejores ingenios de España en diez y seis autos a lo divino y diez y seis loas y diez y seis entremeses, 76n.

Neoclassicists, 17-18, 29, 31, 170. See also Moratín, Nicolás Fernández de.
Net, Parable of, 19n.
non-kingdom parables, definition of, 32. See also Good Samaritan, Lost Sheep, Prodigal Son, Rich Man and Lazarus.

Obra da Geraçao Humana. See Vicente, Gil.
Obra llamada los desposorios de Cristo, 138, *145,* 147, 174, 183.
Olmedo, Félix G., 51n.
Origen, 20, 171.
Oveja perdida, 51, 52-55, 58, 145, 173, 183.

parable, allegorical interpretation of, 18-20, 84-87; "form critics" interpretation of, 20-22; didactic purpose of, 24-26; "hardening theory" of, 25-26; artistic value of, 30-31; as ready-made material for *auto,* 33-35, 87-88. See also Kingdom parables, Non-kingdom parables.
Parabola Coenae, 139, *142-145,* 146 148, 155, 156, 174, 177, 182, 183.
Parabola Samaritani, 63, *64-65,* 66, 67, 176, 183.
Parker, Alexander A. 9, 10, 15-16, 17, 20, 23-24, 31, 124n, 135n, 170, 171, 193n.
pasos, 14.
Paz, Julián, 10, 36, 76.
Pedro Telonario, 76, 77
Pfandl, Ludwig, 75.
Philo of Alexandria, 20.
Post, Chandler, 24, 26.
Prodigal Son, Parable of, 31, 34n, 35-49. See also *Auto del hijo pródigo, Auto del hijo pródigo* (Valdivielso), *El hijo pródigo.*
Puente, Luis de La, 62n.

Quién hallará mujer fuerte, 160n.
Quijote, 37, 166.

Ramón, Alonso, 36, 37.
Representación de la parábola de Sant Mateo a los veinte capítulos de su sagrado evangelio. See Horozco, Sebastián de.
Restori, Antonio, 93.
Révah, I. S., 63.
Rich Man and Lazarus, Parable of, 74-83. See also *El rico avariento.*
Rodríguez-Puértolas, Julio, 88n.
Rojas Zorrilla, Francisco. See *El rico avariento.*
rôques, 16-17.
Rouanet, Leo, 35. See also *Aucto del hijo pródigo.*
Rueda, Lope de, 14.

Sanvisens, Alejandro, 65n, 89n.
Sanzoles, Modesto de, 93, 96, 97, 103n.
Smalley, Beryl, 28n.
Sorrento, Luigi, 39.
Sower, Parable of, 19n, 32, 84, 85, 87, 108. See also Weeds, Parable of.
Sueños hay que verdad son, 32n.

tarasca, 16-17.
Tares, Parable of. See Weeds, Parable of.
Ternario spiritual, 51.
Ternarios sacramentales, 51, 138.
Tertulian, 20.
Thomas, Lucien-Paul, 102n, 112n.
Ticknor, George, 93, 97n.
Timoneda, Juan de, *183.* See also *La oveja perdida, Obra llamada los desposorios de Cristo.*
Tragoedia Patris Familias de Vinea, 120n.
Treasure and the Pearl, Parable of, 32, 86, *161-169.* See also *El tesoro escondido, La margarita preciosa.*
Triunfar muriendo. See *La segunda esposa y triunfar muriendo.*
Tu prójimo como a ti, 64, *68-73,* 175, 187, 190, 192.

Valbuena Prat, Angel, 9, 10, 15-16, 17, 20, 23n, 64, 76n, 89, 90, 91, 108, 110n, 118, 119, 139, 140, 145, 154n, 159, 160n, 161, 162, 170, 171, 191, 192, 193.
Valdivielso, José, *183-184.* See also *Auto del hijo pródigo, El peregrino.*

Vega Carpio, Lope Félix de, 23, 27, *184-186*. See also *El heredero del cielo*, *El hijo pródigo*, *El pastor lobo y la cabaña celestial*, *La margarita preciosa*, *La oveja perdida*, *La siega*.
Vicente, Gil, 14n, 63.
Vidal Salvador, Manuel, 37.
Villagarcía. See *Auto de la oveja perdida*.
Villalpando, José, 140. See also *El convite general*.
Vinedressers, Parable of, 32, 87, *117-137*. See also *El heredero*, *El heredero del cielo*, *La viña del Señor*.

Wardropper, Bruce W. 9, 13n, 16-17, 28n, 29n, 38, 46, 57n, 124n, 170.
Wedding Feast, Parable of. See Great Supper, Parable of.
Weeds, Parable of, 19n, 32, 85, 86, 87, *88-107*. See also *El juego del hombre*, *La siega*, *La semilla y la cizaña*.
Wilson, Edmund M., 100.

Young, Margaret Pauline, 153n.

Zabaleta, Juan de, 75.

NORTH CAROLINA STUDIES IN THE ROMANCE LANGUAGES AND LITERATURES

I.S.B.N. Prefix 0-88438

Recent Titles

ESSAYS IN HONOR OF LOUIS FRANCIS SOLANO, edited by Raymond J. Cormier and Urban T. Holmes. 1970. (No. 992). -892-1.

JACQUES DE LA TAILLE'S. "LA MANIERE," A CRITICAL EDITION, by Pierre Han. 1970. (No. 93). -893-X.

THE MAJOR THEMES OF EXISTENTIALISM IN THE WORK OF JOSÉ ORTEGA Y GASSET, by Janet Winecoff Díaz. 1970. (No. 94). -984-8.

CHARLES NODIER: HIS LIFE AND WORKS, by Sarah Fore Bell. 1971. (No. 95). -895-6.

LOPE DE VEGA "EL PEREGRINO EN SU PATRIA," edición de Myron A. Peyton. 1971. (No. 97). -897-2.

CRITICAL REACTIONS AND THE CHISTIAN ELEMENT IN THE POETRY OF PIERRE DE RONSARD, by Mark S. Whitney. 1971. (No. 98). -898-0.

THE REV. JOHN BOWLE. THE GENESIS OF CERVANTEAN CRITICISM, by Ralph Merritt Cox. 1971. (No. 99). -989-9.

THE FOUR INTERPOLATED STORIES IN THE "ROMAN COMIQUE": THEIR SOURCES AND UNIFYING FUNCTION, by Frederick Alfred De Armas. 1971. (No. 100). -900-6.

LE CHASTOIEMENT D'UN PERE A SON FILS, A CRITICAL EDITION, edited by Edward D. Montgomery, Jr. 1971. (No. 101). -901-4.

LE ROMMANT DE "GUY DE WARWIK" ET DE "HEROLT D'ARDENNE," edited by D. J. Conlon. 1971. (No. 102). -902-2.

THE OLD PORTUGUESE "VIDA DE SAM BERNARDO," EDITED FROM ALCOBAÇA MANUSCRIPT ccxci/200, WITH INTRODUCTION, LINGUISTIC STUDY, NOTES, TABLE OF PROPER NAMES, AND GLOSSARY, by Lawrence A. Sharpe. 1971. (No. 103). -903-0.

A CRITICAL AND ANNOTATED EDITION OF LOPE DE VEGA'S "LAS ALMENAS DE TORO," by Thomas E. Case. 1971. (No. 104). -904-9.

LOPE DE VEGA'S "LO QUE PASA EN UNA TARDE," A CRITICAL, ANNOTATED EDITION OF THE AUTOGRAPH MANUSCRIPT, by Richard Angelo Picerno. 1971. (No 105). -905-7.

OBJECTIVE METHODS FOR TESTING AUTHENTICITY AND THE STUDY OF TEN DOUBTFUL "COMEDIAS" ATTRIBUTED TO LOPE DE VEGA, by Fred M. Clark. 1971. (No. 106). -906-5.

THE ITALIAN VERB. A MORPHOLOGICAL STUDY, by Frede Jensen. 1971. (No. 107). -907-3.

A CRITICAL EDITION OF THE OLD PROVENÇAL EPIC "DAUREL ET BETON," WITH NOTES AND PROLEGOMENA, by Arthur S. Kimmel. 1971. (No. 108). -908-1.

FRANCISCO RODRIGUES LOBO: DIALOGUE AND COURTLY LORE IN RENAISSANCE PORTUGAL, by Richard A. Preto-Rodas. 1971. (No. 109). -909-X.

RAIMOND VIDAL: POETRY AND PROSE, edited by W. H. W. Field. 1971. (No. 110). -910-3.

RELIGIOUS ELEMENTS IN THE SECULAR LYRICS OF THE TROUBADOURS, by Raymond Gay-Crosier. 1971. (No. 111). -911-1.

THE SIGNIFICANCE OF DIDEROT'S "ESSAI SUR LE MERITE ET LA VERTU," by Gordon B. Walters. 1971. (No. 112). -912-X.

PROPER NAMES IN THE LYRICS OF THE TROUBADOURS, by Frank M. Chambers. 1971. (No. 113). -913-8.

STUDIES IN HONOR OF MARIO A. PEI, edited by John Fisher and Paul A. Gaeng. 1971. (No. 114). -914-6.

DON MANUEL CAÑETE, CRONISTA LITERARIO DEL ROMANTICISMO Y DEL POSROMANTICISMO EN ESPAÑA, por Donald Allen Randolph. 1972. (No. 115). -915-4.

THE TEACHINGS OF SAINT LOUIS. A CRITICAL TEXT, by David O'Connell. 1972. (No. 116). *-916-2.*

HIGHER, HIDDEN ORDER: DESIGN AND MEANING IN THE ODES OF MALHERBE, by David Lee Rubin. 1972. (No. 117). *-917-0.*

JEAN DE LE MOTE "LE PARFAIT DU PAON," édition critique par Richard J. Carey. 1972. (No. 118). *-918-9.*

CAMUS' HELLENIC SOURCES, by Paul Archambault. 1972. (No. 119). *-919-7.*

FROM VULGAR LATIN TO OLD PROVENÇAL, by Frede Jensen. 1972. (No. 120). *-920-0.*

GOLDEN AGE DRAMA IN SPAIN: GENERAL CONSIDERATION AND UNUSUAL FEATURES, by Sturgis E. Leavitt. 1972. (No. 121). *-921-9.*

THE LEGEND OF THE "SIETE INFANTES DE LARA" (*Refundición toledana de la crónica de 1344* versión), study and edition by Thomas A. Lathrop. 1972. (No. 122). *-922-7.*

STRUCTURE AND IDEOLOGY IN BOIARDO'S "ORLANDO INNAMORATO," by Andrea di Tommaso. 1972. (No. 123). *-923-5.*

STUDIES IN HONOR OF ALFRED G. ENGSTROM, edited by Robert T. Cargo and Emanuel J. Mickel, Jr. 1972. (No. 124). *-924-3.*

A CRITICAL EDITION WITH INTRODUCTION AND NOTES OF GIL VICENTE'S "FLORESTA DE ENGANOS," by Constantine Christopher Stathatos. 1972. (No. 125). *-925-1.*

LI ROMANS DE WITASSE LE MOINE. *Roman du treizième siècle.* Édité d'après le manuscrit, fonds français 1553, de la Bibliothèque Nationale, Paris, par Denis Joseph Conlon. 1972. (No. 126). *-926-X.*

EL CRONISTA PEDRO DE ESCAVIAS. *Una vida del Siglo XV,* por Juan Bautista Avalle-Arce. 1972. (No. 127). *-927-8.*

AN EDITION OF THE FIRST ITALIAN TRANSLATION OF THE "CELESTINA," by Kathleen V. Kish. 1973. (No. 128). *-928-6.*

MOLIÈRE MOCKED. THREE CONTEMPORARY HOSTILE COMEDIES: *Zélinde, Le portrait du peintre, Élomire Hypocondre,* by Frederick Wright Vogler. 1973. (No. 129). *-929-4.*

C.-A. SAINTE-BEUVE. *Chateaubriand et son groupe littéraire sous l'empire.* Index alphabétique et analytique établi par Lorin A. Uffenbeck. 1973. (No. 130). *-930-8.*

THE ORIGINS OF THE BAROQUE CONCEPT OF "PEREGRINATIO," by Juergen Hahn. 1973. (No. 131). *-931-6.*

THE "AUTO SACRAMENTAL" AND THE PARABLE IN SPANISH GOLDEN AGE LITERATURE, by Donald Thaddeus Dietz. 1973. (No. 132). *-932-4.*

Symposia

LOS NARRADORES HISPANOAMERICANOS DE HOY, edited by Juan Bautista Avalle-Arce. 1973. (No. 1). *-951-0.*

When ordering cite *ISBN Prefix* plus last four digits given with each title.

Send orders to:
International Scholarly Book Service, Inc.
P.O. Box 4347
Portland, Oregon 97208
U.S.A.

The Department of Romance Studies Digital Arts and Collaboration Lab at the University of North Carolina at Chapel Hill is proud to support the digitization of the North Carolina Studies in the Romance Languages and Literatures series.

www.ingramcontent.com/pod-product-compliance
Lightning Source LLC
Chambersburg PA
CBHW030236240426
43663CB00037B/1152